baking
BOOT CAMP

baking

BOOT
CAMP

Five Days of Basic Training at The Culinary Institute of America

THE CULINARY INSTITUTE OF AMERICA
and DARRA GOLDSTEIN

BICENTENNIAL
1807
WILEY
2007
BICENTENNIAL

JOHN WILEY & SONS, INC.

The Culinary Institute of America
PRESIDENT Dr. Tim Ryan
VICE-PRESIDENT, CONTINUING EDUCATION Mark Erickson
DIRECTOR OF INTELLECTUAL PROPERTY Nathalie Fischer
MANAGING EDITOR Kate McBride
EDITORIAL PROJECT MANAGER Mary Donovan
RECIPE TESTING DATABASE MANAGER Margaret Wheeler
PRODUCTION ASSISTANT Patrick Decker

CHEF Alain Dubernard
CHEF John DeShetler
CHEF Francisco Migoya
CHEF Stephane Weber
David Barillaro

This book is printed on acid-free paper.

Published by John Wiley & Sons, Inc., Hoboken, New Jersey
Published simultaneously in Canada

LIBRARY OF CONGRESS CATALOGING-IN-PUBLICATION DATA:
Goldstein, Darra.
    Baking boot camp: five days of basic training at the Culinary Institute of America / The Culinary
Institute of America with Darra Goldstein.
        p. cm.
    Includes index.
ISBN: 978-0-7645-7279-1 (cloth)
    1. Baking. 2. Culinary Institute of America. I. Culinary Institute
of America. II. Title.
    TX763.G568 2007
    641.8'15—dc22

                                                        2005033609
PRINTED IN THE UNITED STATES OF AMERICA

All photos by Ben Fink
Cover photo by Keith Ferris
Interior design by Vertigo Design NYC

10 9 8 7 6 5 4 3 2 1

For Dean, who has perfect pitch

Contents

Preface viii
Acknowledgments ix
Introduction x

Chapter One
ORIENTATION 2
Orientation Begins 4
Navigating the Campus 7
Our Boot Camp Gear 10

Chapter Two
THE CREAMING METHOD 12
Chef Kate and the Day's Production 15
Into the Bake Shop 21
Afternoon Lecture: Bread 28
Dinner at Ristorante Caterina
   de' Medici 34

Chapter Three
**THE RUBBED DOUGH
METHOD** 38
Ensuring Tender, Flaky Crusts 40
Pie Fillings and Meringues 43
Making Our Own Crust 47
Beyond the CIA Campus 54
Dinner at the Escoffier Room 55

Chapter Four
ENRICHED DOUGHS 58
The Role of Butter, Eggs, and
   Milk in Doughs 60
Making Challah 63
Baking as a Process 68
Afternoon Lecture: Baking Science 69
Dinner at the American Bounty
   Restaurant 77

Chapter Five
LEAN DOUGHS 80
The Day's Production 82
Baking Boot Camp Graduation and
   Going Home 86

Chapter Six
CUSTARDS 88
The First Session 90
Chef Paul Demonstrates 96
Dessert Before Lunch 104
Dinner at St. Andrew's Café 107

Chapter Seven

THE FOAMING METHOD 108

Using Eggs as Leavening 110

Fruit Tarts 116

Afternoon Lecture: Chocolate 118

Dinner at the Ristorante Caterina
de' Medici 124

Chapter Eight

PUFF PASTRY 126

Laminated Doughs 128

Buttercream 136

Afternoon Lecture: Dessert Wines 140

Dinner at the Escoffier Room 145

Chapter Nine

**MOUSSE AND BAVARIAN
CREAM** 146

Bavarian Creams and Mousses 149

Shaping Puff Pastry 156

Afternoon Lecture: Coffee and
Tea Tasting 158

Dinner at the American Bounty
Restaurant 161

Chapter Ten

**QUICK AND ELEGANT
DESSERTS** 162

Decorative Chocolate Shapes 164

Dessert Sauces 164

Decorating Cakes 166

Soufflés 168

Pastry Boot Camp Graduation 169

Chapter Eleven

WHAT WE BAKED 170

Quick Breads and Cakes 172

Yeast Breads 199

Cookies 211

Pies and Tarts 219

Desserts 232

Pastries 244

Sauces, Glazes, and Creams 258

Conversions and Equivalents 268

Index 272

Benefactors 277

Preface

When we first had the idea of creating boot camps on our Hyde Park campus, we knew that we wanted to keep learning at the forefront of a great experience. We were determined to be sure that our "campers" not only learned impeccable foundation techniques but were exposed to our entire campus, from the public restaurants to student dining, the classroom to the kitchen, the library to the recreation center.

Over the years, we've found that two of our most popular offerings—baking boot camp and pastry boot camp—echo the distinctions bakers and chefs make about the kind of work they do. Baking, most agree, is more precise and more methodical than the culinary arts. But when attendees at our baking boot camps really begin to see how bakers and pastry chefs work, they see that there is more to baking than science, ratios, or even a baker's scale. There is every bit as much artistry and creativity in making a good pie dough as there is in making perfect petits fours.

One of the most important (and enjoyable) parts of any boot camp is the meals the campers share. Whether during the morning break, where they learn to appraise their morning croissant and muffins with a professional eye, at lunch made by our full-time students, or during dinner in our restaurants, they begin to talk about baked goods and evaluate them, looking for signs of quality in everything from hard rolls to tortes. Afternoon lectures that cover topics such as dessert wines, baking science, chocolates, and teas, as well as excursions into the Institute's storeroom, give our students a rounded exposure to everything involved in today's baking and pastry arts.

Boot camps aren't demonstration classes, and our boot camp graduates will tell you that they felt real pressure to produce, just as a professional baker or pastry chef does. Whether learning to temper chocolate or braid a loaf of challah, they have to accomplish the same things we expect of any of our full-time students.

As instructors for these boot camps, we are in a privileged position. We get to bring the art and craft of baking and pastry to life. We get to debunk the myths that sometimes get in the way of great baking. And we get to share our passion for the baking and pastry arts with the wonderful students who come to Hyde Park, New York.

We hope to see you at a boot camp soon!

KATE CAVOTTI
PAUL PROSPERI

Acknowledgments

Since a chance conversation with Pamela Chirls led to the writing of this book, I'd first like to thank Pamela, my visionary editor at Wiley, for the opportunity to experience boot camp at the CIA. Thanks also to Angela Miller, my dedicated agent, and to Mary Donovan at the CIA, who shepherded this project from beginning to end with equal doses of wisdom and humor. I'm enormously grateful to my CIA instructors, Kate Cavotti and Paul Prosperi, who gave unstintingly of their time and expertise. Final thanks go to my husband, Dean Crawford, whose editorial brilliance and unflagging support brought this book to fruition; and to our daughter, Leila, who accepted my long hours at the computer with good cheer and tried not to laugh at me in my toque.

Introduction

Who could resist telling friends and family that she is about to enlist in CIA boot camp? The response is inevitably slack-jawed disbelief. Only after a beat does the punch line come: no, no, there won't be any cloaks and daggers, just toques and knives! As for covert action, sous cloche is about as undercover as it gets, though (seriously) there's no denying the course's rigor. Welcome to The Culinary Institute of America, where you can get a taste of the professional chef's life.

The Institute's promotional materials make much of the military metaphor. Boot Camp 1, or Basic Training, offers students instruction in the fundamentals of cooking. At this camp, students share "war stories" with other "recruits"; they "prepare to excel in [their] own battleground"—presumably the kitchen. Baking boot campers are "armed" with a textbook and "baking fatigues." (After completing my own, exhausting basic training at baking boot camp I ascribed new meaning to the word *fatigues*!)

The army rhetoric seems less appropriate when you arrive at the beautiful campus of the CIA. Perched high on the bluffs overlooking the Hudson River, the Institute occupies the grounds of a former Jesuit semi-nary, St. Andrew-on-Hudson. The imposing main building, Roth Hall, constructed of red brick and marble, dates back to 1901. For sixty-odd years this retreat was where Jesuit priests on the East Coast were trained. The Culinary Institute of America bought the property in 1970 and over the years has transformed it into the nation's premier culinary school. Roughly 2,400 students are enrolled to earn associate's or bachelor's degrees in culinary arts management or baking and pastry arts management. The school also has an active Continuing Education division, which sponsors the boot camps. These mainly weeklong programs cover topics such as Basic Training, Skill Development (an accelerated two-day program), Baking, Pastry, Healthy Cuisine, Gourmet Meals in Minutes, Small Dishes Big Flavors (appetizers and hors d'oeuvres), and Italian Cuisine.

I enrolled—enlisted, I should say—in two separate boot camps, baking and pastry. The opportunity to refine my baking skills thrilled me. Ever since my first childish attempts at mud pies (not the decadent southern dessert, but the real thing, made of mud) I've enjoyed baking. Although I never had any formal training, that wasn't by design. After my sophomore year of college

I'd signed up for a two-day baking course at the original Cordon Bleu cooking school in Paris. The class was to be the highlight of my summer. Those were the days when young women could still hitchhike more or less safely around Europe, and I had left plenty of time to travel from Finland to France—or so I thought. But I arrived in Paris two hours late, after the class had already begun, and no amount of pleading could convince Cordon Bleu to allow me to take the second day of the course. I'd had to forfeit not only the tuition but also my immediate dream of learning how to bake from a master French chef. Now I finally had a chance to make up for that youthful mistake.

Like those early courses at Cordon Bleu, the boot camps at the CIA are open to anyone—no experience necessary. They take place year-round, but to me, winter seemed the best time for baking: I could enjoy the ovens' heat while blizzards raged. I had no intention of becoming a professional baker—not with that profession's early morning hours! Like most CIA recruits, I suppose I just wanted some tricks of the trade, the sleights of hand that magically produce billowy meringues and croissants so flaky that they litter your face and hands. To be honest, though, I didn't really care how much I learned. A week of uninterrupted baking was temptation enough!

chapter 1

ORIENTATION

Our boot camp orientation was held the night before classes began. I made the two-hour drive from home in leisurely fashion, thinking about how the Culinary had changed over the years. I had first heard about it thirty-some years ago, when my sister's college roommate enrolled there after graduation, horrifying her parents by choosing a cooking school over a more prestigious course of study. In the early 1970s, becoming a chef was definitely not the thing for an Ivy League grad.

A couple of years later, I experienced the CIA for myself when I attended college at Vassar, just down the road from Hyde Park. The CIA's highly structured, professional curriculum could not have differed more from my free-wheeling liberal arts studies. Perhaps that's one reason why the school felt so much like a place apart. The few forays that I made to Hyde Park did feel almost illicit—as though I might encounter dangerous characters who would tempt me with tasty morsels until I lost all perspective and control. These days, the CIA's image couldn't be more different, I mused as I turned onto familiar Route 9. Now it's the elite destination for any student interested in food; now the profession of chef is revered, celebrated on television. Still, the male-female ratio is nearly two to one at the school, so perhaps there were still dangers awaiting young women. I was eager to find out.

ORIENTATION BEGINS

I had wanted to stay in the CIA dormitories, if only to get the full student experience, but no rooms were available. So I settled on a quiet, secluded inn in Poughkeepsie, about twenty minutes down the road, which turned out to be a perfect retreat from the intensity of boot camp. After checking in, I headed back up the highway. The thermometer on my car registered 8°F, arctic. Roth Hall, named after the CIA's founder, loomed large as I drove into the main parking lot. The orientation meeting was to be held in the Anheuser-Busch Theatre in Roth Hall. As I made my way through the now-barren courtyard I realized, with a bit of a jolt, that everything at the CIA was branded, from the Heinz Plaza I was traversing to the J. Willard Marriott Continuing Education Center that sponsors the boot camps and the new Colavita Center for Italian Food and Wine, which also houses the Torani Bar (named after the well-known syrup company). You can track the corporate donations as you wander the halls.

The Anheuser-Busch Theatre is actually a small, gently lit amphitheater. I felt as though I had entered a hallowed space, and it was blessedly warm inside. I eyed the handful of other people in the room, trying to figure out where they had come from and why they might have been drawn to boot camp. The range was broad, from perfectly coiffed and bejeweled matrons to guys in work clothes. I decided I'd better not speculate. Lisa Paquin, the program manager for the Continuing Education division, introduced herself as our orientation guide. Though very friendly, she was also no-nonsense and commanded full attention despite her diminutive size.

Lisa began by apologizing for being in her "civvies"—out of uniform. Apparently the military model pervaded all of the CIA, not just the boot camps. Sixteen graduation ceremonies take place throughout the year at the Culinary, she informed us. The next session would begin tomorrow, but today was a "down day"—the Monday following a graduation, when no students were on campus. That meant the administration could relax the usual strict standards of dress. It

Anheuser-Busch Theatre

occurred to me that the uniforms might have less to do with military training than with the classical French kitchen, where hierarchies and sartorial signifiers are still very much part of the game.

Lisa cut immediately to the issue of parking, a sensitive subject at the CIA. She was, in fact, just about to introduce a security officer when she changed her mind and rushed us out of the theater, explaining that there was a problem with the heating system and she was afraid we'd roast before the orientation meeting was over. I could deal with the suspense of the parking rules but hated to leave the cozy warmth of the theater. We headed down one corridor after another. No one spoke, except for the chatter of two older women who seemed to have come to boot camp together. We traded the grandeur of Roth Hall for the new J. Willard Marriott Continuing Education Center, where we seated ourselves at tables in a plain dining hall.

The first thing I had to adjust to was the number of acronyms Lisa threw at us. CE was clear enough—continuing education—but we also learned that our baking boot camp instructor, Kate Cavotti, was an AOS instructor in the baking program at CIA, not a regular member of the CE program. All I could think of were the other AOS acronyms I knew, which can involve the *other* CIA from time to time—affidavit of support or adjustment of status for immigrants. Here at this more benign CIA, AOS stands for associate in occupational studies, the basic degree program. The AOS is distinct from the BPS—the bachelor of professional studies, which

requires thirty-eight months of study as opposed to the twenty-one months necessary for the associate's degree. Lisa then informed us that there's actually an FBI at the CIA— a comment she knew was always good for a laugh. That's the Food and Beverage Institute, she explained.

This rapid-fire information was only a preamble to the main issue Lisa wanted to get back to: parking. The CIA, we learned, was undertaking a large construction project, building townhouses to increase dormitory space for the students. She warned us that parking was fraught; most students commuted to campus since there weren't enough dorms. By 9 a.m. all of the spaces were usually full—the early shift of students had already taken them. She then introduced us to Officer Rob from Campus Security, the shift supervisor from 3 to 11 p.m., who told us that campus security is in business 24/7 and warned us that if we didn't park in our designated area we'd get "a little pink thing"—a ticket, which would set us back a pretty penny. The designated area was at the far end of the north lot, which he jokingly referred to as "Siberia." None of us laughed. He then told us that a security officer mans the north gate all night, so even if we were to try to sneak into the lot early, someone would be wise to our tricks, and that we had better park where assigned so that "no one falls into a hole like Jimmy Hoffa." I realized he was trying to soften his message with humor, but I could feel the anxiety that this last little joke aroused among some of the boot campers. "What if there are no places left?" one woman anxiously whispered.

But Officer Rob didn't hear her. He had already moved on to the next safety issue, the sheer drop of twenty to thirty feet to the Hudson River from the cliff behind Rosenthal, one of the dorms. "The DSO patrols it, but they won't find you for a while," he quipped. The DSO, it turns out, was the Deputy Sheriff's Office. I could feel the ladies behind me growing increasingly anxious. First we have to park in Siberia; next we're warned not to fall off a cliff. From their whispered conversation I'd gathered that they were commuting to boot camp, and that on top of everything else the weather report was predicting sixteen inches of snow for the next day. I could feel the temperature in the room rising—it was lucky we had left that overheated amphitheater. Officer Rob gave a cheerful goodbye, his parting words a reminder that no smoking was allowed in campus buildings. I don't smoke and never have, but I briefly considered taking it up.

NAVIGATING THE CAMPUS

Lisa returned to the front to explain what her job entailed. As operations manager, she was in charge of ordering and buying for the kitchens, coordinating five lecture halls, three kitchens, and three studios, and in general making sure that everyone had everything they needed pre-

cisely when they needed it. No wonder she was so organized!

Then it was time for a brief tour of Roth Hall. We began with the hospitality center, located across from a bookstore now run by Barnes and Noble. In addition to cookbooks and the usual sorts of college supplies, this concession stocks lots of kitchen gadgets and gifts, from aprons to grilling utensils to recipe cards. Next we peered through the picture windows of the Apple Pie Bakery kitchens, newly opened in 1999, where students turn out delicious baked goods to serve in the next-door café. Lisa urged us not to miss their devastatingly rich Mudslides cookies. If we wore our name tags, she said, we would get a 10 percent discount at the bakery, which sounded like a good idea—little did we know that by the end of the week the last thing we'd want was baked goods. We proceeded down the hallway to the American Bounty Restaurant, one of the CIA's four training restaurants, and then saw the Escoffier Restaurant at the other end of the long corridor—the oldest and most formal of the CIA's dining rooms. Here, a meal can take two and a half hours.

Lisa pointed out Farquharson Hall, the pride of Roth Hall with its dramatic vaulted ceiling and gorgeous stained glass. Now the student dining room and the site of graduation ceremonies, this room once served as the seminary's chapel. Farquharson Hall recently underwent a $2 million restoration, overseen by the same company that restored Grand Central Station in New York. The original stained glass was cleaned and repaired

Apple Pie Bakery kitchens

and the huge chandeliers reconfigured so that they could be lowered to the floor for cleaning—an advantage the monks never enjoyed. Over the doorway a lion rampant with sword in paw adorned a carved and painted wooden plaque announcing "Fide et fortitudine," "By fidelity and fortitude," the motto on the Farquharson family crest.

Lisa reminded us to wear our name tags at all times, especially if we wanted to breakfast in Farquharson Hall, where the students eat family style at large round tables. Several of us groaned when she told us that the doors to the dining hall open at 5:45. She encouraged us to arrive early for breakfast, because by 6:30 the breakfast line usually stretches down the hall to the front doors of Roth Hall, and we'd risk being late to our 7:00 class. It was worth the early hour, Lisa assured us, because we'd enjoy a wonderfully hearty breakfast—though in the next breath she cautioned us not to eat too much, since the boot camp pastry break would begin promptly at 8:15, following each morning's lecture. None of us imagined how inflexible this schedule would be.

As we headed for the exit, Lisa expressed consternation that some tables and chairs and equipment had been left out in the halls—an obvious breach of the orderly procedures that characterize the CIA. "That shouldn't be!" she exclaimed with annoyance, assuring us that the mess would be gone by tomorrow and had been neglected only because it was a "down day." We exited onto Heinz Plaza, where, when the weather is nice, food festivals and other functions are held.

Across the plaza stood St. Andrew's Café. This informal restaurant boasts a healthy menu for which the food is prepared without any cream sauces, and often with an Asian flair.

Our tour continued with entry into ML CE—in CIA-speak that's the Middle Level of the Continuing Education building—where we were greeted by a large American flag. Down a long corridor we came to a smallish kitchen labeled "K17: Cuisine of the Americas," a pantry where Lisa told us our lunch would be served each day promptly at 11:00. Already I didn't like this acceleration of meal times. An early breakfast was fine, but why couldn't we have lunch at a normal hour? It hadn't yet occurred to me that with so many students to feed, the Culinary had to squeeze the boot campers in.

The second floor of the Continuing Ed building housed impressive bake shops and a confectionery studio, also with picture windows for visitors to view the students at work. We exited the building on the river side and walked across a small square to the new Colavita Center, where Lisa pointed out the Ristorante Caterina de' Medici, the newest of the four restaurants, as well as the classroom and kitchen where we'd be spending our boot camp week.

Our final stop was at the Conrad N. Hilton Library, with its exceptional holdings of books and periodicals relating to food and drink. The library also owns more than twenty-eight thousand menus, including many from railroad companies and shipping lines, dating back to 1883. And it houses a collection of rare books with titles by such culinary luminaries as François Pierre de La Varenne, François Massialot, Nicolas de Bonnefons, Charles Francatelli, and Amelia Simmons. In this building are also the student computer center (Lisa assured us that we could check our e-mail from there) and the Danny Kaye Theater, where lectures and cooking demonstrations are held. I recognized this space from a lecture I'd given several years earlier, on Russian cuisine. It felt humbling to be wearing the student's shoes this time around.

OUR BOOT CAMP GEAR

The tour over, we returned to the orientation room, where we were issued our uniforms and gear: a deep green duffel bag sporting the CIA logo and containing the book *Understanding Baking: The Art and Science of Baking,* a neon-green CIA logo thermal coffee mug, a Silpat sheet for baking, two pairs of houndstooth chef's pants, two chef's jackets, and two white neckerchiefs. We each also received a chef's kit, complete with a bench scraper, a plastic dough scraper, a swivel peeler, a set of measuring spoons, a paring knife, a chef's knife, a serrated knife, a whisk, an offset spatula, a rubber spatula, a pair of tongs, and a simple wooden spoon.

By six-thirty, the orientation was over, and we were free for the evening. Only about half of the students who had signed up for our boot camp had appeared for the orientation. Lisa mentioned that there had been some last-minute cancellations due to the predicted storm. It was obvious that she disapproved. Like the children's-book postal service that delivers mail through rain and snow, sleet and hail, the CIA is not slowed down by the weather. The Institute never closes, because the students have to eat. I felt a sense of imminence, as I often do before storms. At home, people would be rushing to the grocery store to stock up on milk and flashlight batteries. Had Lisa done any extra ordering in advance? I was too shy to ask.

I wondered whether my missing classmates would arrive before the storm. I also wondered whether those of us commuting to boot camp would make it up the highway through the snow. At that moment I wished I shared Lisa's dauntlessness. She waved us off, adding that she looked forward to seeing us bright and early the next morning. As I walked to my car—illegally parked, as I now realized—I could hear the wind beginning to pick up. Adventure was in the air. This was going to be a memorable week!

Heinz Plaza

chapter 2

THE CREAMING METHOD

Things did not bode well for my induction into the CIA. Despite perfect pillows and a comfortable bed, I had not slept well. What if my alarm didn't go off? What if the monster snowstorm arrived as predicted? I had no idea whether the local highway department plowed the roads well. If they didn't, would my car be able to make it through the snow? I was starting boot camp—so why, oh why, had I left my boots in the car? I had decided that it was important to jump right into the boot camp experience with a full breakfast, a protein punch that would carry me through what I thought would be long hours ahead. That meant arriving at Roth Hall by 6 a.m. to avoid long lines. Then I could enjoy my meal and still show up promptly for class at 7:00.

My alarm did indeed go off right on time, at 5 a.m., and I awoke to a world transformed. Over twelve inches of snow had fallen overnight, and it was still coming down hard. Snowstorms are beautiful as long as you don't have to drive in them. The morning news announced school closings everywhere—everywhere except at the CIA.

I hurried to get dressed. The twenty-minute drive might easily take an hour. That's when I experienced my second bad moment of the day. I didn't just slip into my boot-camp-issued uniform, I slid. My five-foot-three frame was lost in the billowing houndstooth pants and the rigid, double-breasted chef's jacket. Even after rolling up the cuffs on both jacket and pants, I looked like a clown. All right, maybe I'm vain, but this was not how I wanted to present myself to the world. What could I do, though? I decided to stay in my civvies for the time being—the snow was enough to deal with. Bootless, I waded through snowdrifts to the

car. At least I had the scraper! By 5:15 I was crawling out of the unplowed parking lot, grateful for those Swedish engineers who design cars to be undaunted by snow. On the highway the plows were out in full force, casting eerie lights in the darkness. The world felt sci-fi, populated by giant machines whose rumbling motors were muffled by the snow.

On such a day it seemed appropriate to park in "Siberia"—the name students give to the CIA's distant north lot. I donned my boots and made my way to what looked like a castle on a hill, looming darkly through the snow. Slogging across the tundra of the parking lot, eyes half closed against the snow, I felt spurred on by the promise of the hearty breakfast awaiting me in Roth Hall. I shouldn't have worried so much about getting to the dining hall in time. The snow had obviously slowed people down, so I was able to walk right up to the counter. Both "eggs any style" and French-style omelets tempted me, but in the end I settled on a bowl of steaming oatmeal. I learned that offerings on other days include breakfast burritos, blintzes, huevos rancheros, chocolate chip pancakes, sausage-stuffed French toast, corned beef hash, and funnel cakes. All are prepared by students as they rotate their way through the Institute's cooking classes.

I was anxious to stop by the supply room in the desperate hope of finding more flattering garb. I did find some extra-small chef's pants and a jacket, but they still seemed sized for Gullivers rather than Lilliputians, and the balloon cut of the pants was disastrous in any size. I took a deep breath and resigned myself to looking comical all week.

CHEF KATE AND THE DAY'S PRODUCTION

Though properly attired, I felt claustrophobic from the neckerchief pressing against my skin. I saw myself as a character in a bad comedy, racing down the corridors and dashing through a snowy courtyard to reach class in time. My fellow campers were already gathered in the Colavita classroom, where our instructor, Kate Cavotti, was fiddling with a computer. Chef Kate had come to the Culinary after years of cooking in New York City restaurants. She taught baking in the Culinary Arts program, where students earn an associate's degree in occupational studies, but she was also moonlighting with us for the week. *Moonlighting* is probably the wrong word—*overtim-*

ing is more like it. After Kate finished our six-hour class, she went to her regular afternoon sessions. After that she went home to her three children. Her plate was very full.

Perhaps because she was used to juggling so much, Chef Kate was wonderfully calm and impressively organized. Nothing fazed her, as we immediately discovered when she turned on the computer for a PowerPoint presentation. Instead of her class notes, her personal e-mail popped up on the screen, but she just laughed it off, her humor dispelling the nervousness of our group. There were twelve of us seated at Formica-topped tables arranged in long rows facing a blackboard. The room was bright but sterile—no softening touches anywhere. It felt odd for me to be on the other side of the desk after twenty-some years in the classroom, and I could feel nervous tension in my classmates, too, as we smiled warily at each other. Introductions would soon take place, but first we had to pay attention to Chef Kate, who began the class promptly at 7:00.

Kate did not fit the stereotypical image of a chef—her face was too kindly, without any hauteur. She seemed fit and strong, and from the first hello, her no-nonsense, precise manner was evident. Kate had pinned her hair up under her chef's hat, and I noticed with a pang that not a wisp poked out. The disposable paper toques we'd been issued were obviously not designed for people with wild hair like mine. No matter what I did, I couldn't contain the curls that kept finding novel ways to escape. Not only did I look like Charlie Chaplin, I was unkempt besides.

Chef Kate's professional yet motherly managerial skills soon became apparent. When the computer screen displayed the list of baked goods we'd be preparing that day, she explained that we would divide into four groups of three. At this announcement our anxiety was palpable: you could see the bodies tense, the hands clench. Would we get into our first choice? Everyone wanted to be in Group 1, Pound Cake and Peanut Butter Cookies, and feared being placed in Group 2, Zucchini Bread and Oatmeal Cookies. Clearly, this class of campers leaned toward indulgence! Bob, whom we immediately pegged as the joker among us, wondered if we weren't also bean-sprout averse. Bearded and bearlike, he was a jolly sort, a local who had earned a nice retirement package from the phone company where he'd worked for years. He'd decided to continue his education by attending CIA boot camps and had already been to a few. Chef Kate reassured us that no matter which group we were placed in, we would all share our food and everyone would get to taste everything, whether we liked zucchini or not.

I lucked into Group 4, Cranberry Bread and Chocolate Chunk Cookies. My partners were Emily and June. Emily was a nutritionist who taught at the CIA. She was taking the class simply to learn more about baking. There was a notable calm about her, and she seemed unusually comfortable with silence. June couldn't have been more different. In her mid-sixties, she had flaming red hair and a regal carriage. Emily and I seemed swallowed up by our uniforms, but June modeled hers. She was stunning. The mother of five grown children, she had recently retired from teaching psychology at Mount Sinai Medical School. I was enthralled to learn that she had been a pioneering sex therapist and had known Masters and Johnson. She, too, was a repeat boot camper. From the minute she joined Emily and me she announced her likes and dislikes. June was used to taking charge and expected others to listen. That didn't sit too well with me, but I decided to see how things played out.

Our first lesson involved the most basic of skills, creaming. I was surprised that a whole class would be devoted to something that seemed so intuitive to me, but here at the Culinary, creaming was serious business. Chef Kate cautioned us that before we entered into the nitty-gritty of baking, we had to learn a few important skills, such as how to get organized. I couldn't help thinking of the opening sentence of *Mrs. Beeton's Book of Household Management*, published in 1861: "As with the COMMANDER OF AN ARMY, or the leader of any enterprise, so it is with the mistress of the house." As Kate explained, in order to master the kitchen, we had to master ourselves; only then could we master our work or supervise others. Such mastery begins with the mise en place, a French term that means "putting in place"—otherwise known as getting everything you need ready ahead of time, so that you don't have to stop and search for some ingredient in the middle of a crucial step in the baking process.

Chef Kate also stressed the importance of weighing ingredients rather than measur-

ing them by volume. Cooking can be a free-for-all, but baking is surely a science. Proportions of fat and liquid and leavening must be accurate and in accord; if they're not, the final product will fail. The magic of baking lies in the chemical reactions that take place among ingredients, which will bubble, curdle, or turn silken or billowy depending on how you handle them. This first lecture turned out to be largely about food science. Creaming, that most basic of methods used to mix batters for cookies and cakes, is a process by which sugar and fat are combined to incorporate air. Air is the leavening agent, though chemical leaveners can also be added, as they regularly have been since baking powder was formulated in the mid-nineteenth century.

For making standard cookies, pound cakes, and quick breads, four basic ingredients are needed: fat, sugar, eggs, and flour. As Chef Kate explained it, the ingredients mesh together and build one big team. Then they work together as a team to expand under heat into a delicious product. There is a little wiggle room—slight variations in proportions will produce different kinds of products, and the very same ingredients put together by different methods will also yield various results. But when making basic cookies, pound cakes, or quick breads, you must use leaveners and eggs or they will, quite literally, flop.

The four basic ingredients can be separated into two groups: the liquefiers and the stabilizers. The liquefiers are the fat (butter, shortening, or oil) and the sugar. This division does not seem intuitive until you consider that when fats and sugars are heated, they melt. Fat tenderizes the mixture to yield a nice crumb, and both types of liquefiers also add important flavor—the "mouthfeel" that helps you feel sated. The stabilizers are the eggs and flour, which hold the product together. When heat is added to the stabilizers, the opposite reaction occurs: instead of melting, they set up or coagulate, lending structure and stability and, in the case of flour, gluten to the mix.

Chef Kate stressed the importance of having the ingredients at the right temperature. Butter should be at 75°F, liquids at 80°F to 90°F. If the butter is too warm, it will melt and fail to absorb air, making it impossible to cream into a light mass. But don't start with butter right out of the refrigerator, or the mixture will not incorporate well.

We all know that cookie cravings suddenly materialize from out of nowhere. What to do then? Kate had a ready answer for this, as for every emergency: If you've forgotten to take the butter out of the refrigerator and can't wait to start baking, put it in the microwave for 30 seconds per pound to soften it, or beat it gently with the paddle attachment of the mixer until it has warmed up sufficiently.

When making a creamed batter, the idea is to form an emulsion—a stable mixture of two ingredients that don't naturally mix. We think of this phenomenon when mixing oil and water for a vinaigrette, but it happens to be a principle in baking, too. Curdling will hurt the texture of cookies or cakes. It can occur if there is too much liquid, or if the liquid is added too quickly, before an emulsion can form.

The temperature of the liquid is equally important. It should not be cold, to avoid curdling the mixture. Eggs should be at room temperature, but if they come straight from the refrigerator they can always be heated by placing them briefly in warm water. Or you can crack them into a bowl and stir them over steam to warm slightly, but be careful not to cook them!

Chef Kate explained that the idea behind creaming is to have a level playing field. In the kitchen that means that all ingredients should be similar to each other in terms of temperature and density so that they don't experience too much shock on contact. So if you're using a firm ingredient such as almond paste, you should soften it first with a little water or egg to make it more like the creamed batter it will be stirred into.

Except when making the most delicate cakes, most American home bakers have not sifted flour for decades. But we learned that it is, in fact, a good practice to sift the dry ingredients, not so much to get rid of lumps as to incorporate air, which will make the finished product lighter.

Chef Kate advised us that sifting can be skipped for baked goods in which some density is desirable. She also warned us that more mixing is not always better. Batter should never be overmixed, or too much gluten will develop, resulting in a tough product. Liquid batters, as for muffins, should even have some lumps. The more liquid the batter, the tougher it can become from too much handling.

We paged through our course handouts until we got to the recipe for pound cake, which had been adapted from the original that gave the cake its name—a pound each of butter, sugar, and flour. All of the measurements were in ounces, except for the salt and baking powder, which were given in teaspoons. Everyone in the class had the same gut reaction: to convert those ounces to cups, so that we could see how much of each ingredient we needed. And our impulse was the point of the next segment of Kate's lecture: to teach us the value of weighing out ingredients, and to make us feel comfortable using scales. I thought of Fanny Farmer and the domestic science movement of the late nineteenth century, which revolutionized cooking in America. Farmer's insistence on using volume measures rather than weight has proved to be a disservice. Not only have generations of young cooks been brought up on precise measurements that thwart creativity, but bakers have a hard time getting accurate measures, since flours vary in weight depending on their moisture content.

Boot camp runs on a strict schedule, so when it was time for our 8:15 coffee break, we trooped outside into the still-raging snowstorm and across the square to the Continuing Ed dining room, where a beautiful spread of freshly baked croissants, blueberry and corn muffins, and Danish pastries awaited us. No one was hungry, having filled up on breakfast a mere two hours earlier, but the baked goods

smelled so enticing that we dove in and were not disappointed.

Over coffee I met Paige, from Williamsburg, Virginia, yet another seasoned boot camper who was back for more, a gift from her husband who no doubt was glad to be the beneficiary of the baked goods she loved to make in her spare time. Tall and attractive, Paige exuded an air of competence, which may have been explained by her job as an anesthesiologist. She spoke with a soft southern lilt. Unlike most of the campers, who were staying in the Super 8 Motel just down the road, Paige had a room in a CIA dorm. She confessed to having had a rough night, though her reasons were different from mine: she wasn't used to the undergraduate dorm life that gathered steam in the late evening hours.

I also met the lovely Nicole, who lived on New York's Upper East Side and worked as a fund-raiser for the nonprofit Robin Hood Foundation. Something in her face suggested pain or loss, yet this quality was appealing rather than distancing. We made small talk, each of us trying to explain in just a few words who we were and why we were there. The week at boot camp offered a return to the classroom, which for most of the group was welcome. For me, it felt like a haven from the narrow confines of academia—I would get to play in the kitchen! This was not my usual crowd, and I enjoyed that. Before we knew it, half an hour was up, and it was time to head back to class.

INTO THE BAKE SHOP

We now moved from the classroom into the kitchen, where Chef Kate gave us a quick tour. The kitchen was truly impressive in its organization. We saw the pot storage rooms, with all imaginable sizes of bowls and pans for stirring, whipping, boiling, baking, and

other processes that wouldn't be covered in our course; the dry storage room, lined with mega boxes of baking soda, baking powder, salt, and oats, massive jars of peanut butter and cans of shortening, giant blocks of almond paste and chocolate, and tubs of apricot jam; the immense walk-in refrigerators with slabs of sweet butter, whole flats of eggs, and bottles of milk and cream. Out in the kitchen, separate bins held granulated sugar and confectioners' sugar, all-purpose flour, pastry flour, cake flour, and bread flour. Each was carefully labeled. We learned which bins were for trash and which held food waste for recycling. Each group chose one of the butcher-block workstations that straddled either side of the massive gas stoves. Already we felt the heat from the pilot lights, which were never extinguished. We donned our paper toques, chef's aprons, and side towels.

Next came another surprise. I had assumed that since boot camp focused on basic skills, we would be creaming and mixing by hand, as I usually do at home. I prefer to mix by hand for several reasons. First, I enjoy feeling a connection to my ingredients that is not mediated by a machine, the noise of whose motor also diminishes the pleasure of my kitchen experience. Second, things can get messy when adding dry ingredients to a KitchenAid bowl, as flour tends to fly around the room and settle in your hair. Third, I like the workout that creaming by hand affords—it keeps my forearms taut and strong. But I have to admit that even with my workouts I don't have the patience that women once had to stir cake batter for one hundred vigorous strokes or beat biscuit dough for a full hour

to break down the gluten and make them tender. So my homemade pound cake batters are never as fluffy and light with air as those made with a stand mixer, and by the end of boot camp I had to concede that my home batters were never quite as tender, with as delicate a crumb, as those we prepared in class. It's the difference between a fine product and one with a professional edge. In the context of restaurant production, no chef would consider mixing batters by hand, but gradually I came to see the value of stand mixers even in the home kitchen.

Chef Kate had us gather at the weighing and mixing stations, where she explained the idiosyncrasies of the 20-quart Hobart heavy-duty mixers—we had to be sure to set the speed before turning on the machine. Kate was very good about using analogies to help us understand what we needed to do. Just as in a car you have to depress the clutch in order not to strip the gears, so with the Hobart we had to be sure not to change gears with the motor running. Some of the older mixers had timers and were programmed not to run at all if the timer was set at zero. The newer models had security cages that I found alienating in the way that they distanced the baker from her ingredients. No doubt they were the result of some random accident that had ended in litigation. From the mixers we moved on to the scales, which were of three kinds: balance, spring, and digital. The spring scale seemed far more straightforward than the balance, which required that we remember always to set the bowl on the left-hand balance, with the counterbalance on the right. For amounts over 1 pound, we would need to add weights. Not

surprisingly, we liked the small digital scale best, especially for its precision in amounts less than ¼ ounce.

Before we headed to our workstations, Chef Kate demonstrated a pound cake batter. She weighed out 12 ounces of butter and 12½ ounces of sugar, dumped them into the mixer bowl, and then proceeded to cream them, all the while explaining how patience is one of the greatest attributes a baker can have. At this Bob piped up that he didn't want to have to wait to cream things properly—he'd rather just dump everything into the bowl at once and be done with it. Nicole chirped in with a good-natured "Glad you're not on our team!" Bob's teammates looked worried.

When the mixture turned light, it was time to add the eggs. Again, they were measured not by unit but by weight. The recipe called for 9½ ounces of eggs, which seemed overly fussy to us. Whether Kate added the eggs too quickly or they were not at the proper temperature, I'm not sure, but they upset the balance and the mixture curdled slightly. No problem for Chef Kate! She brightened at the opportunity to show us a solution. She carried the bowl over to the stove and heated it slightly right over the gas flame until the mixture warmed up a little, all the while whisking it by hand. She cautioned us not to heat the batter too much or it would liquefy and we'd lose all the air we had just beaten in. Her implicit message seemed to be that baking was a matter of becoming comfortable with your ingredients, getting to know their properties and how they would react under different conditions.

The batter's balance restored, Chef Kate sifted the flour by tapping it through a tamis—a fine sieve—a process that is much faster than using a sifter with a handle or crank. She emphasized the importance of scraping the batter as it mixes. Especially in professional mixers, when ingredients are added from above, the batter on the bottom and sides of the bowl must continually be scraped to the top so that everything will be fully incorporated. The paddle should be scraped, too. I loved Chef Kate for doing that with her fingers.

At this point we met our assistants, the kitchen angels who made dirty dishes and pans disappear. They worked over three deep sinks: one to soak the pots in detergent, the next to rinse them, the last to dip them in disinfectant. One of the components of a CIA education is an externship of eighteen or more weeks, which each regular student must complete to earn a degree. Our assistant Suky had done hers at Thomas Keller's French Laundry restaurant in Napa Valley. She was wonderfully competent and loved everything about being in the kitchen. Patty, a student in the Pastry and Baking program, was very sweet and eager to help. Nell was just the opposite— resentful, sullen, and dour, the kind of scullery maid I'd always envisioned from Dickens novels, whose hands may not have been chilblained but whose nose was eternally out of joint. No amount of coaxing could bring her out of her funk.

We broke up into our groups; mine set to work making Cranberry Quick Bread. First we had to prepare the pans by greasing them with butter or shortening and dusting them with flour. The CIA has nifty preshaped loaf pan liners made of parchment, but even a flat piece of parchment or brown paper placed in the bottom of the pan will ensure that the loaf will slide out unscathed. Next we blithely began to cream our butter and sugar. It had all looked so easy in Chef Kate's hands, but no sooner did we add eggs to the batter than we were faced with a curdled mess. Undaunted, we repaired the batter by holding it over the flame, as Kate had taught us. I call that a successful lesson.

As a regular denizen of the CIA, my teammate Emily knew about the famous Mudslide cookies sold at the student-run Apple Pie Bakery Café. They were awesome, she said, so with Chef Kate's approval we decided to make those as well as the Chocolate Cherry Chunk. The Mudslides were a great choice: this was definitely a pop-in-the-mouth, scrape-the-bowl, lick-the-spoon kind of batter. And no wonder—it held nearly 3 pounds of chocolate. I offered to melt the chocolate and butter, taking a shortcut that I knew was not condoned in this kitchen: I put them right over the gas flame instead of in a double boiler. By stirring constantly over very low heat I knew I could keep the chocolate from scorching, but I still hoped that Chef Kate wouldn't see me melting it this way as she made her rounds among the groups. Meanwhile, Emily fetched the remaining ingredients, and June mixed them in the big Hobart. With a giant spatula, we deftly folded in the dry ingredients by hand and portioned the cookies on baking sheets

that we had spread with parchment. Then we put them in the freezer to firm up.

Emily, June, and I were now on a roll. In fact, we worked so smoothly together that we finished early and decided to make a variation on the basic pound cake by adding almond paste. We creamed the paste with a little of the butter to make it less stiff and easier to incorporate. Then we creamed the butter and sugar and added the almond paste and remaining ingredients. No sooner had we scraped the last of the batter into the prepared pans than it was 11:00—time for lunch! We all groaned. We hated to interrupt the rhythm of the morning, but at the CIA, schedule is sacrosanct. We would have liked to skip lunch, but Chef Kate promised to stay in the kitchen to make sure that our cookies and cakes and quick breads didn't burn.

We had no choice but to take off our aprons and toques and head back to the Continuing Ed building, where we fell into line with the regular students. Each three-week class session features a special dining theme. Our boot camp was lucky enough to coincide with the theme Cuisines of the Americas. Today was New England day, with a choice of Johnnycakes with Mushroom Sauce, Cod Cakes, or Pot Roast, all served as a full plated meal. We gave our order to Chef Phil Delaplane, the expediter who called it into the kitchen and then, with much barbed humor and bantering, handed out the plates covered with stainless-steel cloches to keep the food warm. Two tables had been reserved for our class in the dining room. There, we could request our choice of two soups or a salad, and

1. Granulated sugar smoothes out the fat and leaves tiny air holes behind, which lighten the baked product. Batters should be creamed on medium speed, using the paddle attachment. It was a revelation to learn that not all baked goods are creamed to the same degree. If you cream the mixture until it is nearly white and very fluffy, it may bake up drier than you'd like. If you don't cream the batter enough, it will be heavy. This is where the art lies—knowing exactly when to stop mixing. Although the degree of creaming is important for baked goods such as pound cakes, we were relieved to learn that it is less crucial when making cookies.

2. Add eggs gradually, 25 percent of the total at a time, so that the liquid doesn't overwhelm the batter. It is important to scrape after each addition to make sure that all of the ingredients are well mixed. Any additional liquids are added slowly, often in alternation with dry ingredients. The dry ingredients are added first, then a little liquid, and then more dry, and so on, ending with the dry ingredients. This gradual process keeps the mixture from curdling.

$\mathcal{3}$. Cookie batters that can simply be dropped from spoons onto a baking sheet are often referred to as drop cookies, but we learned that you can take certain steps to make sure you've got cookies ready to bake at a moment's notice. Instead of dropping the dough, mound it on a piece of plastic wrap or parchment paper and roll it into logs. Let the logs of dough chill, either in the refrigerator or in the freezer, until they are firm. Then simply slice the dough into rounds about ½ inch thick and bake.

$\mathcal{4}$. Baked goods aren't really finished baking until they've cooled. Give the cookies a minute or two to settle a little, then lift them from the pan to cooling racks. Cookies can bend or stick to each other when they are hot, so don't stack them up until they have reached room temperature.

The recipe for Chocolate Chunk Cookies, shown here, is on page 211.

feast on the breads and desserts arrayed the length of the tables—the fruits of the morning's baking classes.

Over lunch we learned more about our fellow boot campers. Alyssa was commuting to camp from a town just across the Mid-Hudson Bridge from Hyde Park. She worked part time as a speech pathologist in the public schools but also ran a bed-and-breakfast inn. She had signed up for baking boot camp because she was tired of making the same things for breakfast and wanted to perfect her bread-making techniques. Her boyfriend had given her the package as a Hanukkah gift.

James and Susan made an inseparable pair. Old friends from eastern Massachusetts, they had traveled to boot camp together and insisted on being in the same work group. James published a chain of weekly newspapers; Susan was an avid home cook. Both had already taken the cooking boot camp and were back for the baking round. They were, in fact, cooking-class junkies, having just come from a weekend bread-making course at the King Arthur Flour kitchens in Vermont. In the trunk of their car they had some pain au levain dough that they planned to bake in the CIA ovens.

Lunch was over at noon, and we trudged back through the courtyard to the Colavita kitchen. The wild snowstorm still raged, but back inside the sleek stainless-steel kitchen, everything had its place. I felt as though we were in a strange inversion of a snow globe, where the snow swirled outside the artificial space within.

While we were gone, Chef Kate had set out the baked quick breads, pound cakes, and cookies for us to admire and taste. Not that we had much appetite after such a large, and early, lunch, but somehow we managed to eat those cookies. The Mudslides were the hands-down favorite.

Chef Kate asked us to look closely at the pound cakes. She pointed out how the batter will crest if the oven is hot, because the sides bake fast, pushing the center of the batter up into a dome. She also pointed out sugar speckles on the top of some of the pound cakes and quick breads, a sign that the sugar had not entirely dissolved in the mixing—something we should try to avoid in the future. Kate admonished us to keep the edges of the pan clean after the batter has been poured in so that it doesn't get hung up on the pan as it attempts to rise.

All in all, said Chef Kate, sounding like the perfect mother and teacher, we had done well and she was pleased with our results. We cleaned up the kitchen, tossed our aprons and side towels into the laundry bin, and set our toques aside for the next day.

AFTERNOON LECTURE
BREAD

Our guest lecturer for the afternoon was Chef Eric Kastel, who had come to tell us all about bread. The minute he entered, I saw that his toque was different—it came to a point on top rather than being rounded like Chef Kate's. Back in the early nineteenth century, the great French chef Antonin Carême had insisted on a hierarchy of toques to distinguish the chefs from the lowlier cooks. The taller the toque, the more important the wearer—Carême's own toque was said to have been eighteen inches high. So here was the hierarchy of chef's hats in action, nearly two hundred years after Carême!

The CIA, it turns out, is traditional in other ways, too. The late-nineteenth-century chef Auguste Escoffier followed Carême in affirming the importance of uniforms in the kitchen, and this tradition remains very much in evidence at the Culinary today. Proper dress is a mark of professionalism, and students are faulted for tying their neckerchiefs improperly or for failing to wear their paper toques. Etiquette is similarly important. Even among themselves, the chefs address one another as "Chef." Uniforms, ranks—the idea of boot camp made sense to me when I thought about the school's near-military model: rigid order is maintained in the storerooms and kitchens, uniforms are kept neat, students and faculty are perfectly punctual. They are also unfailingly polite and cognizant of rank.

Perhaps it was because of his tall toque, but we felt a frisson when Chef Eric entered the classroom. A lecturing instructor in baking and pastry arts, he had previously worked at a number of noteworthy places, including Daniel Leader's artisanal bakery, Bread Alone, in nearby Boiceville, New York.

Chef Eric began by echoing Chef Kate's early-morning admonitions about the importance of scaling—weighing the ingredients instead of measuring them by volume. After the British Commonwealth converted from the imperial system to the metric system in the 1970s, attempts were made to introduce metrification to the United States as well. But they failed miserably. American home cooks cling to their battered aluminum cups, their teaspoons and tablespoons, which offer a nostalgic connection to kitchens of the past. Little do they care that a cup of one flour is unequal to a cup of another, that their weights can differ tremendously depending on moisture content and degree of refinement. Scaling is imperative in professional baking, however, since it always yields consistent results.

After reiterating this point, Chef Eric began to talk about the breads we were going to make: baguette, ciabatta, multigrain rye, semolina, honey-walnut whole wheat, durum semolina, sourdough buttermilk wheat, and sunflower-seed rolls. What all of these breads from different traditions have in common is the use of a poolish, a pre-fermentation technique that helps the bread develop more flavor. This odd-looking word refers simply to a mixture of flour and water (usually in equal proportion) and a little yeast, which is allowed to sit overnight to ferment slightly. A poolish differs from another flavor booster, the Italian biga, in that it is more liquid. Home cooks will recognize a poolish as a starter or sponge.

Chef Eric's passion was infectious. He rhapsodized about bread, and about butter on bread. He rued the then-popular low-carb movement that was giving bread a bad name: "It's not the bread, it's the lack of exercise!" If "flower power" was the mantra for some of us who came of age in the sixties, "flour power" was Chef Eric's refrain. He considered flour to be like a god in its ability to create the sustenance of life. Because flour is the most important component of baked goods, and of lean bread in particular, where there are no fats to add flavor, the quality of the flour is critical. Chef Eric proceeded to give us a crash course in the many different kinds of flour available, from a variety of wheat flours, both hard and soft, to flours made from other grains, such as rye, barley, and buckwheat. We learned that flours made from hard wheat contain 11 to 15 percent protein, with more gluten and less starch. By contrast, soft wheat flours contain 6 to 10 percent protein and therefore are better for tender baked goods such as pastries and layer cakes, in which the vigorous action of expanding gluten would toughen the product. Soft-wheat flour with its lower gluten and higher starch content is used for cake flour and pastry flour. Cake flour has 6 to 7 percent protein, while pastry flour has 8 to 9 percent. Pastry flour looks a bit more crumbly than cake flour. Serious bakers play around with different flours to discover the exact proportions of hard and soft wheat flours they like, or, in the case of bread making, of wheat and other flours. That way they can control the final texture and taste and get the crumb that they're looking for.

Chef Eric had prepared an array of different flours for us to examine, and the differences in texture were amazing. I scooped up a handful of bread flour and squeezed it in my fist, as Chef Eric instructed us to do. Starch, as we had learned from Chef Kate that morning, is a stabilizer that binds, and because of its low starch content, the bread flour did not hold together in my hand as the pastry flour did. All-purpose flour, the kind most home cooks use, is a blend of half bread and half pastry flour (in other words, half hard wheat and half soft wheat flour), with a protein content of around 10 percent. Chef Eric explained that his own personal bugaboo is bleached flour—he's a bread man, after all—and that's why he disdains cake flour, which is always bleached. Because bleaching leaches the flavor from flour, it's disastrous for good bread, where the taste of grain must come through.

To make his point, Chef Eric walked us through the commercial bleaching process. I felt as though I were listening to a contemporary version of Upton Sinclair's *The Jungle*—here was a scary industry adulterating our food, but this time it was the flour mills rather than the meat processors. Granted, Chef Eric didn't talk about rodents in the flour, but in his account the chemicals loomed equally horrific. He told us of a German study that demonstrated how bleaching at factories near the Rhine contributes to environmental pollution, and how the chemicals even get into the water piped to children's day care centers. Meanwhile, the pesticides used in farming the wheat also get into the food chain, perhaps contributing to the development of some cancers. His tales were pretty grim. Chef Eric insists on using flour made only from organic wheat. At his urging, I took up a handful of unbleached flour. I really did see its pale golden beauty and sniff its wheaten scent. By contrast, the bleached flour did not have an earthy smell—it had virtually no odor at all.

The texture of bread is, of course, also affected by the leavening agent, which in bread

Types of wheat flours (clockwise from upper left): whole wheat, rye, pastry, cake, buckwheat, bread, and all-purpose (center)

making usually means yeast. Chef Eric's feelings about yeast were as strong as they were about flour. He does not like the newfangled rapid-rise yeast that is touted as a time-saver for harried folks who want to bake. Rapid-rise gives a quick burst of energy, but then it dies. Chef Eric far prefers other yeasts that develop more slowly. We were treated to a detailed lesson on the different kinds of yeast and learned that Eric is partial to fresh compressed yeast, which gives bread a wonderful aroma. Unfortunately, this type of yeast has a shelf life of only eight to ten weeks, making it least suitable for bakers who just like to bake an occasional loaf of bread.

Compressed yeast should be tan in color, not gray, as gray indicates the beginning of spoilage. It should also be crumbly, due to the 66 percent water it contains. Next in the hier-

archy comes instant dry yeast, which when properly stored will last for a year. Only one-third the amount of dry yeast is needed in proportion to fresh yeast. Chef Eric feels that instant dry yeast works just as well as compressed, even if it doesn't yield quite the same depth of aroma. Finally, there is active dry yeast, which Chef Eric likes least. To activate the living cells within, this type of yeast must be moistened, so it is always mixed beforehand with water.

Eric gave us a formula for figuring out substitutes for the different kinds of dry yeasts: 4 ounces of active dry yeast $\times$ 0.83 = 3.32 ounces of instant dry yeast. In other words, you need 17 percent less instant dry yeast than active dry yeast. We muddled over this equation for a while—none of us had expected a math class—and decided that one reason professional chefs like their digital scales so much is that they can register fractions of ounces or grams, making conversions automatic. Otherwise the calculations can be pretty confusing. Chef Eric ended his discussion of yeasts with a description of the European dry yeasts SAF gold and SAF red. SAF gold is preferred for breads that are high in fat, such as brioche; high in acid, such as sourdough; or high in sugar, such as breakfast buns. SAF red is good for regular dough. Although the gold also works, SAF red is better for breads that are more difficult to leaven.

We thought that we had the ingredients for bread down pat at this point, but Chef Eric warned us that the water we use in making bread is important, too. It can affect the final outcome of the loaf. If hard water is added, its high mineral content can slow down fermentation. Eric recommended using filtered or softened water, though he cautioned that if the water is too soft the dough won't hold together as well. Other liquids can be used in place of water, but they are generally for enriched, rather than lean, breads.

At last it was time to mix! Like a consummate scientist, Chef Eric extracted his digital thermometer from the loop on the sleeve of his chef's coat to take the temperature of the dry flour. It was 69°F. Then he tested the water, which at 62°F was considerably cooler. The next step was to decide which kind of yeast we wanted to use. Compressed yeast had to be mixed with water first to break it up, while active dry yeast would need to be rehydrated in water before being mixed with the flour. Only instant dry yeast could be

added directly to the flour. Chef Eric cautioned us that at this initial stage of mixing, it's important that the yeast not come into direct contact with any ingredients that might slow down its action, including salt, eggs, or fats. I was quickly disabused of my romantic notions of baking as a Zen-like activity, a meditative interlude in an otherwise frantic day, as Chef Eric turned to the large stand mixer that would not only mix the dough but knead it.

Eric began mixing on low speed to disperse the yeast, then gradually added water. He explained that he likes to mix the dough this way for 4 minutes or so, because low speed creates less friction and shows less aggression toward the dough. Periodically he stopped the mixer to scrape the bottom of the bowl, the only way to be sure that the dough would be evenly mixed. When the dough began to pull away from the sides of the bowl, Chef Eric increased the speed to medium to begin developing the gluten. He took the dough's temperature again. It was 73°F. He was aiming for 80°F, a goal that would take 12 to 15 minutes to reach by hand. But after only 2 or 3 minutes of machine mixing on medium, the dough was already at 77°F. Chef Eric could sense what we were thinking: why not get up to the desired temperature even faster by mixing on high speed? That, he told us, was a definite no-no. Under no circumstances were we to use high speed. We were to be patient as the machine mixed on medium to develop the gluten into elastic strands. I guess this was where the Zen came in.

At that point he taught us a helpful visual cue. We were to look for a "window" that tears when the dough is stretched. This "window" is really just a thin membrane of dough translucent enough to allow light to filter through. The minute it forms, the dough is ready. Too much mixing, and the color of the dough will begin to change from a nice golden shade to whitish, and the dough will feel tough. If the temperature rises much beyond 80°F, you've entered into a danger zone. If it approaches 84°F, then the bread is close to breaking, which means that all the long strands of gluten that you have so carefully developed will collapse, and the dough will no longer be buoyant.

As soon as the dough is well mixed, shape it into a ball—gently, so that all the air isn't knocked out. Place the ball in a lightly greased bowl and cover with plastic wrap so that a skin doesn't form (a skin will prevent the dough from expanding, so it won't rise well). The bowl should be large enough to give the dough plenty of room to expand. Leave the dough to rise in a warm, but not hot, place for a couple of hours. You'll know when the dough has risen sufficiently when pressing it with your finger leaves a deep indentation that does not fill itself in. Contrary to everything I had been taught, Chef Eric said that dough should never be punched down before its final shaping. If you punch it, you'll expel all of the gases that formed as it rose. You want to leave some of them in. "Always handle dough gently!" he admonished.

After the loaf has been shaped, it's a good idea to brush it gently with an egg wash made by whisking a whole egg and a yolk with a little water and salt. The egg wash seals the bread and promotes expansion. If you want a shiny crust, coat the loaf two times, and then brush it twice more before the bread goes into the oven. When the bread is ready to bake, score the crust so that it will expand evenly. Professional bakers use a lame, a sharp razor-like knife, but any sharp knife will do. Score the top of the loaf at a 45° angle—don't just make a slit.

Chef Eric conceded that bread turns out much better in professional ovens, but he shared a few tricks to help us produce loaves with good crumb and crisp crusts at home. First, just before baking the bread, place a couple of ice cubes in a hot pan in the bottom of the oven. As they melt, they'll gradually create steam. To get the best rise, the oven should be well vented, especially toward the end of the baking. The problem with modern ovens is that they're so well sealed that breads and soufflés don't rise as well as they would in a less airtight environment. To counteract this design, open the oven door slightly when the loaf is about three-quarters browned (caramelized) on top. This will allow for a little airflow and ensure a good crust. If you don't open the door, the steamy environment will yield a soft crust, which may be appropriate for some enriched breads but is undesirable for lean doughs.

Chef Eric shared one final tip. If you want bread that tastes freshly baked but don't have time to make any, freeze an extra loaf the next time you bake, then allow it to thaw, unwrapped, at room temperature. Heat the bread directly on a rack in the oven for 8 minutes at 450°F, and voilà! Everyone will think that you've spent the day in the kitchen.

DINNER AT RISTORANTE CATERINA DE' MEDICI

After Chef Eric's lecture I felt a new respect for flour and yeast, and also for temperature, which can determine the success or failure of the baked goods. We gathered our binders and notebooks. Chef Kate had told us that we could accelerate our learning by going to the library to watch instructional videos on baking, but I had had enough. I was beat, yet after the intensity of the day the free hours until dinnertime seemed almost purposeless. Just as we were getting into our coats, Lisa Paquin appeared in the classroom to propose a master storeroom tour, an offer I couldn't resist. The Culinary is justifiably proud of its storerooms, which house amazing quantities of foodstuffs and materials for the Institute's thirty-nine kitchens. The purchasing, storage, and expediting of ingredients must be expertly coordinated so that each class has what it needs for a successful day of cooking or baking. The evening before a class, it's up to the instructor to let the expediter know how many pounds of butter, bags of raisins, and blocks of chocolate are needed for baking cookies. If inspiration strikes in the middle of class, it can be problematic if ingredients are not on hand.

My head pounding from the day's information, I wanted nothing more than to go for a run after the storeroom tour. But that proved impossible. Although the snow had stopped, few paths had been cleared. I decided to visit the student recreation center instead. This new center was built in part to address the need of students to work off some of the extra calories that are an inevitable part of their study. It has state-of-

the-art weight rooms, a jogging track, tennis and racquetball courts, and a six-lane swimming pool. The center's large spaces are converted into lecture and dining halls for the numerous conferences held at the Culinary every year. I took advantage of my special status to key myself into the faculty/staff locker room instead of using the grungier student facilities. The jogging track looped around an upstairs balcony that overlooked a large hall. Down below, students were busy setting tables and arranging a lavish buffet under the watchful eye of their instructor, who boomed out instructions about the proper placement of cutlery, napkins, and glasses.

The run felt good, a shower even better. Despite my early-morning haste, I'd had the foresight to bring a change of clothes from the hotel, knowing that I wouldn't want to drive back again through the snow. What a relief to put on a tight, flattering skirt and a clingy sweater! I was starting to feel like myself again. I made my way back to the Colavita Center in time for our 6:30 dinner. Most of the other campers were already there. Was I the only one who would have liked to wait to eat until 7:30 or 8:00? I was hardly hungry, but as I had discovered earlier in the day, at boot camp mealtimes are accelerated, as well as inviolable.

One of the attractions of boot camp is the opportunity to dine at a different CIA restaurant each night. That first evening we ate at the newest one, the Ristorante Caterina de' Medici. We were particularly looking forward to the meal because all day Bob had waxed rhapsodic about the huge Tuscan grilled ribeye steak he had eaten there during his last boot camp. We gathered at a long table in the restaurant's private dining room, whose deep yellow hue felt warm and inviting. Menus were distributed. All of the dishes were listed in Italian, with English translations below. I was immediately drawn to Crudo di Tonno alla Battuta—Thinly Sliced Raw Tuna with Capers, Herbs, Lemon, and Olive Oil—but couldn't decide easily on an entrée. The Branzino con Cavolo Nero alla Chiantigiana—Striped Bass with Tuscan Kale, Pancetta, and Chianti Sauce—certainly looked good. Most of us were silent as we contemplated the menu, but not poor Bob. His ribeye was no longer on the menu! He had to settle for a strip loin steak, which he washed down with copious amounts of red wine. Bob's appetite was large, his delight in food even larger. His expansiveness seemed to know no bounds as he finagled tastes of most of our meals and ordered an extra serving of rosemary potatoes. A few of us exchanged worried looks: what if he suddenly had a heart attack from so much rich food? On the other hand, what's life for if not living it large?

Our group of twelve included three other campers I hadn't gotten to know earlier in the day. Mary, a 1983 CIA graduate now working as an editor there, had long been curious about the boot camp program, so she decided to experience it for herself. Nancy and Lenore, at sixty-something the oldest in our class, were devoted friends. Their hair was coiffed in traditional styles, and they clearly took pains with their appearance.

They had worked together for years in Pennsylvania, but then Nancy had remarried and moved to a town not far from Hyde Park. Lenore had just retired. She was visiting Nancy, now also retired and an active soup kitchen volunteer. This was Lenore's first time at boot camp, and she seemed tentative, but Nancy was a veteran; as she gaily announced, "I do boot camps!" She also announced, "I can't bake, but I make a great pot roast." That's why she had decided it was time she learned how to work with flour. Nancy and Lenore spent a lot of time tête-à-tête, laughing together about things the rest of us were not privy to. When we commented on their mutual delight, Nancy explained that "husbands can never replace girlfriends." And she said she should know, since she'd had two of the former.

The student servers were a little unsure of themselves, being on the first day of their rotation, but what they lacked in aptitude they made up for in charm. We were each poured a glass of Orvieto to begin the meal. My tuna carpaccio arrived glistening and lovely, but too heavy a hand had been used with the olive oil and lemon dressing, so the flavor of the tuna was lost. For my main course I wound up choosing Pollo al Mattone—Chicken Under a Brick, pressed and grilled until crisp. Everyone's hands-down favorite was the broccoli rabe sautéed in olive oil with garlic. At Bob's urging, we ordered extra servings for the table.

Contemplating my fellow campers, I could already see allegiances forming. Nancy and Lenore seemed like long-lost sisters.

They decided to forgo dessert and leave early because of the weather. James, Susan, and Bob were accustomed to keeping others at bay with their quick repartee. Calm, centered Emily gravitated toward gentle Nicole, who seemed to be seeking a haven in the camp. June strode along fairly oblivious to everyone else, which surprised me, given her background in psychology. And me? I'm not sure what the others thought. I was tense, and so I might have seemed stuck up. I worried that I wouldn't be able to shed my academic skin enough to relate well to everyone. But the main reason I was having a hard time relaxing was that I hadn't revealed my role at the boot camp. I felt duplicitous, like a spy on some secret assignment that would result in an exposé. I decided I had to announce who I was and what I was doing. So, heart pounding, I just blurted out: "You all will probably be interested to know that I'm actually here because I'm writing a book about the boot camp experience. You'll star in it. I hope you'll share your impressions with me!"

Reactions were mixed, from delight to wariness. Bob seemed suddenly to clam up, though that may have been my imagination. Alyssa was excited to meet a writer but wanted practical information: What was I looking for? What kinds of things would I say about them? Of course I had to admit that I didn't yet have a clue. Paige took the news in stride. In surgery, she's used to dealing with more mortal issues. Nicole loved the idea but feared that her life wasn't glamorous enough. She wanted me to write that she had been a Hollywood stripper who saw the light and gave up the den of iniquity for work helping others. James stiffened. When we left the table, he drew me aside to tell me that I couldn't possibly use his real name—he had a professional reputation to uphold.

It was time for dessert. We were each poured a glass of sweet Asti di Nobile, a lovely wine that loosened our tongues. Suddenly complaints came pouring out. Several campers felt disgruntled that the wine was doled out so sparingly—a notice at the bottom of our menus said that anything beyond the single glass offered per course would be at our own expense. Considering that the boot camp cost nearly $1,850, this policy felt stingy. We'd had a grueling day, it was the dead of winter, and we wanted to indulge. This complaint led to other gripes—the fact that Barnes and Noble runs the CIA bookstore and offers a 10 percent discount only to regular students and not to us, and that we were made to park in Siberia, even in a snowstorm. For the cost of the course, shouldn't we be allowed to park nearby?

Gripes behind us (for now), our conversation gave way to a discussion of the other boot camps that several campers had attended. All of them agreed that the cooking boot camp was much more strenuous, and considerably more stressful, since testing and competition were built into the course. They found the baking boot camp to be much more low-key. I was stunned. From my perspective, the day had been intense—but then, this group of people was intense, too. The week was not going to be mellow and low-key. Already many of our group had demonstrated a need to perform. But perhaps things would settle down tomorrow. We said our goodnights and inched home over the slick, snowy streets.

Dining room of the Ristorante Caterina de' Medici

chapter 3
THE RUBBED DOUGH METHOD

After the rigors of the previous day I decided to bypass the lavish breakfast for a few extra minutes of sleep. I would simply grab a cup of coffee and hold out for the delicious pastries that I knew would be awaiting us at the morning coffee break. Even so, when the alarm went off at 6:00, I found it nearly impossible to shake myself from sleep. Pulling on my chef's uniform, I was determined to spare myself a glance in the mirror—though that might have woken me up.

Siberia seemed neither as remote nor as forbidding as it had in the snowstorm the day before. Once inside Roth Hall, I downed my coffee and headed to class along the labyrinthine corridors that already seemed familiar. Chef Kate looked as cheerful and energetic as ever. By contrast, my classmates seemed anxious, which surprised me—last night's dinner had broken the ice, and I expected greater ease among us. It soon became clear that the nervousness had nothing to do with group dynamics. Everyone was simply afraid of making piecrust, the lesson of the day. Since we were now masters of creaming, it was time to learn a second basic baking method: rubbed dough. Each group would practice making pie dough, and then half of us would make biscuits, the other half scones.

Pies happen to be my favorite thing to bake. In the spring, as soon as the first rhubarb shoots up in our garden, I transform it into pie. In summer I pile crusts high with strawberries or blueberries or raspberries. Winter finds me making lemon meringue and cream pies, the richer the better to soothe the dark days. But it's at Thanksgiving

when I really lose control. Since I can never choose among apple, pumpkin, buttermilk, pecan, maple syrup, and pear pies, I usually end up making them all. And since people have always admired my crusts, I didn't feel nervous about the lesson, just curious about what I would learn.

ENSURING TENDER, FLAKY CRUSTS

Chef Kate explained what the rubbed dough method entails: incorporating large amounts of fat into flour to achieve a tender result. Fat is cut into flour for piecrusts, biscuits, and scones. Piecrusts can be flaky or crumbly, but they should never be tough. The texture of the baked crust depends on the size of the pieces of fat that are left in the flour: the larger the pieces, the flakier the crust. As she had done in her lecture on the creaming method, Chef Kate taught us the science behind the art. When the fat melts during baking, it leaves pockets of air, which expand as the temperature rises. It's only logical, then, that larger pockets of air would yield a lighter finished product. Smaller air pockets give rise to a more crumbly texture. In any case, the fat should be cold so that it will melt during the baking process, not before, and thereby lighten the dough.

One of the things I liked about Chef Kate was that she wasn't at all doctrinaire. With three young children, a demanding job, and a husband into "muscle cars" (as she put it), she was all for taking shortcuts when necessary. We all gasped when she told us that she is not above using cake mixes. Her cardinal rule is not to pooh-pooh what fits into your life. Such practical advice was welcome, if unexpected, in a course designed to teach from-scratch methods. Expanding on her belief that saving time is a good thing, Kate told us that she often cuts butter into tablespoon-sized pieces, which she freezes for future use. When she wants to make a piecrust in short order, she can work the butter right into the dough without thawing it first.

The morning lecture over, we trooped upstairs to the coffee room, where I was not disappointed by the array of breakfast pastries. I was glad for the morning break—not only was I hungry but I needed a second cup of coffee to perk me up. The coffee was strong. The pastries included muffins as well as apricot and cheese Danish. As I bit into a blueberry muffin I realized that I was already judging the pastries in a new way. The day before I had merely concerned myself with how good they tasted, but today I was testing the crumb—was it sufficiently tender?—and examining the caramelized top of the muffin to find any telltale sugar speckles. Our group chatted easily. I learned that Alyssa's boyfriend was an amateur home brewer. Susan's parents owned a large baking supply house; she had grown up surrounded by fine equipment and couldn't bring herself to use flimsy pans. Bob's elderly mother had recently moved close by so that he could take care of her.

Back in the kitchen, it was time for Chef Kate's demo. She weighed out 3 pounds of all-purpose flour on the balance scale, then dumped it onto the table, making a well in the center of the pile. Into the well she dropped 2 pounds of butter that she had previously cut into chunks. Kate noted that she sometimes uses a mixture of butter and chilled shortening, in which case she cuts in the harder butter before adding the shortening. The advantage of using some shortening is that it's softer than butter, and therefore easier to handle, but it doesn't have good flavor and can leave a waxy feel in the mouth. So Chef Kate advised us not to use shortening alone, or even predominantly, for our piecrusts.

She used her bench scraper to cut in the butter. Actually, her movements were much more like chopping than cutting. She wasn't at all gingerly with the dough, which surprised me. I'd always thought that the real secret to a tender crust was to handle the dough as little as possible, but Chef Kate wasn't timid. The other surprising thing was that she left the butter in large, walnut-sized chunks. I had always thought that the fat needed to end up in pea-sized lumps that were more fully incorporated into the flour, so that the mixture looked sandy, or like cornmeal, as recipes often describe it. Kate called this kind of sandy mixture a "mealy" pie dough and acknowledged that some people prefer its melt-in-the-mouth crumb to the flaky texture of the pie dough she was demonstrating. In "mealy" doughs, fat coats the flour, thereby preventing much gluten from forming; in effect, the fat shortens the protein strands by restricting their development. The end result is a tender crust but not a flaky one. Suddenly a light went off in my head. I had never attached literal meaning to the word "shortening" before.

When cutting—or chopping—the butter into the flour, Chef Kate was careful not to use a stirring or mixing motion, which would develop the gluten. Likewise, she sprinkled the water gradually onto the butter and flour mixture, cautioning us not to use too much, because water also encourages the development of gluten strands. She advised us not to use our fingers to work the mixture because our body heat would melt the fat. At this, June, the psychologist, called out, "My mother was wrong about even more than I realized!" But no sooner had Kate made her pronouncement than she took the dough in her hands and worked it until it more or less held together. I thought about challenging her on this apparent contradiction but figured it was part of her non-doctrinaire approach. The mixture looked like a shaggy mass, not at all what I considered ready, but Kate emphasized that it's important not to overmix the dough. I realized then why she

hadn't used the stand mixer: the machines are so powerful that they could reduce the dough to a tough lump in twenty seconds flat. She wrapped the dough tightly in plastic wrap and then pressed it into a disk, once again using more force than I would have thought prudent. But Kate was the teacher, and I admired her bold technique. She set the dough aside to rest, or "relax," as she called it. At home, she said, she might put it into the freezer to use anytime in the next six weeks.

Chef Kate explained that a brief period of rest before rolling out the dough keeps the piecrust from shrinking because it relaxes any gluten strands that might have developed. Although the dough we made didn't have to be refrigerated before baking, for maximum rise it's best to keep it cold so that the fat will be hard and melt only when exposed to heat. Alyssa, who owned the B&B, asked why pie dough can't simply be patted into the pan, like a shortbread crust for bar cookies. Kate answered that the action of rolling helps to develop the layers of flour and fat. Under heat, these layers expand and separate to make the crust flaky. The same chemistry occurs with puff pastry, though much more dramatically.

The shameful truth is, I just didn't feel like making apple pie. Was I becoming a difficult student? I had spied some tart Morello cherries in the freezer, and even though it was the dead of winter, I was drawn to them. One of the advantages of baking at a professional school is that a wide range of products is constantly on hand, ones to which the home cook would not necessarily have access. I always bake a cherry pie for the Fourth of July, not out of patriotism but because that is when the tart New York State cherries come on the market. Here, in mid-winter, I thought it would be fun to have a cherry pie for Washington's birthday, and Chef Kate graciously agreed. Besides, I wanted a chance to try my hand at the lattice crust we'd just learned to make.

PIE FILLINGS AND MERINGUES

No matter what type of pie or pastry crust we planned to use, we still had to learn the intricacies of various fillings and toppings for pies.

The recipe for apple pie filling printed in our manual called for 2 pounds of EPQ apples. EPQ, or "edible portion quantity," was another new expression for me. It's a food-service term for the usable part of the apple—apples that have already been peeled and cored. Two pounds of EPQ apples differs from 2 pounds of apples with peels and cores still intact, since the peels and cores make up part of the product's weight. The recipe suggested a mixture of Granny Smith and Golden Delicious for the best flavor and texture: Granny Smiths are firm and tart, while Golden Delicious apples are soft and sweet. Other combinations would work well, too, Kate noted, depending on how custardy a texture we like in our pies. She often uses Northern Spy.

I was surprised to find two thickeners listed among the ingredients: both cornstarch and tapioca starch (which is simply finely ground tapioca). I asked Chef Kate why there would be two starches, and whether tapioca starch yields a different texture than cornstarch. She couldn't answer the question. The mark of a truly confident teacher is the willingness to admit what she doesn't know, followed by the initiative to find out. Chef Kate sat right down and shot off an e-mail to Peter Greweling, a fellow CIA chef. Greweling answered immediately, and Kate printed out his response. I was struck first by his professional jargon, and then by the depth of his knowledge:

> *Hey, that is the formula that I developed for the apple pie opening. The advantage is that by using a root starch and a seed starch, you get some of the advantages of each: that is, the cornstarch retrogrades upon cooling, resulting in a gelled texture so that you can cut a slice and it will hold its shape. Too much of this effect, though, leaves you with a cloudy, too firm, short-textured filling that expels moisture...not a pleasant thing. The root starch does not retrograde nearly as much, so it stays clear and somewhat fluid upon cooling. If you use only root starch in a pie filling, it will get a mucilaginous texture and will not slice cleanly, also not a great result. By using some of each, I have approxi-*

mated a modified starch, creating a mixture that will gel but remains mostly clear. I selected tapioca because it does not tend to become as snotty as other root starches, and cornstarch for its availability and price. Hope this helps.

I knew I'd be rereading this intricate answer more than once before I fully understood it. But, in the meantime, I loved the image of "snotty" root starches.

I sampled a cherry. It was so tart that I had to keep adding sugar to reach a degree of sweetness that didn't make me pucker. I just poured the sugar in, without weighing it first or even measuring. Definitely a no-no! I felt as though I was adding too much, but I didn't want to risk a sour pie. A second problem was that the frozen cherries didn't behave as nicely as fresh ones; they gave off a lot of liquid as they thawed. When I filled my piecrust I had to use a slotted spoon to scoop up the cherries so that they wouldn't be drowning in juice.

While I made my cherry pie, other groups worked on pecan pie and pumpkin pie. Chef Kate advised us to use cheese pumpkins, which have firm, sweet flesh. The pumpkins grown for Halloween are insipid and watery, so it is better to use canned pumpkin than a jack o'lantern from the farm. With fresh cheese pumpkins, it's easy enough to prepare them for pie: just cut them in half, scoop out the seeds, and bake them until the flesh is tender. Mix the baked pumpkin with spices, eggs, and cream, and your filling is ready.

We dispatched the cherry, pumpkin, and pecan pies into the ovens with little ado (and,

I should add, my cherry pie turned out delicious). Then it was time for the lemon meringue pie. As it happens, lemon meringue was the first pie I ever baked, when I was around seven years old. I wanted to make it for my father since lemon meringue was his favorite. The meringue wept. Over the years, in the various kitchens I've cooked in throughout the country, with their varying degrees of humidity, my meringue toppings have sometimes wept—and I along with them. Other times they have turned out miraculously well, but no matter what I do I can't ensure success every time, even with all the usual tricks of the trade: don't overbeat the eggs, don't use old eggs, don't refrigerate the pie, pile on the meringue while the filling is still warm. I now learned from Chef Kate that to prevent weeping, all I had to do was make a more stable meringue, an easy enough task once I understood the science behind sugar and egg whites.

The meringue I had been making over the years, it turned out, was the classic French style, which likely contributed to my topping's tears. The common French meringue consists simply of 2 parts sugar to 1 part egg whites, an amount of sugar not quite large enough to ensure the mixture's stability. To make a French meringue, you whip the egg whites until they start to foam, then add the sugar gradually and beat the mixture until it forms stiff peaks. Here Chef Kate shared a wonderful tip: if you add confectioners' sugar, the mixture can absorb more sugar and therefore will be more stable. Still, a French meringue is not the best choice for pie toppings that are only briefly browned under the broiler or with a blowtorch, for the simple reason that neither method ensures that the egg whites get cooked. And in these days of salmonella poisoning, raw eggs can be a concern.

To ensure food safety, a meringue is needed in which the egg whites are either warmed or cooked. So Chef Kate taught us about Swiss and Italian meringues. A Swiss meringue is the next step up from the French in terms of complexity. The egg whites and sugar are placed together in the top of a double boiler, then heated over boiling water to at least 145°F to pasteurize them. The temperature is gauged with an instant-read thermometer, a tool Chef Kate advised us never to be without. When the mixture reaches sufficient temperature, the whites are whipped to stiff peaks. Our Swiss meringue turned out beautiful and billowy. We spread it on top of the still-warm lemon filling to minimize the risk that it would break down from contact with a cool surface.

The third type of meringue that we learned to make is the Italian, used in buttercream icings. Here the sugar is first cooked to 240°F, the soft ball stage. Then it is poured in a stream into the raw egg whites, which are beaten to stiff peaks. This method yields the most stable meringue of the three, one that will not break down. It also has the advantage of being completely food-safe.

Alyssa asked Chef Kate why so many meringue recipes call for the addition of cream of tartar. Acid, Kate replied, such as cream of tartar, lemon juice, or even a little vinegar, facilitates expansion of the egg whites—but it is not necessary. What is crucial is to make sure that the bowl in which the egg whites are whipped is entirely free of fat. This you can do by wiping down the bowl with vinegar or lemon juice to remove any traces of fat. If a bit of egg yolk falls into the whites, as sometimes happens, it too can prevent them from whipping to full volume. The best way to remove the yolk, Kate explained, is with a piece of eggshell, to which it will adhere. This was another great practical tip.

After the dough had rested, Chef Kate kneaded the disk slightly by hand to make it pliable. Then she dunked it right into the flour bin to coat it on all sides with flour—no mere sprinkling for her. She rolled it out ⅛

Soft peak (left), medium peak (center), stiff peak (right)

inch thick, working rhythmically and evenly, expertly turning the round of dough as she rolled so that she ended up with a perfect circle. Kate put the crust into a disposable foil pie tin, then placed another foil tin on top of it to weight down the crust. If the crust is sufficiently weighted, there's no need to prick it to allow air to escape when baked "blind," without filling; it will cook evenly rather than puff up in some places and not others. An alternative way to ensure an even crust is to fill it with dried beans all the way to its rims, not just place the beans in a shallow layer on the bottom. After the crust has baked through three-quarters of the way, remove the beans and finish baking.

Chef Kate placed the piecrust, now sandwiched between the two tins, upside down in the oven, with the bottom of the pie tin facing up—another little trick of the trade that would ensure even baking.

MAKING OUR OWN CRUST

After this demo, it was time for us to move to our stations. First, though, James and Susan called our attention to the pain au levain dough they had made over the weekend at a bread-baking workshop at King Arthur Flour in Norwich, Vermont. They had frozen the dough and placed it in the trunk of their car for the drive to New York. Thanks to the frigid weather, it had remained hard as a rock. Once they arrived at their Super 8 Motel in Hyde Park they'd put the dough in the bathtub to thaw. Now they made a show of calling us all over to see the dough as they set it out to rise. They rather importantly explained why bread such as pain au levain, made with a wild yeast starter rather than commercial yeast, is superior. But their passion for baking was infectious.

Emily, June, and I set about making a 3-2-1 pie dough, so called because, like a pound cake, it was originally measured by weight, not volume. The proportions refer to the flour, fat, and liquid: 3 pounds of flour, 2 pounds of fat, and 1 pound of ice water. It seemed odd to measure the water by weight, but we poured it into a plastic jug (which we weighed first to get the tare) for scaling. For ease of cutting the fat into the flour, Chef Kate suggested that we replace a quarter of the butter with shortening. The butter used at the CIA is Plugrá, an unsalted European-style butter containing less water and more fat (82 percent compared to the standard American 80 percent). Plugrá (a brand name that plays on the French *plus gras,* "more fat") yields excellent texture and flavor. Following Kate's lead, we worked the flour, butter, shortening, and water together into a still-shaggy mass. I was sorely tempted to keep mixing, but, remembering Chef Kate's admonitions, I refrained. I suppose that to be absolutely precise I should have followed Chef Kate's instructions to the letter, but since I felt comfortable with pie dough I didn't worry about taking a few shortcuts, such as not having the shortening perfectly chilled. I figured I'd be able to handle the dough anyway. A kind of performance anxiety seemed to have overtaken June, who kept asking, "Are you sure that's right?" and "Don't you think it should be done differently?" That led to a bit of tension between June and me, but luckily Emily was calm enough to defuse it.

We discovered that 1 ounce of dough is needed for each inch of a standard pie tin's diameter. Thus, for a 9-inch pie we would need 9 ounces of dough for a single crust, and twice that much if we wanted a top crust. Because the foil pie plates we were using were 10 inches in diameter, we carefully weighed out 10-ounce balls from the 6 pounds of dough we had made and flattened them into disks.

Piecrusts complete, it was time for us to make biscuits and scones. My group was assigned cream scones, which Emily and I decided to jazz up with chocolate chunks and dried cherries.

1. Chef Kate suggested that we roll the dough for the lattice top of our cherry pie just slightly thicker than we did for the bottom crust for greater body and ease of handling. We rolled the dough into a 10-inch circle and cut sixteen strips from it. Kate demonstrated how to lay out the strips. (You can work directly on the pie filling, but for a very neat lattice, assemble it on a cake circle.) She picked up every other one and laid them evenly from one edge to the other. That way, the shorter strips are on the sides and the longer strips are in the center. Follow the same order as you start to weave the lattice.

2. To weave the lattice, fold alternate strips halfway back on themselves, then place a new strip across the center of the pie, perpendicular to the existing strips for a square pattern or at an angle for a diamond pattern. Unfold the folded strips and fold the ones that had been flat. Add another strip running parallel to the one you just added. Continue making the lattice by placing new strips all the way to the edge of the pie. Once one-half of the lattice is complete, turn the pie and repeat the process on the other half, again working from the center out.

3. If your lattice is woven on a cake circle, slide it carefully onto the pie filling. Finish the lattice pattern by turning the rim of the pie up over them rather than tucking the strips under. This way you will get an elegant edge, and the lattice will look as though it has disappeared right into the pie. Nancy worried aloud that she was likely to work so slowly that the dough would become too soft to manage. Kate countered that the dough can always be refrigerated at any point if it gets too soft.

4. The pie emerged from the oven with perfect golden lattice strips intact. The filling had thickened beautifully, and the promise of those tart cherries seemed fulfilled. But even professionals occasionally have pies that bubble over, so Chef Kate reminded us to put a pan underneath the pie to catch the drips before they fell onto the oven floor.

The recipe for Cherry Pie, shown here, is on page 220.

Our final task before lunch was to bake cookies. The day before, June, Emily, and I had baked our Mudslides after chilling the dough briefly, but the other groups had shaped their cookie dough into logs, which they left in the refrigerator overnight. I was beginning to see just how much this course focused on efficiency and production, a boon for busy people who might find the time to mix up some cookie dough but then not manage to bake it right away. Once the dough was formed into logs it could be held in the refrigerator for a few days or in the freezer for three months and then baked at leisure, and the cookies would be no worse for it. The class began slicing the logs into rounds. Some of the rounds looked as though they had crew cuts because they were so flat on top. Chef Kate told us we could avoid this punkish look by pressing down less heavily on our knives. We transferred the rounds to parchment-lined sheets and slipped them into the ovens. None of us were ready to leave for lunch—we wanted those cookies!

GOT TWINKIES?

I later discovered further evidence of Chef Delaplane's humor. As described on Planet Twinkie, the official Web site of Hostess Twinkies, he and his bride made their wedding cake out of Hostess snack cakes, which they had both adored as children. The story of Chef Delaplane's cake is told under the "World of Wackiness" link.

PHIL DELAPLANE DESIGNS SWANKY CAKE FOR SPECIAL DAY

Phil Delaplane of Red Hook, NY is a man with a sophisticated palate. A chef by trade and an instructor at the Culinary Institute of America in New York, Phil teaches chefs who go on to cook in some of the fanciest restaurants in the world.

So when Phil and his fiancée Pam began planning their wedding, he knew the only cake that would make their special day complete was one created entirely of Hostess snack cakes.

Phil and Pam both loved to eat Twinkies and Cup Cakes as children. On their first date, Phil ended a day of golf with a bottle of champagne and Cup Cakes to munch on as they watched the sun set over the Hudson.

It only took Phil one hour to complete his wedding cake. After building the tiers with layers of Styrofoam disks, the only complication was figuring out how to piece the snacks together. Finally, after several design changes, Phil came up with this idea of using a variety of Hostess snack cakes such as Twinkies, Cup Cakes, Ding Dongs, Ho Hos, Suzy Q's, Sno Balls, and Mini Muffins.

Don't be too surprised if this creation ends up on the dessert tray at your nearest swanky restaurant!

But Chef Kate insisted that we go, and promised not to let our cookies burn.

Grumbling a little, we headed to the Continuing Ed dining room, where once again we were offered New England fare. Chef Delaplane was as lively an expediter as before. The Culinary attracts passionate, often eccentric, people. Theirs is not an unbridled kind of pas-

sion or an eccentricity that veers out of control, for the CIA is nothing if not disciplined. But within its rigid strictures there is plenty of room for individualism, and I understood the appeal of a highly structured job that still allows for and even liberates creativity.

In his position as chief expediter of the K-17 Kitchen, Chef Delaplane is one of the Culinary's most memorable characters. He had turned the monotonous job of expediting into a lively one by joking with both the students waiting for food and the line cooks dishing it out. At the same time, there was no questioning his authority. In this space, he was the absolute monarch. You got the sense that if he didn't like you, he'd make sure you wouldn't get your first-choice entrée for lunch, even if it was available.

I couldn't quite decide between Johnnycakes with Mushroom Sauce or New England Pot Roast for lunch. I decided to go with the johnnycakes. No sooner had I sat down at the table than I heard a loud groan from Bob, followed by an expletive. He had experienced a calamity: the front of his uniform was streaked with gravy that had dribbled onto his chest! And Chef Kate had warned us to be prepared for a group photograph after the meal. No amount of dabbing could restore the uniform to its previous pristine white, and Bob returned to the Colavita kitchen in a panic. Luckily, the photo session had been postponed, but the accident occasioned an excellent new lesson: we learned that chef's coats are double-breasted for a good reason. If the front gets dirty, they can simply be buttoned the other way to replace the soiled surface with a clean one.

Though we didn't have much appetite, we were eager to taste the results of our morning's labors. The scones were melt-in-the-mouth tender, not only our chocolate-and cherry-studded ones, but also the savory cheddar cheese and jalapeño scones that another group had made.

What we learned: SCONES

1. First we gathered our mise en place. We dumped all the dry ingredients—flour, salt, baking powder, and sugar—into a sieve and sifted them together. This step prevents clumps of baking powder from spoiling the scone's flavor. While Emily and June were scaling these ingredients, I cut up nearly a pound of cold butter into medium dice, then weighed out and mixed together the eggs, egg yolks, and cream. It still felt unnatural to weigh 2½ ounces of eggs instead of thinking about them in units.

2. Using the paddle attachment, we cut in the butter on low speed, then added the liquids in a steady stream. The basic idea is to mix briefly and gently for tender results. Professional bakers refer to the dough as having reached a "shaggy mass" stage. It is evenly moistened and just barely holds together. At this stage, we briefly, and very gently, mixed in the cherries and chocolate chunks by hand.

3. Chef Kate suggested that we try two different ways of shaping the dough, so we divided it in half. One half we patted out to a 1-inch-thick, 8-by-8-inch square on a baking sheet that we had lined with parchment paper and lightly floured. We refrigerated the dough for ten minutes to firm it up before cutting out triangular scones. The other half we rolled into a 4-inch-wide log, then flattened it slightly before slicing off triangles. Both methods are much faster than the one I use at home, which involves carefully rolling out the dough into a circle before painstakingly cutting it into wedges. The methods Kate showed us are far superior for production.

4. The scones are finished baking when they are crisp on the outside. So much cream and butter in the dough gives the interior a lovely, rich crumb. Chef Kate noted that it is simple to adjust the flavorings. Dried fruits are classic choices, but so are more savory items, such as ham, scallions, and cheese. And even though we hardly needed to gild the lily, she also mentioned that a sugar glaze, made from powdered sugar and a bit of water, is a nice way to finish them off.

The recipe for Glazed Chocolate Cherry Scones, shown here, is on page 186.

Next, we moved on to the cookies. Cookies carry such warm and fuzzy associations: think of aproned grandmothers dishing up comfort along with cookies and a glass of cold milk. But something counterintuitive happened with our group. Instead of bringing out people's soft and cuddly side, the cookies precipitated competitive and aggressive behavior that hadn't been evident before. None of us were hungry after lunch, so we realized that we couldn't begin to consume the many dozens of delicious cookies we'd made. As soon as Chef Kate suggested that we pack them in boxes, the race was on to see who could grab the most perfect-looking cookies, those without overly browned edges or burnt bottoms. Bob was like a linebacker in his maneuvers, and he won the game, ending up with three densely filled boxes that he said he was taking home to his mother. Only the ever-gentle Nicole declined to engage in this rampage.

BEYOND THE CIA CAMPUS

No lectures or lessons had been scheduled for the afternoon, and our cookie scrimmage was an odd way to end the day. We must have been ready to spend some time alone, because when a couple of students came by the classroom to offer us a tour of the Institute, there were hardly any takers.

Instead of joining the tour, I decided to drive to Warren Cutlery, a cookware store in nearby Rhinebeck. I hoped to find a tamis to replace my now-ancient sifter; I also wanted to treat myself to a nifty digital scale that would register both metric and standard measures down to a single gram. Despite the snowy streets, the drive offered respite from the intensity of the day, and had I not still been overly conscious of my chef's uniform—which, coupled with a down parka and a sprinkling of flour in my hair, made me look all the more like the Pillsbury Doughboy—I would have been able to relax completely. Warren Cutlery sits forlornly on the highway out of town, in a rather nondescript building. But inside are treasures galore. Three large rooms burst with knives, pots, pans, pottery, place mats, and all kinds of kitchen gadgets from muslin bags for lemon slices (to keep the pits from being squeezed out into one's tea) to larding needles to dozens of decorative metal tips for pastry tubes. Alas, the only tamis they had was nearly two feet in diameter, not at all right for domestic use, but I did find the scale I was looking for, plus a professional half-sheet pan and some precut parchment liners. Satisfied with my shopping spree, I returned to the inn to decompress.

DINNER AT THE ESCOFFIER ROOM

We learned a lot more about each other at dinner that night, which was held in the most formal of the CIA's restaurants, the Escoffier Room, named after the great French chef who codified classical French cuisine in the early twentieth century. Unlike the Mediterranean-hued Ristorante Caterina de' Medici, the main dining room of the Escoffier is done up in dark reds that bespeak a quiet elegance. It reminded me of an old-fashioned hotel dining room, a bit on the stuffy side. For this meal we were not all seated at the same table but divided between two large round ones. I sat with James, Bob, Susan (the three of them were already inseparable), Alyssa, and Nicole. Susan remarked on how few men there were in our class, and how lucky we were to have them at our table. The rest of us pondered this observation in silence. Then Alyssa talked about wanting to learn to make different breakfast items for her B&B—she was very earnest, eager to turn her boot camp experience into something of practical use. Nicole, almost in passing, told me that she'd had a personal crisis in graduate school and decided that she needed to live her life quietly and not be caught up in a stressful career. Although I was curious and felt that there was something more to it than grad school experience, I didn't want to pry. Meanwhile, Bob and James, the two guys, engaged in competitive banter, showing off their dueling wits, encouraging each other to come up with increasingly outrageous rejoinders.

A waiter arrived to ask whether anyone wanted a drink before dinner, reminding us that whatever we ordered would be on our own tab. James ordered a Sazerac made with Maker's Mark bourbon. The waiter dutifully took his order but within minutes returned, rather embarrassed, to say that the bartender didn't know how to make that drink. James offered to show him, so off he went to the bar. I found the whole episode amusing, since just a week before, *Saveur* had run a feature on the Sazerac, naming it the cocktail of the hour. But I also happened to know from the article that the classic twentieth-century *Sazerac* is made with rye whiskey, not bourbon, so James's air of authority seemed a bit misplaced. I managed with some effort to bite my tongue.

With our first course we were served a Muscadet wine, which James pronounced "slightly effervescent," at which Bob quipped, "Yeah, they added baking soda." Bob was in raptures over the meal, audibly groaning over the fine food. He had ordered Beef Wellington, an elaborate (and old-fashioned) preparation in which a fillet of beef is spread with foie gras and mushroom duxelles, then encrusted with puff pastry and roasted. A rich Madeira sauce is served on the side. I didn't quite see how this recipe fit into the restaurant's billing of "French recipes...prepared true to the principles of legendary chef Auguste Escoffier, but with a light, contemporary touch," especially since Beef Wellington doesn't appear in Escoffier's *Guide Culinaire*. But no matter. Bob was in his element, exclaiming about how much he likes red meat (which we knew from the night before) and hot dogs. For dessert he ordered Chocolate Excess Cake, which seemed to epitomize his exuberant approach to life.

The conversation shifted to June. "Isn't she getting on your nerves?" someone asked. Others seemed to agree. June's outspoken insecurities had also irritated me, but it didn't seem right that people were singling her out. She and I were in the same platoon, and besides, she was sitting right at the next table, within earshot, I was afraid. But it was clear that her manner had not endeared her to the class. True, she was used to getting attention, she demanded it. Yet despite the peculiar manifestation of her type A personality, I couldn't help admiring her—anyone who has mothered five kids while pursuing a demanding career gets credit in my book, and I said so. My classmates countered that she was always interrupting, always challenging Chef Kate. Maybe, but because I've spent so many years in the classroom I saw it dif-

ferently: she just asked a lot of questions. June was unconstrained by inhibitions; anyway, Chef Kate could handle her. The criticisms persisted, and I was left troubled. Nancy also asked a lot of questions, but there was something so self-deprecating in her manner that no one got annoyed. Unlike June, Nancy had a desire to please and to do things right; on the other hand, she didn't want to have to struggle with anything. Her favorite refrain was "How long will this take?" With June, it was always about performance, about being on top. "What grade would you give this?" she constantly asked. Yet, even though she was always judging things, she never turned down a challenge; in fact, the more complex the task, the more it engaged her.

As the conversation went on, I thoughtfully chewed my Joues de Veau Braisées aux Mandarines. Catty remarks seemed out of place in this temple to gastronomic pleasure.

The Paul Bocuse Kitchen in the Escoffier Restaurant

chapter 4
ENRICHED DOUGHS

Another early morning! At 7 a.m. I am not at my most sparkling, and my fraught relationship with acronyms only added to my bewilderment. Before Chef Kate even began her lecture, James asked about the RCF. What was that, I wondered—an obscure government agency or a patented electronic device? It turns out that RCF stands for "recipe conversion factor," an important consideration in culinary math. Was I the only one in the class whose heart sank at his question, or did my fellow students also silently groan? I couldn't read their emotions—they looked as dopey as I felt. Chef Kate, however, was daunted neither by the technical question nor by the early hour. She launched right into an explanation of the formula.

Even though I convert recipes all the time, this formula made a fairly intuitive process seem much more complex. First, you have to divide the number of servings you want by the number of servings that the recipe makes. This yields the conversion factor. You must then multiply each ingredient amount in the recipe by this factor. If you're using volume measures, you can round up or down, but when baking it's better to use a digital scale so that the proportions remain precise. That said, Kate stressed the importance of subjectivity. Ultimately, the finished product depends on the environment (what is the temperature of the room? how high is the humidity?), on the type of equipment you use (what material are the pans made of? how hot is your oven?), and, of course, on the ingredients you're working with. To guarantee success you should go by experience and feel, not by a rigid calculation. I took some comfort there.

THE ROLE OF BUTTER, EGGS, AND MILK IN DOUGHS

Chef Kate began her lecture by talking about some of the specialty equipment in the Colavita kitchen, such as the Dutchess Divider, used for mechanically portioning dough into a specified number of pieces of equal weight. This machine (apparently named after Dutchess County, where Hyde Park is located, because it was invented in nearby Beacon) looks like an enormous cookie cutter. I wondered whether it had been originally patented by the Nabisco Company, which once had a large baking facility in Beacon, in the vast space now transformed into the Dia:Beacon museum of contemporary art. The Dutchess Divider looked scary, so I was just as glad that we would be portioning our dough by hand.

We had already learned quite a bit about bread baking from Chef Eric's class the first afternoon, but today Chef Kate wanted to focus on enriched yeast doughs, those containing roughly 20 percent milk, eggs, or butter, either singly or combined. As we had learned in our lesson on piecrusts, fat serves to shorten the gluten strands and thus tenderize the dough. Although enriching products add nutritional value, they can make the dough difficult to work with. Some highly enriched doughs, such as brioche, are therefore left to rest overnight to recover from the mixing process. And what an intense mixing process it is! The dough needs to be mixed until it is as smooth and shiny as satin. "It should be like a baby's bottom. When I walk past I just have to pat it," declared Kate, who had patted several babies' bottoms in her time. She added that she had been the first CIA chef ever to teach while close to term—so pregnant that she couldn't tie her apron around her middle!

Chef Kate taught us two different methods for mixing bread dough. For the straight dough method, all of the ingredients are put into the bowl at once and mixed until the gluten develops. For the modified method, all of the ingredients except for the additional butter are mixed together. Then the extra fat is added slowly so that an emulsion forms. In order for this second method to work, the fat must be warmer than room temperature.

We set to work making challah, brioche, a soft dough for dinner rolls, and a sweet dough for sticky buns or cinnamon rolls. My group was assigned the sticky buns, which pleased me, as I have a notorious sweet tooth. Mixing the dough proved to be straightforward by either method, and shaping it was definitely fun. We rolled out the dough ¼ inch thick, keeping in mind that the wider we made the rectangle, the larger the buns would be. If we wanted smaller buns (though whoever would?), we'd have to make the rectangle narrower. Emily brushed the dough with egg wash in a 1-inch swath along the length of its upper edge so that it would seal well after being rolled into a log. Then June smeared on a rich mixture of butter, brown sugar, flour, corn syrup, cinnamon, eggs, and vanilla, all the way to the edges, avoiding only the strip that had been brushed with egg. Next came my turn: I carefully began to roll the dough into a log, beginning with the long bottom edge, trying all the while to keep it tight and to keep the edges from pulling in. Despite my best efforts, the log ended up slightly lopsided, so we gently tugged on it to try to even it out. As with the other doughs we had made, we let the log relax for 5 minutes before cutting it into 1½-inch-thick rounds with a serrated knife.

Meanwhile, we mixed more butter, brown sugar, corn syrup, flour, and vanilla for the pan smear, which we spread over the bottom of the pan. When the dough was ready, we placed the rounds right in the smear and left them to rise until doubled. We slid them into the oven with great anticipation—we'd have hot sticky buns! While they were baking, we began shaping the dough for our next project, dinner rolls. The kitchen was so well ventilated that even my super-sensitive nose couldn't detect the smell of the buns baking, which disappointed me—part of my pleasure in baking lies in the aromas that waft through the air. On the other hand, we were supposed to be adults here, so I had to restrain myself from constantly running over to the oven to check on those sticky buns.

When it was finally time to retrieve the pan, we gathered at the oven. The buns were blobs, a complete disaster! In our enthusiasm, we had used far too much pan smear. It had oozed out over everything and kept the large buns from baking all the way through. Basically we had created a gooey mess, which not even I, with my sweet tooth, wanted to bite into. We ran to Chef Kate to see if there was some way to salvage them. She suggested returning the pan to the oven—at least that way the buns would bake through. We did as she recommended, but the buns still ended up much less than perfect. This was our first failure, and it didn't feel good. June, especially, did not take it well. She actually stomped her foot, a small, precise movement. Alas, there was no time to make another batch. At the CIA, schedule rules.

Luckily, we had an easier time with the soft dough for dinner rolls, which we learned to shape in all sorts of ways: a single knot, a figure eight, a braided roll, a butterflake, a double knot, a square knot, a Parker House roll, and a cloverleaf. I liked the butterflake best. To make this style, we rolled the dough out into a rectangle, then cut it into four or five strips. Each strip was buttered and then stacked. We sliced the stacks into squares and set them upright in muffin tins. This method yielded a wonderfully rich roll (thanks to all that extra butter), which was also fun to pull apart to eat. Chef Kate next encouraged us to try the famous "Cavotti knot," which turned out to be whatever shape we wanted. This liberation was welcome after having meticulously formed so many classic shapes. Most of the Cavotti knots ended up looking like lumps, however.

We had other shaping techniques to learn for brioche and challah—large, distinctive loaves of enriched bread. I was a little troubled to read in our class manual that "brioche is associated with the Brie region in Burgundy, and with the dairy regions of northern France (such as Normandy)." The dairy regions make sense, since brioche is loaded with butter and eggs, but the association with Brie is a false etymology. I made a mental note to suggest that the CIA hire a food historian to vet the materials they provide. Although the Institute's offerings are nearly flawless in terms of technique and food science, sometimes the history is more akin to "fakelore," taken from unreliable sources. In any case, Chef Kate demonstrated how to fit a large ball of brioche dough into a fluted mold. Once it was in place, she made an indentation in the dough, into which she set a small ball to make the tête, or head, of the loaf. She then brushed the loaf with egg wash before baking so that it would emerge from the oven with a lustrous, deep brown sheen. The challah was next.

MAKING CHALLAH

Challah is something that I've been making since childhood, when I helped my mother braid it for our weekly Sabbath meal. As a self-taught baker, I had always just followed my instincts, which meant that I braid the loaves from one end to the other. My challahs consistently turn out looking beautiful, even if slightly off-kilter, with one end thicker than the other. So it came as a revelation to discover that if you braid a three-strand challah from the center of the loaf out, reversing the braiding pattern for the two sides, the loaf will turn out perfectly symmetrical. Another trick I learned is not to flour the surface on which the strands are rolled out. Flour makes the strands flop around; it's so much easier to roll them out when they stick slightly and can be more easily manipulated. Once I saw these tricks, they seemed so self-evident that I felt embarrassed not to have come up with them myself. With this new knowledge under my belt, I decided to try my hand at a six-strand braid, something I had never attempted before (my previous challahs all had simple three-strand plaits).

Chef Kate distributed a handout depicting the necessary sequences for braiding challahs with three, four, five, or six strands. I looked at the diagrams and blanched—I don't grasp schematics easily, even after years of putting together supposedly simple toys. I'm much better at observing actual practice. But I knew that I had to give the instructions a try. I began by shaping six strands and fastening them together at one end, which I numbered in my head from 1 to 6, from left to right. As instructed, I crossed strand 6 over strand 1, noting that this step was considered out of sequence. That made me wonder who had decided to braid six strands in the first place, and how that person had figured out the right pattern. The first motion complete, I crossed strand 2 over strand 6, then strand 1 over 3. The next step was to cross strand 5 over strand 1, and strand 6 over strand 4, but by that time I had completely lost track of which strand was which, and had to start all over again. Nevertheless, I persevered, and after a couple of false starts ended up with what promised to be a dramatic loaf.

What we learned: BRAIDED LOAVES

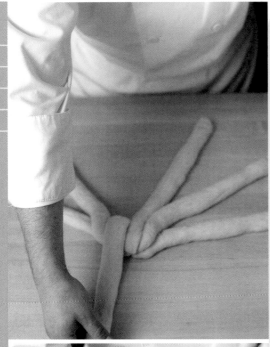

1. Lay the six dough strips parallel to one another. Pinch the strands together at the end farthest from you to hold them in place while you braid, but fan the ends apart to make braiding easier. To begin the braid, lift the strand that is third from the right and fold it back over the pinched-together ends so that it points in the opposite direction from the other strips.

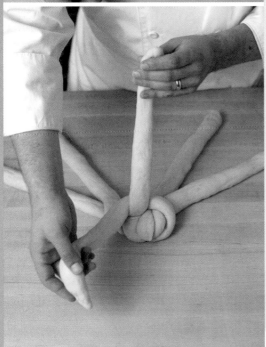

2. Next, lift the strip on the far left and cross it over all the strands of dough, moving that strip from one side to the other. Lift the strip that you folded back in step 1 up and over the strand you just moved from right to left. Set it back down in its original position. The lifting and folding sequence is a little like the weaving sequence of a lattice top.

3. Still holding the strip you moved to the far right in one hand, use your other hand to pick up the strip that is now second in from the right-hand side and lay it over the top of all of the strips to the left. The strip you have moved is now in the far left position. Continue to work gently so the strips don't stretch too much as you work.

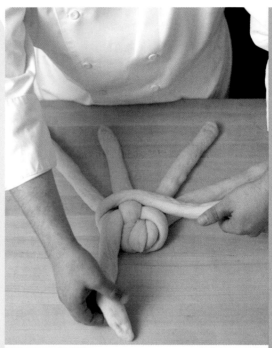

4. Lift the strip in the far right-hand position over the strand you moved in step 3 and bring it down between the second and third strands. The loaf is starting to look like a real braid now. (This is where I had to stop and redo my braid, because I couldn't remember if in our diagrams it was the strips that were numbered or the positions.)

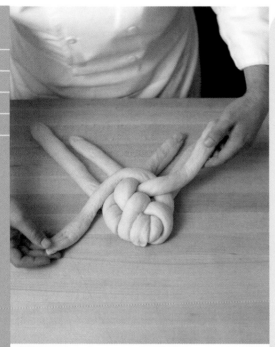

5. The braiding sequence begun in step 1 is repeated again by holding up the strip that is currently the third from the left. With your other hand cross the strip from the far left to the far right. Braid the challah leaving a little space between the strips, but not big gaps. As the dough rises, it will fill in the spaces and make the loaf rise higher. If you braid too tightly, however, the dough will stretch and your finished loaf won't rise as high. If the gaps are too big, the dough might spread out too much as it rises.

6. Lower the strip you were holding back to its original position, in the center of the four strips you aren't currently braiding. At this point, about half of the loaf is braided. If you rotate the loaf so the braided end is closest to you, your loaf will turn out more even. Remember to continue alternating from side to side, however, starting to braid from the left side once the loaf is turned.

7. Keep repeating steps 1 through 6 until all of the dough is braided. Pinch the ends of the braid together to seal the strips in place. Tuck both ends neatly under the braid and gently apply a thin coat of egg wash with a pastry brush before letting the loaf rise. Work carefully so that the egg wash doesn't collect in pools in between the strands of your braid.

8. Put the loaf on a lined pan for its final rise, but don't cover it with plastic; the plastic will stick to the soft dough. After the loaf has risen for the final time and is ready to go into the oven, brush it with egg wash once more. The finished loaves should be dramatic and showy. A fully baked challah feels light for its size and has a rich, eggy flavor.

The recipe for Challah, shown here, is on page 205.

pens to transform raw goods into baked has a rational explanation.

Chef Hinnerk had prepared a detailed handout called "The Art and Science of Baking," which broke the process down into its most basic parts. We began with the simplest terms. *Cooking* is the application of heat to individual items. Foods can also be "cooked" with acid rather than heat, as in seviche, where the addition of lime juice changes the texture of raw fish. *Baking* refers to the application of radiant heat in a contained environment. Cooking, by contrast, utilizes conducted heat, which makes the heat transfer more intense than in baking. Chef Hinnerk explained that within the realm of cooking, roasting is the counterpart to baking. He went on to explain that he considers cooking a more artistic activity than baking because you can play around with things and change them freely up until the very last minute. Baking is more scientific. You must stick to a formula, or at least to certain fundamental proportions, in order for the product to turn out right. And once the baked good is in the oven, that's it—you can't tinker with it.

Having grasped these basic concepts, we moved on to ingredients. Here Chef Hinnerk reiterated what Chef Kate had taught us in her first lecture. While cooking can involve a seemingly limitless number of ingredients, the basic ingredients for baking are very few. Even so, each has a distinct purpose. The three categories of functional ingredients in baked goods are the stabilizers (flour and egg), the liquefiers (fat, sugar, and a range of liquids), and the leaveners (either natural or chemical). Just a few basic ingredients can result in a wide variety of baked goods, depending on how they are used. Each time you substitute an ingredient, change the proportions, or handle the ingredients in a new way, you will get a different result. And that's where both the science and the artistry come in, Chef Hinnerk explained. Then he described each of the basic ingredients in more detail.

Flour gives backbone and structure to baked goods, which results in their characteristic texture and appearance. In addition to working as a binding and absorbing agent, flour also adds flavor, which is why using fresh flour is so important. Finally, it provides some nutritional value. Chef Hinnerk went on to discuss the structure of grain. The endosperm yields starch and protein; the germ yields oil and B vitamins and minerals; and the bran yields fiber and minerals. Each component has an important function. Within the endosperm, starch is embedded in a matrix formed by protein; the germ has the highest energy density and provides food for the growing plant; and the bran contains phytochemicals that are increasingly recognized as important to good health. Chef Hinnerk, like Chef Eric before him, disapproves of overly refined flours in which the nutritious outer layers of the grain have been removed. He explained, though, that while whole grains such as rye and whole wheat have their place in yeast-risen breads, they are too heavy when only a chemical leavener such as baking powder or soda is used. He would never choose a leaden rye muffin for breakfast over a tender blueberry one! Chef

Liquifiers include fats (left column, top to bottom): butter, shortening, oil; and sugars (middle column): granulated, brown, powdered. Stabilizers (right column): all-purpose flour, cake flour, and eggs

Hinnerk invoked Thoreau's phrase "faith in a seed." I wasn't quite sure how Thoreau's ideas about seed dispersal connected to the lesson at hand, but I figured Chef Hinnerk meant to convey his reverence toward the marvelous world contained in a single grain.

He then elaborated on processed flours. Because flour must age before it is ready for use, commercial mills often add chlorine bleach to speed up the maturation process. "Now, is that something you'd want to ingest?" boomed Chef Hinnerk. He and Chef Eric were obviously of one mind. Bromated flour also contains additives: bromate, phosphate, ascorbic acid, or malted barley is added to reduce yeast fermentation time and enable the flour to better withstand the long mixing that encourages gluten development. Finally, to make up for the vitamins and minerals lost in processing, refined flours are often enriched.

We turned next to the other basic ingredients of baked goods: eggs and liquefiers. Eggs give color and texture to baked goods; they also increase volume and provide structure, flavor, and nutritional value. Liquids are important because they hydrate the flour, thus ensuring the protein development that yields the gluten so crucial to a good loaf of bread. Liquids also serve as solvents for water-soluble ingredients. Although we don't usually think of liquids as leaveners, in fact, when water turns to steam it increases in volume an astonishing 1,600-to-1,800-fold, making it a very impressive leavening agent. Liquids can further assist in leavening by rehydrating dry yeast.

Chef Hinnerk enumerated some other ingredients that contribute to the success of baked goods, gluten first among them. Gluten is a new protein that forms when the two existing proteins in wheat flour, gliadin and glutenin, are mixed with a liquid. Mixing and kneading develop gluten's elastic strands—that's why it's so important to knead bread well. Bread with sufficiently developed gluten will achieve greater volume not only because of the lengthened protein strands but also because gluten helps to retain gases.

Chef Hinnerk invited us to do a simple experiment to get more than an abstract sense of what gluten is. He placed before us two bowls, one containing hard wheat flour, the other soft wheat flour, and added some water. I couldn't resist the glossy ball that formed in the bowl of hard flour. I picked it right up. It was better than Silly Putty—springy and tremendous fun to manipulate. The dough stretched effortlessly in all directions, and it was easy to see how it could expand under heat to produce wonderful bread. If the gluten was not well developed, the strands would not be sufficiently elastic and would break, causing the bread to rise poorly. Chef Hinnerk cautioned us not to make dough too wet or work it too much when mixing, or it might collapse on itself. As an aside, he mentioned that seitan is nothing more than the gluten from wheat. No wonder I have never liked its elastic texture!

The next important component of finely textured baked goods is fat. Fat gives baked goods an elusive but all-important mouthfeel. It also lengthens their shelf life by keeping them from getting stale—in effect, fat insulates baked goods from moisture loss, similar to the way in which it insulates our bodies from heat loss. But fat can also turn rancid if kept for too long, so the commercial balance is a delicate one. Fats add nutritional value and volume, but their most important function is to tenderize by inhibiting gluten development.

Sugar or other sweeteners are added to enriched breads not only for their sweetening power. When creamed with fat, sugar helps to leaven baked goods and promote good texture by creating air pockets. It also helps baked goods retain moisture and thus stay fresh longer. The process of caramelization that occurs when sugar is exposed to heat imparts a beautiful golden color to the finished product. Finally, a little sugar added to yeast boosts the fermentation process in bread making. Chef Hinnerk warned us to exercise caution, however: if the product contains more than 50 percent sugar, the yeast will die because sugar is hygroscopic (it takes up water from the environment). Being hygroscopic is a good property for sugar when it's used in jams and jellies—it draws out the moisture from the fruit, thus preserving it—but disastrous if you want your loaf to rise.

Next we looked at the leavening process, which Chef Hinnerk divided into three categories: mechanical, chemical, and

Leaveners can be mechanical: water (left) produces steam; organic (center column, top to bottom) sourdough starter, instant yeast, active dry yeast; or chemical (right column) baking soda, baking powder

organic. *Mechanical leavening* refers to a physical process that either creates or retains gas. In most baked goods, air and/or steam are the mechanical leaveners. Air is an excellent means of increasing volume, as it gets trapped through the processes of whipping, folding, creaming, kneading, sifting, and so on. Unsifted flour is compact and takes up less space so you can get more flour into the measuring cup. Sifted flour takes up more space but weighs less. There can be a difference of up to a full ounce between a cup of sifted and unsifted flour. That's why it is so important to weigh the flour rather than just measure it by volume. The trapped air is made up of gases that expand when heated, a principle that underlies the production of soufflés and genoise cake batters. Steam works somewhat differently. Under high heat, the water present in the batter is converted into steam, which causes voluminous expansion. Examples of baked goods leavened by means of steam include puff pastry, pâte à choux (cream puff pastry), and popovers.

Chemical leaveners work very quickly, so it is not surprising that modern kitchens rely on them. The two most common chemical leaveners are baking soda and baking powder; both produce carbon dioxide gas when acids and certain bases are combined with a liquid. These leaveners are used for quick breads and other fast-rising products such as cookies and cakes, which need a weak gluten structure; otherwise the developing gluten would suppress rising during such a short period.

Baking soda is the everyday term for sodium bicarbonate, a dry alkaline substance. It requires sufficient acid and liquid in order for a reaction to take place. When baking soda is used, the entire reaction takes place immediately. If too much soda is used, not only will the product fail to rise properly, it will also have a bitter and soapy taste. To make his point, Chef Hinnerk told us that baking soda reacts with fats in batter in much the same way that lye (a much stronger alkali than baking soda) reacts with tallow (a fat) in soap making. Furthermore, using too much baking soda can affect the appearance of baked goods: the interior may look rusty, while the exterior can turn excessively brown. Chef Hinnerk explained that the excessive browning is due to the Maillard reaction between proteins and sugars, which favors an alkaline environment. He suggested that devil's food cake may originally have been so named because of the reaction between the baking soda and the batter, which contains alkalized (Dutch-process) cocoa. Dutch-process cocoa has a red tint,

unlike regular cocoa powder; the Maillard reaction that occurs further reddens the batter. The red food coloring often added to enhance the devilish effect is a more recent addition.

Baking powder differs from baking soda in that it is a properly balanced chemical mixture of a dry acid or acids and a base. It often includes cream of tartar, a partially neutralized salt of tartaric acid derived from wine crystals that yields a sour taste but has no intrinsic flavor. The standard formula for baking powder is 1 part baking soda, 2 parts cream of tartar, and 2 parts cornstarch, which acts as a buffer. When baking powder was first developed in the mid-nineteenth century, it was known as "single-acting": only liquid was required for the reaction to take place, and there was one reaction only, which resulted in carbon dioxide gas. The acid part of the mixture was soluble in cold water, and, as with baking soda, 100 percent of the reaction took place immediately.

Single-acting baking powder is rarely used today. Now we favor the double-acting kind, which contains or produces several acids and a base. Unlike the single-acting powder, the double-acting yields two reactions, beginning at 68°F and ending at 140°F (the first is at room temperature, the second under oven heat). Tiny air pockets are produced in the first reaction, which involves 30 percent of the rising; the subsequent reaction expands these pockets by the remaining 70 percent. In double-acting baking powder, 20 percent of the acids are soluble in cold water; they dissolve as the batter is mixed.

When the product is baked, the sodium bicarbonate is neutralized and more acids are produced, resulting in the production of carbon dioxide.

Organic leaveners produce carbon dioxide by means of simple living organisms, namely, yeast. Unlike chemical leaveners, these natural products require a strong gluten structure, which is why they are used primarily for breads rather than for more delicate baked goods. The leavening action of these organisms occurs very slowly, over hours, sometimes days. The yeast is trapped within the gluten and starch structure. When furnished with food, water, and heat, the yeast will, under ideal conditions, produce both carbon dioxide gas and alcohol and thereby expand the existing air pockets.

Sourdough is a yeast dough that has been fermented for a longer period. It has a long shelf life as well as antibiotic properties, something I wasn't aware of. Chef Hinnerk mentioned the old German practice of sprinkling sourdough bread throughout the house to keep bacteria levels down. He told us about his grandmother, who suffered from poor circulation, which caused open wounds to appear on her skin. She was able to avoid serious infection because she kept sourdough bread in her room.

Looking at Chef Hinnerk's still boyish face, I pictured him playing in his grandmother's bedroom, a space that seemed oppressive not just from her illness but also from the heavy drapery and dark, massive furniture I imagined there. How had he turned out to be so sunny, I wondered, and when had he become such a wonderful raconteur, able to make even dry technical descriptions come to life?

Having explained the basic ingredients for baking, Chef Hinnerk moved on to the standard methods of mixing dough, which we had to cover quickly because very little time remained. Chef Kate had already gone over these methods in her lectures, but it was good to hear Hinnerk's commentary. First he tackled the straight dough method, used for bread, in which liquid and yeast are combined to disperse the yeast evenly before adding the dry ingredients. The dough is then kneaded to develop the gluten structure. Chef Hinnerk explained that the longer the dough is worked, the finer the crumb will be. In a very loose dough such as ciabatta, which is initially too wet to be worked as a mass, air pockets automatically form in a process known as autolysis (self-digestion).

Chef Hinnerk kept looking at the clock, no doubt aware that he had already kept us beyond the hour and a half that our strict schedule allowed. But we were willing captives—he was a wonderful teacher. He hurried through the last methods. For the creaming method, the fat and sugar are mixed together, then eggs are gradually beaten in. Hinnerk stressed the importance of having all the ingredients at room temperature to avoid curdling. The fat, sugar, and eggs are blended into a single mass, then one-third of the dry ingredients and one-third of the liquid are added in stages to create an emulsion. During this process it's important to scrape down the bowl continually and add the ingredients gradually until all have been incorporated.

The foaming method is used to make the classic genoise, a light, airy sponge cake that also contains butter. Eggs and sugar are combined in a double boiler and heated to 100°F over boiling water. Then they are whipped on high speed until the mixture triples in volume, at which point the sifted dry ingredients are carefully folded in. The foaming method allows a great deal of air to be incorporated into the batter, which serves as a natural leavener. Sensitive palates can detect the difference between cakes raised by natural means and those that rely on chemical leaveners. Naturally leavened cakes have a purer flavor that contains no trace of the bitterness or soapiness that can sometimes occur when too much baking soda or powder is used.

Finally, the rubbed dough method is used for making piecrusts, scones, and biscuits. Minimal liquid is added so that the starch won't get gummy, which would prevent the crust from being crisp. To make piecrusts by this method, the fat is cut into the flour, as Chef Kate had showed us. Then ice water is mixed in with the lightest of hands. The dough is formed into a ball and rolled out to the desired thickness.

With that, our food science lecture was over. It was nearly five o'clock, and already dark outside. We thanked Chef Hinnerk and packed up our notebooks. He seemed disappointed that the class had to end, lingering as we said goodbye and urging us to be in touch with any questions. Chef Hinnerk obviously enjoyed sharing his knowledge, or, more accurately, his passion.

DINNER AT THE AMERICAN BOUNTY RESTAURANT

After nearly a week of very little exercise and much more food than usual, I felt the need for some exercise before dinner. I usually jog, but the thought of running in circles around the track did not appeal to me, so I decided to go to the weight room instead. The number of machines was impressive, and not being a regular, I found the choices overwhelming. I eventually saw a treadmill that looked straightforward enough, and a stationary bicycle. Soon I was pedaling away, captivated by the MTV on the screens placed prominently throughout the room. I could hardly tear my eyes away from the pulsating bodies! Only then did I realize how removed my life was from popular culture.

I didn't want to be late for dinner, though, since this was our last night at baking boot camp. This evening's meal was at the American Bounty restaurant, down Roth Hall's long corridor at the opposite end from Escoffier. American Bounty did not have a particularly welcoming entrance. It felt dark and a little cramped. A nice bar stood just beyond the entryway, but dinner guests had to make a dogleg to get to the main dining room, which itself felt too contained in its long, narrow space. No matter, though. Our class was ushered into a private dining room with a table so wide that it was nearly impossible to converse with anyone except the people sitting on either side. Yet, despite its initially off-putting architecture, American Bounty turned out to be my favorite of the week's restaurants. The celebratory Ameri-

can menu draws on local foods from the Hudson Valley, and each entrée is complemented by a suggested American wine or beer, including the CIA's own private-label Chardonnay from their Greystone Cellars in Napa Valley. A few of the dishes seemed overly contrived, such as the Grilled Bacon-Wrapped Pork Tenderloin with a Wild Rice Pheasant Tamale on Vanilla-Scented Black Currant Sauce, Sweet Potato Gratin, and Apple-Glazed Beets. But the featured New England winter meal of Roasted Stuffed Breast of Guinea Fowl on Pumpkin Game Jus with Blue Corn Polenta seemed perfect for the season, and it did not disappoint. Neither did my warming starter, a sampler of three soups: Navajo Soup (butternut squash and black bean side by side), Ham Bone and Collard Greens Soup, and Wisconsin Cheddar Cheese and Beer Soup.

Perhaps because the food was so wonderful, or perhaps because it was our last night of boot camp, our gathering was lively and warm. Free of our unflattering uniforms and toques, we were not an unattractive group. The women, especially, looked lovely in makeup and formfitting clothes. Had our uniforms been partly to blame for the awkward group dynamics? In our own clothes, we were definitely more at ease. With a little wine and only a half day of boot camp remaining, we could leave our tensions behind and enjoy a few hours together over a fine meal.

At the far side of the table, Nancy and Lenore were reunited in a private world of friendship and love. Nicole was as quiet as ever, her protective wall intact. Paige was eager to rejoin her husband and young son and try out her new skills in baking. Seated next to the rambunctious Bob, she seemed even more mature than her years, the school-teacher growing a little weary of her naughty student's behavior. Bob was joking around with Susan because his sidekick, James, was talking to me. James turned out to be a wonderful dinner partner—witty, provocative, interested in everything. June, by contrast, seemed subdued, set apart from the rest of us. I wondered how deeply the challah incident had affected her. Both she and James were anxious to impress, yet now I could see James's charm, whereas June was unable to shine on this evening, in this venue. Spending time as I do in a world of academics always trying to impress one another with their knowledge and accomplishments, I certainly understood the need to stand out. Did boot camp attract intense personalities or bring out people's competitive tendencies? I had expected to encounter people who led leisured lives, who had extra time and money on their hands and nothing to be anxious about. I wondered briefly what kind of students would enroll in my next course, and how the relationships in pastry boot camp would play out. For now, though, I was enjoying the company. The waiters at American Bounty were attentive, and the food was great. I settled back and relaxed.

The Hilde Potter Dining Room
in the American Bounty Restaurant

chapter 5

LEAN DOUGHS

Maybe it was my imagination, but I felt an undercurrent of excitement as I entered the classroom this last day of baking boot camp: the end was in sight. All we had left to learn was how to make lean doughs. These doughs, Chef Kate explained, are made simply of flour, water, yeast, and salt, four basic ingredients that give rise to a surprising variety of breads. With so little to work with, it is important to keep the ingredients in balance. As everyone knows, too little yeast will not allow bread to rise properly, but too much yeast is just as bad, yielding a sour, overly porous loaf. Too much salt can retard the growth of the yeast cells and not allow the bread to reach full volume. Chef Kate recommended that we use either kosher or fine sea salt in our bread making, since both are additive free. To boost the development of the yeast and increase the moisture content, she sometimes adds a little sugar to the initial yeast and water mix (ah, yes, I remembered, that's because sugar is hygroscopic). Kate added that just because a dough is lean doesn't mean that it can't contain a little fat—a little olive oil will shorten the gluten strands and make the bread more tender.

THE DAY'S PRODUCTION

Today everyone worked harmoniously— we had all checked our egos at the door. We didn't chitchat, just focused on the task at hand. June, Emily, and I set to work making sunflower-seed rolls with whole wheat flour. The straight dough method was a breeze, and we mixed and shaped the rolls in what seemed like no time, having decided to forgo fancy shapes for simple balls more in keeping with the rolls' rustic style. The Hobart mixers effortlessly brought the dough to the perfect degree of elasticity. Mixing is easy when no human muscle power is needed.

Feeling confident, we turned to ciabatta. Ciabatta is a traditional Italian loaf shaped in the form of a slipper (hence its name, which means "slipper"). Ciabatta is meant to be a holey loaf, perfect for soaking up olive oil. Unlike other lean bread doughs that are firm, though not hard, to the touch, ciabatta is utterly gooey, a near-liquid blob. Our class had already prepared the poolish, or starter, which we had left to rest overnight (we were taught to say "fester," though that term reminded me of open wounds and sounded unappealing). Our mixture of bread flour, water, and yeast

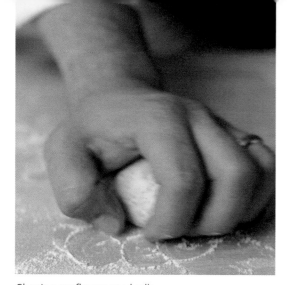
Shaping sunflower-seed rolls

had been refrigerated since the previous afternoon (it can be refrigerated for up to 20 hours or left at a warm room temperature of around 80°F for 12 to 14 hours). If the poolish is left for too long, Chef Kate cautioned, too much acid will form, which not only will keep the gluten from developing properly—and good gluten structure is imperative for lean doughs—but will also have a negative effect on the bread's taste. We felt a little panicky—wasn't it too wet? But Chef Kate assured us that we did not want too firm a dough, because it would not have the requisite light texture when baked. Using large spatulas, Emily, June, and I took turns scraping the mass out onto the work surface, then used our bench scrapers to more or less fold it in thirds from either side. We sprinkled flour on top and covered it with a plastic bag to relax for half an hour. Chef Kate explained that the idea was to handle the dough as little as possible to avoid deflating the air pockets that had formed during the mixing.

The next step was to cut the dough into pieces so we could shape individual loaves. Bench scrapers in hand, we started to cut the very wet, very jiggly dough. We quickly tried to prevent our baby blobs from spreading by flouring them liberally and covering them again with the plastic bag to rest for another 10 or 15 minutes. This time the verb *fester* seemed just right. I fervently hoped that the pieces wouldn't all melt into a single giant blob again.

Kate suggested that we turn the remaining ciabatta dough into focaccia, an Italian yeasted flatbread. So we placed the dough in pie tins to rise slightly, then brushed it copiously with olive oil and added our choice of toppings: sliced garlic, red peppers, olives, feta cheese. The focaccia emerged sizzling from the oven, making us want to eat it on the spot—our stomachs had grown accustomed to an 11:00 lunch. But as usual, our schedule was set in stone, and Kate told us that Chef Delaplane expected us in the Continuing Ed dining room. We would be able to pack up our focaccias and bring them home. I protested that the focaccia wouldn't be nearly as good then—after all, hadn't we just learned that bread starts to retrograde the minute it's removed from the oven? But my objections were to no avail. Chef Kate ordered us to troop upstairs. We were so eager to finish the class that it seemed wrongheaded to stop for a sit-down lunch. I ate quickly, a reprise of the cheddar cheese and beer soup I'd enjoyed at American Bounty the night before.

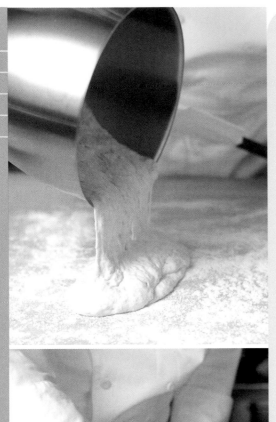

1. Ciabatta is made from a lean dough, but it is made with a greater percentage of water to give the loaf an open, airy texture. We included a poolish in the dough, which means that less yeast has to be added. A poolish also helps the bread remain fresh longer because it adds moisture. We added more bread flour, water, salt, and yeast to our poolish, then turned on the Hobart to do the mixing. This task would have been nearly impossible to manage by hand, since the gooey dough stuck to everything.

2. After the dough had rested, we took our bench scrapers and cut off pieces roughly 3 by 4 inches in size, trying not to smoosh them, a task that seemed nearly impossible since we really had to bear down with the scrapers to make the cuts. No sooner had we separated the pieces than they oozed into new blobs. I had a vision of the 1950s sci-fi movie *The Blob*, where a voracious blob absorbs all the energy forms on Earth: people, electricity, even rifle shots.

3. While the dough rested for a second time, we prepared sheet pans by lining them with parchment and dusting them well with semolina. To my surprise, the relaxation—the "festering"—had done the trick. We were able to pick up distinct pieces of dough and stretch them gently into slipper shapes before placing them on the pan to rise one more time before baking.

4. We held our collective breath as the loaves were removed from the oven. What magic! We oohed and ahhed over the ciabatta, which had turned out beautifully. Chef Kate broke off a piece of one of the loaves. It was light and airy inside, with a crisp crust. She had taught us well. We passed the loaf around, each of us tearing off a piece to taste. We met each other's eyes. Was I imagining it, or was this age-old communal act of breaking bread bringing us closer together?

The recipe for Ciabatta, shown here, is on page 204.

BAKING BOOT CAMP GRADUATION AND GOING HOME

Back in the kitchen, we cleaned up and put everything in order. Then it was time to graduate! With considerable fanfare Chef Kate produced two bottles of champagne. She called each of us up individually to receive a diploma, along with a packet of information about other CIA programs. We also received a copy of the class photo that had been taken a couple of days before. I remembered how Chef Kate had surveyed us before the photo session to make sure that our uniforms were shipshape, with no gravy stains and no pens or thermometers protruding from our pockets. And here was the result.

I loathed it. We looked washed out, like living doughboys, our paleness exaggerated by the grays of the speckled granite countertop and massive stainless-steel hoods and the bright white of our uniforms and tall toques. The only color relieving the drab picture was June's bright red lipstick. She stared out, stunning as ever, from the center of the photo. But the real stars of the photograph were the baked goods arrayed before us on the counter—deep brown challahs, golden biscuits. A few chocolate chunk cookies that had escaped the packing frenzy were also displayed. The only thing missing from the picture was James, who had run out to make a phone call. Bob stood on one end, the lone male in this bakery harem. He looked as cheerful as ever. I noted with despair that my uniform really was unflattering—so that hadn't been empty vanity on my part. I looked tired, and my curly hair had indeed escaped from under my toque. Sigh.

In the photograph, Chef Kate stands confidently front and center. She later confessed that she liked our class: "In some CE [Continuing Ed] classes it seems that the students want to be entertained and don't really want to work, and unlike in my regular curriculum class, I can't yell at them to make them work, so they just merrily roll along through the class. But everyone in your group was very participatory and interested in learning more than the given information." She added that we "all seemed to…embrace [our] differences, sometimes teasingly, but still tolerated each other"—an observation that left me a little surprised. But then students and professors rarely share the same perspective.

We barely sipped at our champagne—at two o'clock in the afternoon, with long drives ahead, we did not want to overindulge. But we were glad to raise toasts to one another and then especially to Chef Kate, who beamed at our praise, then modestly ducked her head. And that was it. Graduation was over. We packed up the leftovers—boxes of cookies, scones and biscuits; challahs and soft dinner rolls; the retrograding focaccia. How would we ever manage to haul all this loot back to our cars in "Siberia"?

I made a couple of trips to the car, then scraped the snow from the windshield and windows. Glancing up at Roth Hall one last time, I wondered: Had I become a better baker? Did boot camp deliver everything I had hoped for? I had expected a kind of heartwarming experience, something that tapped into my romantic notions of baking and comfort, hearths and wholesomeness. Instead, I had learned to focus on issues of production and consistency, and I had gained useful technical skills. We'd been instructed as professionals, learning the value of specialized equipment, its role as a barrier between hands and food, so that people who eat what we prepare won't get sick. We were taught to bake as a service to others; the sensuality of the baking process receded into the background, even though our instructors communicated extraordinary passion.

Boot camp had definitely given me a better understanding of ingredients and methods and how they work together. Our group, too, had learned to work together, operating in teams with people we might not have chosen as our friends and hearthmates. The recipe metaphor for group dynamics didn't escape me, but mainly I considered all the practical lessons that I had learned. I felt sure that with my increased expertise I could now easily build on recipes to create new ones, since I knew what kind of chemical reactions to expect. I had also improved my ability to discriminate among different ingredients and equipment. Yet, even as I enumerated all these excellent lessons, I realized that some part of me was resisting conversion into a more professional baker. My stand mixer will produce a more refined product, to be sure, but I still preferred to make some things entirely by hand. Despite all I had learned, my recalcitrant core remained. I would rather relinquish a perfect crumb than give up my tactile pleasure in dough. Would my experiences at pastry boot camp succeed in giving me a more professional outlook, I wondered, or was I just a recidivist at heart?

chapter 6

CUSTARDS

I had great expectations that the baking moxie I'd gained at boot camp would carry me through the winter, but the demands of daily life soon quashed my hopes of regularly turning out perfect brioches for breakfast or even a quick batch of scones. Just as I was beginning to despair, a message popped up on my e-mail:

> *Please let me introduce myself. I am Chef Paul Prosperi, and I will be your chef instructor at the Culinary Institute of America for your pastry boot camp. I have attached a copy of my bio for your review.*

> *Get ready, recruits! I am looking forward to a great week of learning (and eating). In the meantime, get plenty of rest—the days are long but a ton of fun! Bring your baking questions; no baking questions are off limits!*

I was psyched! I felt sure that a second round of boot camp would give me the necessary fervor to make baking a daily routine.

THE FIRST SESSION

Since I more or less knew the boot camp ropes (or at least where to park), I didn't feel the need to attend the orientation session, though I decided it would be prudent to drive down to Hyde Park the night before classes began. So I was able to show up bright and early for a full breakfast at Farquharson Hall on the first day of pastry boot camp. After lingering over thick slices of French toast drizzled with real maple syrup, I headed to Lisa Paquin's storage room to pick up my duffel bag, which contained yet another set of ill-fitting chef's pants. I gritted my teeth and slipped them on.

The first thing I noticed on entering the Colavita classroom was how many men were already seated at the tables—quite a change from the baking boot camp. In the baking class the students had sat rather stiffly, reluctant to interact at first. But people in this class were already engaged in animated conversation and greeted me with cheerful hellos. I sat down next to Lee, a young Chinese American who had recently graduated from college with a B.A. in biology. His real interests lay with food, though, and he harbored dreams of opening an upscale fusion restaurant—perhaps called Dark Horizon, he said. Lee was wonderfully open and gregarious. He had learned to cook at his parents' Chinese restaurant in New Jersey but wanted to become more proficient in Western cooking traditions, especially desserts, which are not a featured part of the Chinese repertoire. On my other side sat Nick, a TV news producer recently retired from NBC. Nick was still in his fifties, with a lot of time on his hands and a desire to explore something new. Nick seemed as circumspect as Lee was unrestrained.

Chef Paul called the class to attention and asked us to introduce ourselves. I decided to reveal myself right away and announced that I was writing a book about the boot camp experience. This time everyone took the information in stride—no one requested a pseudonym or a pumped-up pseudobiography as an exotic dancer. Then Chef Paul told us about himself. He had retired from the CIA four years earlier, having taught there for twenty years. Before coming to the Culinary he had been a pâtissier at Les Délices in Paris and at Fortnum and Mason in London. He had also been pastry chef and manager of Paul's Pâtisserie at the Essex House in New York City, well before Alain Ducasse opened his eponymous restaurant there. From the illustrious biography Chef Paul had sent us by e-mail, I knew that he had won a grand prize in classical pastry from the Salon of Culinary Art, as well as gold medals from a number of culinary societies. Now, he confessed, his most active days were behind him. He lived in Connecticut and commuted occasionally to the Culinary to teach.

From the start it was clear that Chef Paul liked to tease and make jokes, though his strong French accent kept some of the humor from coming through. What did come through loud and clear was that he ran a no-nonsense kitchen. Even if his demeanor was friendly, he expected us to heed his commands and execute our tasks well. I asked him about his last name, curious whether his family had immigrated to France from Italy. Chef Paul proudly replied that he came from Corsica. This reminded me of another Frenchman from Corsica who hadn't put up with any guff.

Perhaps because Chef Paul was so voluble, his style of lecturing was much less methodical than Chef Kate's had been, and it was hard to take notes. He did drive home several points about precision and sanitation. First, he emphasized the importance not just of measuring but of remeasuring when making pastry. Pastry making, he informed us, calls for even more precision than baking. "Measure twice, cut once" is as good a maxim for bakers as it is for carpenters.

Then he turned to sanitation. Eighty percent of what the pastry chef makes requires 24-hour refrigeration, so it is important to plan ahead and make sure that you have ample space and a good cooling system. Bacteria reproduce rapidly in moist, warm environments. They especially like rich pastry cream made with eggs and milk. So whenever a batch of pastry cream is made, it should be dated before being placed in the refrigerator to chill. Although the cream will last for up to a week, it's far better to toss a suspect batch than to risk making a customer or a friend sick. Chef Paul told us that government inspectors always check a kitchen's pastry cream first by testing a sample for the presence of bacteria. If the pastry cream is well handled, then chances are the rest of the kitchen is also up to snuff.

Chef Paul talked a blue streak, making the lecture feel more like a conversation than an academic exercise. His style contributed to the laid-back feel of this class, which was characterized by eagerness, not anxiousness. Instead of asking pointed questions, we bantered. I felt a little frustrated not to get hardcore information about ingredients or techniques. I didn't yet realize that Chef Paul's true gifts lay elsewhere.

After the lecture, we headed upstairs for our pastry break, where I got to know Carrie. Trained as a psychologist, she had set aside her career to raise her son, now three and a half. Even though she was devoted to her little boy, she felt conflicted about not working outside the home, and she worried that her mind would atrophy. She was putting considerable energy into a home baking and catering business and had come to pastry boot camp to develop her skills. Also at our table was the third woman in our class, Lavinia, an office administrator for a large orthopedic practice in Jacksonville, Florida. She had studied pre-med in college but then married a surgeon and raised a family. Unlike Carrie, she was completely at peace with her decision to give up her career for family—a difference that marked their generations as much as their temperaments.

Lavinia was like an earth mother, warm and embracing, who simply radiated love. She had big hair (which, I later noticed with some amazement, she managed to contain under her toque). Over pastries she told Carrie and me that she had a family Bible from the early 1900s for which she was having a special stand made. The Bible itself would be under a Plexiglas cover, opened to verses 1–13 from 1 Corinthians 13, which are all about love. "It's all about love," she repeated.

At twenty-three, Lee was the youngster of our group, and he was excited about everything. He couldn't wait to open his own restaurant and was working hard to secure funding. Nothing seemed to daunt him, which is why, when we returned to the classroom to get our

Basic pastry components (clockwise from top): crème anglaise, simple syrup, pastry cream, pâte à choux

assignments, I was thrilled to learn that he would be my partner. Since there were only seven students in our class we would be working in groups of two, two, and three.

The anxiety that had attended the baking boot camp assignments was absent here, since we were all slated to make the same basic things: pastry cream, crème anglaise (vanilla sauce), pâte à choux, and simple syrup. Then we could choose crème brûlée, crème caramel, bread pudding, or petits pots de chocolat, and Chef Paul didn't even mind if two groups made the same dish. I glanced at the recipes in our course binder, struck by how deeply French most of them were. Even the very English vanilla custard sauce was graced with a French name to give it cachet. I wondered whether French would continue to rule the twenty-first-century kitchen.

Chef Paul reminded us to don our paper toques before going into the kitchen—a matter of ever-important hygiene. I decided to try fastening mine in a new way in the hope that my hair wouldn't escape as it had during baking boot camp. Instead of turning out the edges to make the toque sit tall, I simply set it on my head in its foreshortened form. Toques in place, we went to our assigned worktables. Chef Paul introduced us to our kitchen assistant, Ciji, who was friendly and efficient.

Our first task was to tackle pastry cream, the foundation of the pastry kitchen. Chef Paul talked while we worked, explaining that pastry cream can be either used alone or mixed with other ingredients to make a luscious filling. He noted that crème anglaise is simply pastry cream without additional starch to thicken it. Though pastry cream must be sturdy enough to hold its shape, it should never be gummy or leathery. Cornstarch is typically used for thickening, although some recipes call for arrowroot, tapioca, or even flour.

Not surprisingly, Chef Paul emphasized issues of food safety. The trick to a safe cream is to cool the boiled mixture quickly and then get it right into the refrigerator. Chef Paul called us over to one of the tables for his first demonstration. He wanted us to visualize an important consideration in pastry making: temperature. There are plenty of occasions when cooks and chefs need to temper their ingredients. A good temper means that there aren't wild extremes. A bad temper means that you could end up with a curdled, useless mass, whether you are making pastry cream or chocolates.

Ciji had already set out all of the necessary ingredients, including separated eggs; this was Chef Paul's mise en place. First he made a slurry by mixing the cornstarch with a little cold milk. The rest of the milk he poured into a pan to heat, then added half the sugar and all of the salt and vanilla. He stirred the egg yolks into the cornstarch slurry along with the rest of the sugar. This mixture, he explained, is a "liaison," an all-important stage in the mixing process. Because all the ingredients must be at like temperature to avoid curdling, half of the hot milk is whisked into this egg yolk mixture, then the tempered mixture is stirred into the hot milk remaining in the pan. This process ensures that the egg yolks won't cook on contact with the hot milk. Chef Paul brought the milk mixture to a boil, stirring constantly to make sure that it didn't burn. He allowed it to boil for 10 seconds only, just long enough to kill any bacteria. Then he stirred in some butter and immediately poured the pastry cream into a hotel pan. "Be sure to date the container!" he reminded us.

As we worked, Chef Paul made his rounds, stopping by each group's workplace to observe and comment on a false movement here, a good technique there. As he approached Lee and me, I thought I detected a flicker of disapproval. And to my dismay, *I* was the source of it. Chef Paul strode over and yanked the toque from my head, admonishing me to fold it properly. Here was my first real lesson of pastry boot camp: uniforms count. Where Kate had been motherly, Chef Paul was a martinet. I was already in his doghouse, no doubt pegged as an unserious female for whom vanity was more important than propriety.

What we learned: **PASTRY CREAM**

1. Chef Paul reminded us to be precise in our measurements, to weigh out everything the recipe called for, even the salt. We aspired to a complete and organized *mise en place*. I offered to fetch the butter from the refrigerator and chop it into cubes while Lee expertly separated the eggs and stirred the yolks lightly together.

2. Then we tempered the hot milk into the yolk mixture. The first step was to heat the milk with sugar and vanilla. Next we had to blend the hot milk into the yolks to warm the yolks up. Skipping this tempering step might result in scrambling the yolks. We ladled in about half of the hot milk, a little at a time and whisking all the while.

3. The eggs were added back into the pastry cream, and all that remained was a brief cooking period, just long enough to thicken everything and to be sure that the eggs were properly cooked. The fact that pastry cream contains starch and sugar means that you can bring the eggs to a higher temperature without fear of overcooking them. Still, it is important not to cook the cream too long.

4. Instead of using a bowl, professional chefs cool the cream by pouring it into a hotel pan, set in a second pan that is partially filled with ice. This cools the pastry cream as quickly as possible so that it is safe to store in the refrigerator. If you don't have a hotel pan, make sure to use a stainless-steel container, not plastic, which will insulate the cream rather than permit it to cool instantly. Cover the cream with plastic wrap to prevent a skin from forming.

The recipe for Pastry Cream, shown here, is on page 261.

CHEF PAUL DEMONSTRATES

After we had produced our own perfect batches of pastry cream, which Chef Paul praised, he called us back to his table for a demonstration of the Paris-Brest, a wheel-shaped pastry named after the famous 1,200-kilometer bicycle race run every four years since 1891 between Paris and Brest, in Brittany. Pâte à choux, or cream puff dough, forms the basis of the Paris-Brest. I was surprised to see that our recipe called for bread flour, with its higher protein content, rather than pastry flour, made from soft wheat. I had always made cream puff dough with all-purpose flour, but Chef Paul said that the higher gluten content of bread flour would help the dough expand in the oven. He added that a mixture of milk and water in equal proportion yields the best pâte à choux, though either liquid may be used alone. One has to be careful when using only milk, however, since its sugar content will cause the pastries to brown more quickly.

As he prepared to shape the Paris-Brest, Chef Paul spelled out details he hadn't included in his morning lecture, and I suddenly understood why: his genius lay in his hands. And what hands they were! They moved fluidly and gracefully, with total assurance. Chef Paul left perfection in his wake; there was no messing up à la Julia Child, no "Oops! Don't worry about that." Chef Paul let us know that everything makes a difference, and he was here to teach us the correct way from the start.

Chef Paul demonstrated cream puffs, for which he chose a star tip larger than that used for the Paris-Brest. He held the pastry tube close to a sheet of parchment, then squeezed to release the dough, turning the pastry tube in a circular motion to make a nice mound. It all looked so easy in his hands. He was about to put the pastries into the oven when Lee begged him to make some éclairs. The rest of us seconded this request—éclairs, we discovered, were everyone's favorite. Chef Paul showed us how to prepare a baking sheet for éclairs by folding a piece of parchment paper in quarters lengthwise, then unfolding it so that the fold marks remained. Along the length of each fold he piped 3-inch logs of dough, spacing them 1 inch apart. The folds helped him make the éclairs consistent in size—an important consideration in commercial production, when the weight and size of the product must be maintained. Ciji slid the baking sheets with the cream puffs, the Paris-Brest, and the éclairs into the oven. As they disappeared into the depths, Chef Paul explained that steam would act as the leavening agent to puff them up. They should be baked until most of the moisture evaporates, he advised, otherwise they'll be soggy, but he cautioned us against baking them too long: if they become crisp, they'll lose their distinctive texture.

Cream Puffs, page 254

What we learned: **PARIS-BREST**

1. Chef Paul mixed the water and milk in a saucepan with salt, sugar, and cubes of unsalted butter and brought the mixture to a rolling boil. He dumped in the flour all at once to precook it before baking, stirring vigorously until the dough pulled away from the sides of the pan.

2. He then carried the saucepan over to the Hobart mixer and scraped the mixture into the bowl. Again I felt a sense of disappointment at this reliance on machines, even though I recognized that a professional chef who must produce multiple items can't take the time to mix everything by hand. After beating the mixture until it had cooled slightly, Chef Paul added the eggs gradually, continuing to beat until the mixture turned shiny. He cautioned that the pâte à choux should be rather soft and not too thick so that it can easily be piped.

3. He took a pastry tube and fitted it with a round tip. With a pen he traced circles on a piece of parchment paper, then flipped the paper over to ensure that no ink would penetrate the pastry. He scooped dough into the pastry tube, then squeezed it once to expel any air. Working quickly, he piped along the inside of the circle. When the sides were the right height, he released the pressure on the pastry bag and pulled the "tail" out to avoid unsightly peaks.

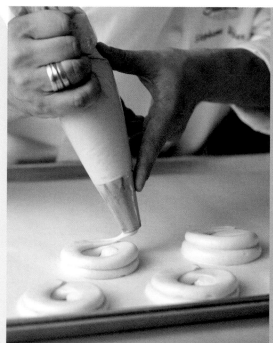

4. He sliced the baked pastry circle in half horizontally, revealing a perfectly empty interior created by the steam. He then reached for a small piece of parchment paper and cut out a triangle, which he rolled up to make a diminutive pastry tube with a tiny hole. From this tube he piped raspberry jam onto the pastry. He took a larger pastry tube, filled it with Chantilly cream, and piped that over the raspberry jam. He added some sliced strawberries, topped the Paris-Brest with the other half of the pastry, and voilà! It was spectacular, definitely worth a 1,200-kilometer ride.

The recipe for Paris-Brest, shown here, is on page 257.

Soft ganache (top), medium ganache (middle), hard ganache (bottom)

While the pastries were baking, we turned to the ganache for icing the cream puffs and éclairs. Ganache is simply bittersweet chocolate melted with heavy cream. It can be either hard, for glazing, or soft, for filling a cake, and it's a cinch to make. Lee retrieved a block of chocolate from the pantry and chopped it finely while I heated heavy cream with a little corn syrup to give the ganache a shiny texture and make it more stable. When the cream came to a boil I poured the hot liquid over the chocolate in a bowl; Lee stirred until the chocolate melted, and that was that. We worked well as a team. Chef Paul told us we could store the ganache in the refrigerator and melt it again when we were ready to use it.

We still had to make crème anglaise and simple syrup. Crème anglaise is an excellent accompaniment to fresh fruits and is frequently used as a base for ice creams and Bavarian creams, which Chef Paul told us we would be making later in the week. I was a little surprised at how much time we were spending on all these different creams. In my mind *pastry* meant dough. I was especially eager to learn how to make the perfectly flaky croissants and rich Danish pastries that I couldn't buy in my small New England town. When I voiced my impatience, Chef Paul repeated that creams are a vital component of any pastry shop. He assured us that we would get to the various doughs later in the week.

To make the crème anglaise, Lee got a heavy-bottomed saucepan from the storage room. I poured in some whole milk, then added a vanilla bean, half the total amount of sugar, and a little salt. We brought the mixture to a boil, stirring constantly so that it wouldn't burn. So far, this course had us using the stovetop much more than the ovens. The burners were wonderfully responsive, but because they were so powerful we had to keep a close eye on whatever we were heating. As we had done for the pastry cream, we made a liaison by mixing the egg yolks with the remaining sugar, a process Chef Paul called "burning." Before we knew it, little lumps of sugary egg yolk had formed, which we whisked smooth before adding a little of the hot milk mixture. We tempered this liaison just as we had for the pastry cream, although this time there was no starch slurry to mix in. While I stirred, Lee poured the liaison back into the pan with the remaining milk. We wanted to bring the mixture to the nappé stage, the point where it coats the back of a spoon. From Chef Paul we learned that this stage is reached at 180°F. To be precise, we should test the temperature with an instant-read thermometer, he said, especially since this moment is so critical. The nappé stage is reached only 15 seconds before the mixture reaches the next stage, when it curdles, so it has to be watched very carefully. If the mixture begins to boil even slightly, it will curdle and be lost.

I could feel my heart pounding as Lee and I hovered over our pan, watching the digits on the thermometer rise. This scientific method certainly took the guesswork out of the process, but for some reason it didn't alleviate my nervousness. The instant the thermometer registered 180°F we pulled the pan off the heat. Success! Our crème anglaise was beautiful, silken and smooth. Chef Paul came by to remind us to date the storage container. Crème anglaise has a shelf life of only 4 days, he said, since it hasn't been boiled, providing bacteria a perfect environment in which to grow.

Finally we turned to the simple syrup, another workhorse of the pastry kitchen, used to keep layer cakes moist. The name describes precisely what it is: a simple mixture of sugar and water, roughly in equal proportion, that is boiled gently until a syrup forms. Sugar syrup can be flavored in myriad ways. It keeps for a long time in the refrigerator and is very useful to have on hand. Lee and I boiled up our syrup and set it aside to cool.

We had accomplished so much that I was surprised to discover that it was only ten o'clock. We still had an hour until lunch! Now Chef Paul wanted to put the finishing touches on the baked goods we had made. He asked for some pastry cream, which was by now sufficiently cooled. While Lee ran to retrieve our batch, Chef Paul quickly whipped some heavy cream to soft peaks. He explained that to avoid overbeating—which can happen in an instant—he prefers to whip the cream partway in the industrial mixer and then finish it off by hand. The peaks can be soft, medium, or stiff, depending on how firm you want the cream to be. For mixing with pastry cream it's best to keep the peaks at medium firmness for ease of handling, but if you plan to fill cream puffs with whipped cream alone, then it's best to whip the cream until the peaks are firm so that the pastries will hold their shape.

Because the pastry cream had stiffened in the refrigerator, Chef Paul beat it by hand until pliant. He noted that the cream could be flavored at this point with a liqueur such as Grand Marnier or Kirsch or with a flavoring extract. He weighed out some of the pastry cream, took an equal amount of whipped cream, and proceeded to fold it into the pastry cream. The lightened texture was immediately visible. This, he told us, was known as Diplomat Cream.

"Then what is Chantilly?" asked Carrie.

"Just whipped cream mixed with sugar and vanilla," he replied.

To fill the éclairs, Chef Paul poked holes in the bottom of each one with a pastry tip, then piped in the Diplomat Cream. They looked much more elegant than the pastries I'd seen with holes filled from the side. We each took turns filling the éclairs while Ciji heated some ganache. Then we dipped the éclairs in the warm ganache, and there they were, glistening darkly and beckoning to us! We couldn't resist—we had to have a taste. They were ethereal, the filling simultaneously light and rich, the dough perfectly moist but not soggy.

Chef Paul didn't let us linger long over our treats. It was time to finish the Paris-Brest. After splitting and filling the pastry, he carried the lesson to its final expression, not yet satisfied with his artistry. Plating is part of the pastry chef's oeuvre, he explained, and a large part of his pleasure. He told Ciji to grab a plate from the pantry. He then took a strawberry and, holding it horizontally against the table, made thin, rapid slices right up to the stem. With his thumb and forefinger he spread the slices out into a fan shape. Then, using a serrated knife, he cut into the Paris-Brest. We oohed and ahhed as the luscious filling was revealed. Chef Paul placed the slice of pastry on the plate, garnished it with the fanned berry, and carefully sifted some confectioners' sugar onto the top, noting as he worked that confectioners' sugar in the United States contains starch so that it won't clump, making it easy to sift. That's one thing he likes better about American kitchens, Chef Paul added.

He suggested that we think about pastry in terms of seasonality. In the past, before modern refrigeration, neither a Paris-Brest nor cream puffs would have been served in the summer for fear of spoilage. He directed us to practice making strawberry fans and to plate the remaining Paris-Brest, as well as the cream puffs and éclairs. We would bring these desserts up to the dining room at lunch to share with the regular students.

DESSERT BEFORE LUNCH

A single task remained before lunch, this one of our choosing. As acknowledged chocolate lovers, Lee and I immediately agreed upon petits pots de chocolat. How nice that we were so compatible! We figured we could make them in a snap—after all, petits pots are just Frenchified chocolate pudding. We'd have no trouble at all. But when we opened our course manual, we discovered that the recipe was faulty. It listed only 3 ounces of sugar in the ingredients, but the instructions called for caramelizing 20 ounces of sugar. Which was the proper amount? Three ounces seemed like too little, 20 ounces like far too much. I ran to Chef Paul. In a cool tone he suggested that we try using 12 ounces of sugar, which we did.

Caramelizing sugar is not difficult—it's just a question of melting it—but the procedure demands close attention because sugar can burn in a flash. I slowly stirred the sugar over the heat, trying to be patient. Chef Paul came by to take a look. "Add a little lemon juice," he said.

"Lemon juice?" I repeated. "Won't that cause the sugar to sputter?"

"Trust me," he said.

So I added a tablespoon of lemon juice. And Chef Paul was right—the juice worked wonders, making it much easier to melt the sugar without so many crystals forming. Another nice little trick of the trade, I thought, and one that I would definitely remember for the future.

While I stirred, Lee heated some milk and heavy cream—another instance of tempering. We wanted the temperatures of the caramelized sugar and liquid to be as close as possible so that the sugar would not seize up too much. The minute the sugar reached a dark amber color, Lee poured in the milk and cream. It bubbled madly, but I stirred just as madly, and soon the mixture relaxed into a beautiful caramel sauce. Next I "burned" a little sugar with some beaten eggs and egg yolks. I asked Lee to pour in a little of the caramel sauce while I stirred, once again tempering the two mixtures before combining them. We added this tempered egg mixture to the caramel sauce remaining in the pan, then stirred in some melted chocolate. Although the recipe called for semisweet chocolate, Lee and I decided to use bittersweet, since we like a deeper chocolate flavor. Finally we added some vanilla extract.

To make sure that the pudding was free of lumps, we strained it into ramekins through a chinois, a fine strainer so called because it resembles the shape of the hats that Chinese laborers used to wear. We placed the ramekins in a pan and poured in boiling water halfway up their sides to help the puddings set. Our petits pots didn't take long to bake—only 20 minutes. We removed them before they were entirely firm and placed them on racks to cool before refrigerating.

And then it was time for lunch. Both the routine and the route were familiar to me. We removed our aprons, side towels, and toques, then headed upstairs and out through the courtyard to the K-17 dining room in the Continuing Ed building, where I expected (with some ambivalence) to encounter Chef Delaplane. And sure enough, there he was. The Cuisines of the Americas menu was still going strong. This week I was pleased that foods from the Southwest and Mexico were being featured. As before, the menu distinguished the main courses by cooking method: you could choose among sauté, braise, poach, or roast. I chose the sauté—ancho-crusted salmon with yellow mole. Chef Delaplane handed me my cloche-covered plate, and I crossed the hall to the dining room, where my classmates were already gathering at a long table.

This group was so much more amicable than the last. And this wasn't just superficial friendliness, but something deeper. I tried to figure out what made the difference. For one thing, even on this first morning everyone seemed eager to help and support their classmates. No one had displayed the slightest interest in competing. This realization surprised me, since I had expected the pastry types to be more rigid, if only because pastry demands greater precision. But here were some of the most expansive people I had ever met. Within minutes we were exchanging spirited tales of our travels, of amazing pastries we'd eaten around the world, of our personal lives. I met Daniel, who served as head of operations for a large cable company in upstate New York. He had already taken a few courses at the CIA and was back for more, courtesy of his wife. Ray, a medieval historian from the West Coast and an avid bicycle racer who spent much of each summer bicycling through Europe, loved a good discussion.

We all talked about why we'd come to this boot camp. Ray reminisced about his mother, who used to bake something every day throughout the winter. She'd had a houseful of boys who burned lots of calories, which she'd been determined to replenish. He wasn't sure why he was so interested in pastries and cakes instead of bread, but there it was. He had been to the cooking boot camp and valued the educational experience highly. Daniel added that he, too, was a boot camp veteran. For him, taking this course wasn't just about learning how to make pastry, even though he acknowledged a sweet tooth. It was as much an opportunity to immerse himself in a new social experience among people he didn't know. Suddenly I realized what made this crew stand apart. My classmates really did want to be part of a group. They had come to commune, not just to learn or to show off their skills.

The Chef's Table in St. Andrew's Cafe

DINNER AT ST. ANDREW'S CAFÉ

The only activity scheduled for the afternoon was a tour of the CIA, which I decided to forgo. The weather was beautiful—still cold and raw, as March tends to be in upstate New York, but the sun was shining—so I drove up the highway to the Vanderbilt mansion to walk around its lovely grounds overlooking the Hudson. Hardly anyone else was there, just a few hearty walkers. The isolation was just right after such an intense morning. I followed a slippery path down to the river, where the ice was beginning to break up. The walk invigorated me, and I returned to the inn refreshed.

After changing for dinner, I drove back to the CIA. To my delight, we were meeting at St. Andrew's Café, the only restaurant I hadn't visited during baking boot camp. St. Andrew's has an informal feel. It's brighter and airier than the other restaurants, and the food is intentionally lighter. I liked the internationalism of the menu, from Chicken Yakitori to a

Grilled Ham and Mozzarella Panini. But the Thai-Style Barbecue Chicken Pizza with Aged Jack Cheese and Tomatillo Salsa was far too fusion for me. So I opted for a simple Pizza Margherita, which was very good.

I thought back to the last boot camp group's grumbling over the measured wine at dinner. Boot camp policy had not changed, but this time several of us offered to buy extra bottles for the table so that no one would feel pinched. Not only did this group have a generous spirit, but we were sensitive to each other and careful not to neglect anyone, especially quiet Nick, who, after many frantic years of getting the nightly news on the air right on time, now seemed content just to sit back and watch the evening flow. Lavinia regaled us with stories of her children, now grown. But most of all we were entertained by Lee, whose innocence and idealism were infectious. He was rapidly becoming our pet.

chapter 7
THE FOAMING METHOD

My first thought on waking was how much better I felt on this second day of boot camp than I had at the previous session. For one thing, there was no blizzard to contend with. For another, the March days were longer, relieving me of winter's oppressive darkness. But most of all, I realized that I was eager to start the day and see my new friends. I dressed quickly, drove easily up to the CIA, and arrived in the classroom early. Most of my classmates were already there.

USING EGGS AS LEAVENING

Today's lesson was on the foaming method. It differs from the creaming method, which we studied in baking boot camp, in the amount of air that is incorporated into the batter. Creaming admits some air into a batter but still leaves it rather dense. The foaming method results in the very lightest cakes, such as sponge cakes. It admits so much air that the batter looks frothy. Foamed batters have many more eggs in proportion to flour than other batters do, since eggs have the ability to absorb more air than other ingredients. Because an egg foam is made almost entirely of air, it is very fragile, and that's why so little flour is added: the weight of the flour can burden the foam and cause it to collapse.

Sponge cakes, Chef Paul told us, are rather miraculous. In baking boot camp we had learned that flour and eggs are the two major stabilizers in baked goods. A batter with a low proportion of flour must therefore rely on eggs for structure. When handled gently, not only are the eggs sturdy enough to keep the cake light and airy, but they also allow baked sponge cakes to be rolled up into roulades. Sponge cakes are so versatile that they are an important component of the pastry shop.

I appreciated the way that this boot camp built on the previous one, though I was a little distressed at how much I had already forgotten, and vowed to concentrate harder this time. Chef Paul explained that there are three different techniques used in the foaming method. The first is the cold foaming method, for which the eggs and sugar are whipped together on high speed until they reach maximum volume. He told us that it takes practice to know when this point has been reached. When the mixture attains maximum volume, the eggs will begin to recede ever so slightly. At this point the mixer speed is turned down, and the batter is beaten on medium for a few minutes longer before the sifted dry ingredients (flour and often cornstarch) are folded in by hand. I learned that even for sponge cakes, tempering is crucial. Because a little melted butter is frequently added at the end to give depth of flavor and a nice mouthfeel, the butter must first be gently mixed with a little of the

batter to temper it before folding in the rest. Chef Paul cautioned, however, that if we planned to roll a sponge cake into a roulade we should never add butter, because it would harden under refrigeration and cause the cake to crack when rolled.

For the warm foaming method, the eggs and sugar are beaten over a hot water bath until the mixture reaches 110°F, at which point it's transferred to a mixer and beaten on high speed till it reaches maximum volume. The advantage of this method is that warm eggs can achieve even greater volume. The mixture will also be more stable—if you have to leave it for a little while before folding in the flour, you run less risk of collapse.

For the separation foaming method, the eggs are separated. A third of the total amount of sugar is added to the egg yolks, and this mixture is beaten until it doubles in volume. The whites are beaten separately to soft peaks. Then the remaining sugar is beaten in until a meringue forms. The egg yolk foam and the egg white foam are gently folded together. The dry ingredients are folded in next, and melted butter is added if it's part of the recipe. This method yields the greatest volume of all. These three foaming methods parallel the three methods for making meringues, from simplest and least stable (the French method) to the most complicated and most stable (the Italian).

Chef Paul advised us never to grease the cake pans with butter, because its high water content can make cakes soggy. Shortening is a much better choice. After greasing the pan it's a good idea to lay a round of parchment on it so that the cake won't be greasy.

Chef Paul looked at his watch and saw that it was already 8:15, time for our pastry break. He shooed us upstairs, where we once again selected our favorite pastries to nibble on. Even without much appetite, we were unable to resist the daily offerings of blueberry muffins, almond brioche, and cheese Danishes. I chatted with Lavinia, who gave me valuable pointers on raising teenage girls. "Let them do whatever they want with their hair!" she advised. I could have listened to her for an hour, but it was time to move to the kitchen.

First off, Lee and I wanted to taste our petits pots de chocolat. They had set up

nicely, but the flavor was flat. The intensity of the chocolate was not quite balanced enough with sweetness, and the result was monotone. Perhaps the bittersweet chocolate hadn't been a good idea after all. Lee and I took turns spooning pudding from a single ramekin, hoping to discover more flavor with each subsequent bite, but soon we gave up and left the pudding unfinished.

We turned to the sponge cake recipe. Chef Paul called out that we should add a pinch of salt to the recipe, since a little salt always heightens flavor. Lee and I wanted to make as light a batter as possible, but we didn't feel like going to the trouble of the separation foaming method. So we settled on the warm foaming method. As we worked, Lee entertained me with tales of working in his parents' restaurant and of his struggles as a child of immigrants. From an early age, he and his brother had sorted clean utensils while their parents cooked. As he and his brother grew, they'd graduated to dishwashing, busing tables, working in the garde manger, waitering, and managing the front of the house. Lee was very close to his family and proud of his background, but he was also very much a product of American culture and felt frustrated when his parents resisted new ideas. That was one reason he wanted to open his own restaurant, where he could innovate to his heart's desire. Meanwhile, his brother had gone the other way, neither cooking nor taking an interest in fine dining.

What we learned: FOAMED BATTERS

1. First, we combined the eggs and sugar in a mixing bowl. Although it was ungainly, we used the bowl from the Hobart mixer. That way, we could warm the eggs and sugar in the same bowl we'd use to mix the batter. The trick is to bring it to the right temperature—slightly higher than body temperature, but not so high that the eggs begin to cook. The sugar will blend in completely and you won't feel its grit as you stir with a whisk.

2. Lee and I beat the egg whites on high speed, watching them closely. Sure enough, at a certain point they began to recede ever so slightly, and we knew it was time to turn down the speed. Chef Paul came by our worktable to observe our progress and revealed a trick that seemed like magic: if we continued beating the eggs at high speed or low speed they would collapse, but they could be mixed indefinitely at a moderate speed without collapsing—a boon for a busy kitchen!

$3.$ So we left the mixer on medium and turned to the dry ingredients, which we sifted directly into the bowl through a fine sieve to incorporate even more air. Air, I was beginning to realize, was a key ingredient in baking, even if it was invisible. We folded in the dry ingredients, taking care not to overmix them and risk losing the air we had so assiduously captured. At this point Chef Paul cautioned us not to undermix, either, or the mixture would be too light and collapse in the oven. Lee and I felt sure we had folded our ingredients successfully.

$4.$ We poured the batter into the cake pans we had greased with shortening and put them in the oven. They emerged golden on top, perfectly domed, and ready to use in the cakes and tortes we had dreams of producing for appreciative family and friends.

The recipe for Vanilla Sponge Cake, shown here, is on page 192.

FRUIT TARTS

Our next task was to make fruit tarts. In baking boot camp we had practiced the rubbed dough method for piecrusts, but that kind of flaky crust is not always desirable for fruit tarts, which are enhanced by a rich cookie dough. We opened our manuals to a recipe for 1-2-3 Cookie Dough, so called because the proportions are 1 part sugar, 2 parts butter, and 3 parts flour. Vanilla, eggs, and lemon zest are also added. This dough is made by the simple creaming method, which requires that the butter be at room temperature. Luckily, Chef Paul had instructed us to take the butter from the refrigerator before we started making the sponge cake, so it was the perfect consistency. Lee and I split up the tasks at hand: weighing the sugar, then the flour, retrieving the eggs and vanilla extract, removing the zest from the lemon. By now Lee and I felt like pros with the mixer. We creamed the butter, sugar, and vanilla rapidly, then beat in the eggs one at a time. We added the lemon zest and flour and mixed just until the dough held together. We then wrapped it in plastic wrap and put it in the refrigerator to firm up before use. We would assemble the tarts tomorrow. Ideally, the dough is refrigerated overnight, Chef Paul informed us, but in a pinch you can use it after 3 or 4 hours.

Next on the agenda was a frangipane filling for the tarts. This pleased me, since I love anything almond. We were getting our mise en place ready when Chef Paul called us all over to the demonstration table: it was time to remove the sponge cakes from the oven. He showed us how to unmold the cakes by loosening them around the edges by hand, not with a knife, which might compress them. After running his fingers gently around the edges, he set the cake pan upside down on the table and tapped hard. The cake fell right out. Chef Paul sent us back to our stations to unmold our cakes. He stopped by each worktable to see how we had done. We all held our breath, since Chef Paul could be either lavish in his praise or very critical. He told Lee and me that our sponge cake earned a 10 out of 10, and we beamed.

Still, I couldn't shake the sense that Chef Paul was dismissive of me, a woman in a man's world. Certainly things had changed from his early years at the Culinary, when women were an anomaly. The restaurant industry at that time was still largely based on a European model that excluded women from the kitchen. I sensed that Chef Paul was struggling to adapt to a new reality, one that touched him personally: his daughter-in-law, Courtney Febbroriello, was the author of the book *Wife of the Chef*, an exposé of the rigors of the kitchen and the toll it exacts from one's personal life. Chef Paul told me outright that she would have been better off having children and keeping a home for his son. Perhaps a girl could learn something from a great French chef, but why cultivate female talent when there is a better role for women in the world? I tried to sort out whether I was just reacting to Chef Paul's comments in a gut-level feminist way, even as I wondered what I could do to overcome his condescension, or at least to temper it, as my impression of him had been softened when I saw his brilliant hands-on work.

Still pondering my role in our group dynamics, I wrapped our sponge cake tightly in plastic wrap and set it aside for later in the week. Then Lee and I returned to the frangipane. While Lee got more butter and eggs from the refrigerator, I searched for almond paste in the pantry. The Culinary's professional-quality almond paste was wonderfully intense, far more moist and almondy than the little Danish bars stocked in my local supermarket. I weighed out nearly half a pound of the paste and transferred it to a mixing bowl. Only then did Lee and I remember that the butter and almond paste had to be at the same temperature—that ever-important concept of tempering! So we laboriously creamed the butter by hand to soften it before adding it to the mixing bowl. I was beginning to see the merit of machines. The eggs were supposed to be at room temperature, too, so I ran them under warm water until they lost their refrigerator chill. We creamed the almond paste, butter, and sugar together until no lumps remained, then added the eggs one by one. I folded in a little sifted cake flour by hand, being careful not to overmix and lose the air we'd just beaten in. We scraped the frangipane into a storage container and set it aside.

The pace of the class was picking up. Chef Paul periodically called us over for a quick but always impressive demo. His hands unfailingly worked like magic. He demonstrated the best technique for folding (rotate the bowl as you cut with the spatula so that there is continual motion) and showed us how to pipe butter cookie dough into rosettes. Now I began to feel a little urgency, as we had to finish making our own butter cookies before our 11:00 lunch.

Luckily, Lee had had the foresight to take extra butter out of the refrigerator when he retrieved some for the frangipane. We were beginning to absorb the concept of mise en place and look at all the recipes for the day to see ahead of time what we would need. Honestly, I didn't feel like making butter cookies—I was eager to get on with more complicated projects, such as laminated doughs. But I dutifully worked with Lee to cream the butter and confectioners' sugar with a little vanilla extract and lemon zest. We added an egg and then mixed in some cake flour until just blended, keeping in mind Chef Paul's admonition not to overcream the mixture. Even though we had been working all morning to find ways to incorporate as much air as possible, we now had to make sure not to blend in too much air. Medium creaming was best for the desired texture of these cookies, which were supposed to be somewhat dense. I scraped the mixture into a disposable pastry tube and fitted on a star tip, then handed the tube to Lee, who gleefully began piping rosettes and squiggles onto a parchment-lined baking sheet.

After we'd put the cookies in the oven, we retrieved our cookie dough crust from the refrigerator. After only two hours it was already rock hard. Chef Paul told us not to worry. With a flick of his wrist he tossed flour onto the worktable. (From this simple motion you can easily tell who is a pastry pro.) Chef Paul's flour cascaded gently over the work surface, covering it lightly and evenly. He showed us how to pound the stiff dough with a rolling pin to soften it and then work it by hand to make it pliable. Then he rolled it out, constantly moving the circle of dough to keep the edges even and rolling always in one direction, away from his body. If you roll back and forth, he cautioned, the dough will stick.

We fitted the crust into a tart pan and moved on to the next step. Lee and I chose to make an Apple Custard Tart so that we could enjoy our frangipane filling. Despite our best intentions to have everything ready, we'd neglected to bring the frangipane to room temperature, but it was easy enough to soften in the mixer at low speed. We blended the frangipane with an equal amount of pastry cream to lighten it. I spread the bottom of the tart with a little apricot jam and then dusted it lightly with cake crumbs to keep it from getting soggy. Then I spread on the frangipane mixture. While I prepared the base of the tart, Lee peeled and thinly sliced some apples, which we arranged on top of the cream in decorative concentric circles. I sprinkled the apples with a little sugar to ensure a nicely caramelized finish. And sure enough, the tart emerged golden from the oven. To give it a professional look we made a glaze, using a special gel that is mixed with water and heated. At home I simply heat and strain apricot jam, which works well enough, but Chef Paul had a better idea. He suggested using white grape jelly since its high pectin content gives baked tarts a beautiful sheen.

The morning's work was done! We wiped off our tables, disposed of our dirty aprons and side towels, and headed off to lunch. Standing in the line before Chef Delaplane, I decided to try the braise, a New Mexican green chile stew with Navajo bread. Like all the other lunches I'd had at the K-17 kitchen, the portion was huge, and I barely made a dent. I talked mainly to Carrie about how to juggle family and career, and reassured her that as her little boy grew it would be easier to find a balance in her life. The men meanwhile were engaged in their own conversation—predictably enough, discussing sports. Why did this gender divide seem so inevitable, I wondered, even among a group of like-minded people? I had only just begun to ponder this question when a towering figure materialized at our table. It was Chef Hinnerk, who had recognized several of us from previous boot camps and come over to say hello. He was as affable as ever and glad to see that we had returned for more training.

AFTERNOON LECTURE
CHOCOLATE

In the afternoon we'd been promised a treat: a lecture and demonstration on chocolate. But first we had to get our group picture taken. The day was warm enough to gather outside without overcoats, and the spring sun felt good. In this photograph, no display of baked goods distracts the viewer's eye from our faces. We stand fully revealed, looking a little bowlegged in our baggy chef's pants, but smiling. The three women are strategically interspersed among the men. Chef Paul is clearly the master, even though he is dwarfed by Ray's six-foot frame. Perhaps most significantly, we aren't posing. We lean into one another, not afraid to touch, our shoulders relaxed. Everyone is leaning ever so slightly forward, as though ready to stride right out of the picture and into your kitchen to demonstrate what we can do.

Our guest lecturer for the afternoon was Chef Patricia Mitchell, from the CIA's baking and confectionery program. She began with a discussion of chocolate itself and how it is processed from the cocoa bean into its various forms, including white chocolate (not technically chocolate, since it contains no cocoa solids), milk chocolate, a variety of semisweet and bittersweet chocolates, unsweetened chocolate, and cocoa powder. Chef Patricia explained the term *couverture*, French for "covering," which refers to the processed chocolate favored by confectioners for its excellent melting properties. And no wonder it melts well: to be designated as couverture, more than one-third of the weight of the chocolate must consist of cocoa butter. The best manufacturers blend their chocolates, just as vintners blend fine wines, and once you train your palate you can detect different flavors that reflect both the manufacturer and the chocolate's point of origin. Chef Patricia stressed the concept of *terroir*, or local flavor, which extends to chocolate as much as to wine. A tropical note of bananas is often discernible in chocolate processed from beans growing on cacao trees near banana plantations. She noted that Scharffen Berger chocolate has a distinctly fruity taste, while other brands are more astringent.

Like coffee beans and grapes, cocoa beans are fermented to develop their flavor, a process that requires some artistry. They are then dried in the sun, after which the shell is winnowed from the bean, leaving behind the shattered bits of beans, the nibs. Nibs from one variety of cocoa bean are usually blended with nibs from other varieties to achieve the desired flavor and texture. The blended nibs are then ground to a thick paste, known as chocolate liquor. Hardened into bars, this liquor is the unsweetened chocolate we use for baking.

Chocolate liquor consists of cocoa solids and cocoa fat or butter, Chef Patricia explained. The solids contain all of the chocolate flavor (which is why "white chocolate" is a misnomer, since it lacks true chocolate flavor). Cocoa butter is virtually flavorless, yet it is crucial to good chocolate because it has the wonderful melting properties that contribute to chocolate's sensuous mouthfeel. Sugar, vanilla, and lecithin (an emulsifier) are added to the chocolate liquor to bring it to various degrees of sweetness. For milk chocolate, milk or cream is added. Then the chocolate undergoes a process known as conching to improve its flavor and texture. Chocolate is conched by running it through stainless-steel rollers for up to 72 hours; as the chocolate circulates, it grows smoother and smoother.

Chef Patricia was growing more animated, eager to begin her demonstration. The final step before the chocolate is ready to use is tempering, she announced. There was that word yet again! In the context of chocolate, tempering describes the process of heating and cooling chocolate to recrystallize the cocoa butter that melted during the conching process. The fat crystals in the cocoa butter must be stabilized so that the chocolate will have a sleek appearance and not deteriorate quickly. Tempered chocolate is crisp and shiny, never dull, so it makes beautiful molded candies and glazes. Although chocolate comes tempered from the factory, once it is melted, the solids and the fats separate. So each time it is melted it must be retempered to stabilize it again. The proper temperature depends on the type of chocolate. After initially being heated, dark chocolate is brought down to the range of 89–90°F, while milk chocolate is brought down to 86–88°F. White chocolate must be cooled to 85–88°F before it is brought back up to a higher temperature. No chocolate should exceed 91°F, however, or the cocoa butter will melt again.

Forms of chocolate (clockwise from top): gianduja, dark chocolate, cocoa powder, white chocolate, cocoa nibs, cocoa beans, chocolate liquor, and milk chocolate pistoles (center)

Chef Patricia noted that the tempering process for chocolate is basically the same as that used for steel. I thought of the classic Soviet novel I had been forced to read in graduate school—*How the Steel Was Tempered*, by Nikolai Ostrovsky, the story of a young Communist superhero. Little did I imagine then that I would be thinking about tempering in a vastly new context. I had moved from socialism to chocolate.

I had no time to ponder this existential question because Chef Patricia had already begun to demonstrate how chocolate is tempered. First, she had to heat it. She chopped a slab of chocolate as finely as possible and placed it in a bowl, which she set over a hot water bath. Chef Patricia noted that the water should be kept below boiling, at 120°F. The idea is to heat dark chocolate to between 115°F and 120°F, at which point it will melt. White chocolate needs only to be brought to 105°F. In either case, you want to melt the chocolate gradually to be certain that it doesn't burn. Even the slightest burned spot will ruin an entire batch of chocolate by making it bitter. The work bowl should be large enough so that steam from the pan cannot condense and drip into the chocolate—any water will make the chocolate seize up. If water does happen to drip into the pan, carefully spoon it from the surface. When the chocolate has melted, remove the pan from the heat and dry the bottom of the bowl to avoid any water contamination.

Chef Patricia poured about a third of the melted chocolate out onto a thick marble slab. She told us that the ideal slab size is 2 feet square, to allow plenty of elbow room.

She likes to use an offset spatula or a flexible bench scraper to work the chocolate. As she began to stir the chocolate, Chef Patricia told us that the three most important things to remember are time, temperature, and agitation. When we looked a little confused at the last word in the series, she clarified that she meant not our own agitation, but the agitation or stirring of the chocolate.

Untempered chocolate is "seeded" with tempered chocolate from the slab—in other words, the tempered chocolate is added back into the bowl with the remaining untempered chocolate, and then it is all poured back out onto the slab. This is called the tabling method. The chocolate must be worked and smoothed and scraped continually with the spatula or scraper until the temperature and consistency are right. Chef Patricia showed us how to dig into the chocolate, always keeping the scraper clean so that the texture of the mass remains consistent.

She agitated the chocolate until it turned thick and fudgelike, at which point she was able to build up a little pile in the center of the slab. Tempered chocolate will set in 3 to 5 minutes, Chef Patricia explained, so it's important to keep an eye on things. Chocolate must be kept "in temper" so that it doesn't harden too much. If it gets too hard it can always be heated again over hot water; however, you don't want to create extra work for yourself.

Chef Patricia told us that there is a less labor-intensive way to temper chocolate, though the results are not quite as fine. This method, known as the block or seeding method, requires that two-thirds of the total amount of chocolate be melted; the remaining one-third is cut into chunks. These chunks are stirred into the melted chocolate until they stop melting.

I was totally absorbed in the demonstration when my thoughts suddenly gelled into an epiphany. Our class was compatible because we were "in temper," at one with each other and with our surroundings. Tempering was what group dynamics were all about! Could this class have provided a metaphor for the way to live one's life? I felt agitated, though not in the way Chef Patricia meant. As soon as the demonstration ended, I raced across the courtyard to the library to look *temper* up in the dictionary. I discovered that the verb *temper* comes from the Latin *temperare*, "to moderate, mix," and means "to dilute or soften by the addition of something else." An archaic meaning is "to cause to be well disposed: mollify." Tempering can also mean "to make stronger or more resilient through hardship: toughen," or "to put in tune with something else: attune." What an extraordinary culinary word! Tempering can toughen or soften, yet it inevitably results in a much improved state. I was carried away by the metaphor. The problem in baking boot camp was that we had never tempered our relationships to one another, so we had never succeeded in coming together as a group. In pastry boot camp, by contrast, we were continually aware of ourselves in relation to others, as individual personalities—ingredients, if you will—that lent flavor and texture to the larger mix.

I continued to toy with these ideas after the break as I watched Chef Patricia work with the tempered chocolate. Her expertise and efficiency were impressive. First, she showed us transfer sheets—thin, beautifully patterned pieces of acetate soaked with food coloring that can be cut into decorative shapes or wrapped around the sides of a layer cake. She spread the chocolate on a strip of the acetate. After it hardened, she peeled off the acetate to reveal a lovely color-decorated strip of chocolate with a gorgeous sheen.

Next it was our turn to work with the chocolate. Because it was close to Easter, Chef Patricia had brought some Easter bunny molds for us to fill. We began by painting each interior side of the mold with chocolate to make sure that air bubbles didn't appear on the outside edges. Then we closed the molds, stood them upright, and slowly poured the chocolate in to fill them, tapping them hard on the table to burst any air bubbles that might have formed. For hollow bunnies, Chef Patricia explained, the chocolate is allowed to set up in stages to the thickness desired. Then the excess chocolate is poured out. To see how thick the chocolate is, simply tilt the mold from side to side. For a solid chocolate bunny, the mold is filled to the top with chocolate. Lavinia wondered how to finish the hollow bunnies, since the mold leaves an opening at the bottom. Chef Patricia showed us how to set the unmolded bunny on a strip of chocolate and press down until it adheres. She advised us to polish the mold after each use with cheesecloth or a cotton ball to get rid of all traces of cocoa butter, which could turn rancid and spoil the taste of the next molded chocolate.

Chef Patricia then demonstrated how to make a 2-inch-high ring for a dessert container for berries or mousse. She cut a 6-inch strip of transfer acetate and spread it with chocolate. When the chocolate was firm but still malleable, she picked up the strip and looped it into a ring, overlapping the edges to seal so that the pattern was on the outside. She left the transfer sheet in place until the chocolate was completely set (it can be chilled in the refrigerator for 5 or 10 minutes to speed up the process), then carefully peeled it off. Using the same technique, she next made a 1½-inch-high teardrop shape that could be filled with a disk of cake, or again with mousse. These chocolate containers can be held at cool room temperature for a few weeks.

Our final activity was a chocolate tasting. Chef Patricia asked us to judge various chocolates in terms of aroma (any detectable flavors, such as citrus or vanilla?), break (does it snap cleanly or crumble?), melt or mouthfeel (is it smooth, gritty, or waxy? does it melt quickly or slowly in the mouth?), and taste (how does it develop from start to finish? is it spicy, bitter, musty, etc.?). She noted that just as with wine tasting, you should clear both your palate and your mind and make sure there are no ambient odors to affect the sense of taste. You should also be certain that you haven't recently drunk coffee, which raises the bitterness threshold. Gum chewing and smoking are obvious no-nos. Warm water should be used to rinse your mouth between samples.

We blind-tasted ten different chocolate products, beginning with the sweetest and moving to the most intense. They included a sweet, creamy white chocolate by Cacao Barry, a milk chocolate containing 45 percent sugar, a German chocolate, and dark chocolates ranging between 64 and 70 percent cocoa solids. My favorite was the fruity 64 percent Valrhona with its sensuous mouthfeel. After the chocolate samples we moved on to Scharffen Berger cocoa nibs. They were bitter, with a slight taste of banana, and would add a welcome crunch to sweet baked goods. Next we tried two different kinds of cocoa powders, one a dark reddish brown, the other a light milky brown. Chef Patricia asked which we thought was the superior powder. Almost everyone voted for the darker powder—it looked richer, which meant that presumably it would have a deeper chocolate taste. But this darker powder turned out not to be natural cocoa. It had been Dutch-processed—alkalized to reduce acidity—and in fact its chocolate flavor was not as intense. Chef Patricia suggested always using natural cocoa powder and neutralizing it slightly by adding baking soda to the recipe. We ended the tasting with gianduja, a lovely chocolate and hazelnut paste.

Chef Patricia had thoughtfully brought cellophane bags and bright pink ribbons so that we could wrap up our bunnies to take home. My solid chocolate bunny must have weighed a pound. It looked festive and professional in its wrapper. We thanked Chef Patricia for all she had taught us and then went our separate ways, which for me meant going for a brief run around the campus. Now that there was no snow on the ground I could enjoy the narrow footpaths.

DINNER AT THE RISTORANTE CATERINA DE' MEDICI

Our evening meal was at the Caterina de' Medici restaurant. The menu had changed since my last visit, and I was delighted to find Bob's favorite Bistecca alla Fiorentina, the Grilled Rib-Eye Steak for Two with Roasted Tuscan-Style Potatoes and Broccoli Rabe. At $48, the meal promised excess, but I convinced Lee to split an order with me. Dinner started off quietly. As the academics in the group, Ray and I were a little embarrassed that we had been drawn together by our common scholarly language; for the past couple of days we had been comparing notes about life in academe. Now we were at it again. Lee decided to enter into our conversation. Since he had recently graduated from college, his memory of certain classes was still strong, and he told us how unfair one of his professors had been. Suddenly the whole table got going, each of us

sharing war stories about the cruelest professors we had ever had. It was surprising how deep the humiliation ran, in my case still vivid after thirty-odd years as I recalled a certain French professor who had mocked every student for the slightest mispronunciation. These stories were cathartic but also sobering for Ray and me. Lavinia suggested we shift the conversation to acts of kindness instead of cruelty, and so we went around the table, sharing tales of people who had been especially good to us. We were so caught up in the evening that we didn't want it to end, but we knew that our lesson in puff pastry was scheduled for early the next day, and Chef Paul was no laid-back professor. So we said fond goodbyes and headed out to our cars, parked nearby following our collective protest against Siberian parking in the evenings. It had been a great day.

Dining room of the Ristorante Caterina de' Medici

chapter 8

PUFF PASTRY

I awoke with a great sense of anticipation. Today was the day I'd been waiting for—our lesson in puff pastry! Perhaps more than any other kind of dough, puff pastry distinguishes the chefs from the recruits. Tender, flaky, light as a wisp—if I could make dough like that, I'd be thrilled. So I bounded eagerly to class.

Chef Paul began the day by explaining that only 20 percent of the restaurants in the United States employ a pastry chef. It's an underrated profession, he said, and pastry chefs don't get nearly the respect that celebrity chefs do. This attitude is especially wrong, Chef Paul maintained, because a minimum of ten years' experience after culinary school is necessary to become an executive pastry chef. It's a long, hard road. You either love working with dough or you don't, and pastry making is not something to take on if you don't love dough, because it's difficult work. I suppose we all looked a little skeptical—how could what we'd learned so far compare to being under the gun to produce a perfectly plated meal? It was only when we began working with the puff pastry that we realized how much talent it takes to make the dough respond.

LAMINATED DOUGHS

Chef Paul described the different kinds of laminated doughs. I'd always associated the term "laminated" with plywood. But it made sense that layered doughs would be considered laminated, too. This category of doughs includes croissant dough, puff pastry, and Danish dough, each of which varies slightly from the others. All share a common basis in the creation of many layers of dough and fat through rolling, folding, and turning the dough. When the dough is exposed to heat, steam is created and trapped in the layers of fat. This process causes the dough to rise dramatically, to puff up; hence the name puff pastry. The layers of fat act as natural leavening and, when properly constructed, make the dough tender, flaky, and very light. Without enough fat layers, the steam will escape, causing the pastry not to rise properly. The dough will also fail to rise properly if the layers of fat are not kept distinct from the dough (if the butter is worked too fully into the dough, for instance). Because the fat separates the layers, Chef Paul explained, it's important that the fat remain cold so that it doesn't melt into the dough and merge with it.

At this point Chef Paul decided to truncate his lecture to give us a demo, so that we could visualize what he was talking about. We donned our toques and headed into the kitchen. There are two main steps in making laminated dough, Chef Paul explained. First you have to work some fat into the dough; then you must roll out and fold the dough in order to create distinct layers. There are three methods of incorporating, or "locking in," the fat, a process also known by the French term *beurrage* (from the word *beurre*, "butter"). The locking in is literal—you want to trap the butter in the layers of dough so that when it begins to melt under heat it will create steam to leaven the pastry. The method of locking in depends on the result you want. The "all-in" method, used for blitz, or rough, puff pastry, mixes the fat right into the flour. The two-fold, three-fold, book-fold, and envelope methods fold together two separate doughs—one made with water, the other with butter—and are used variously for classic puff pastry as well as for the other laminated doughs.

Chef Paul directed us to the Classic Puff Pastry recipe in our manual. As expected, the ingredients were listed by weight, not volume, in both standard American and metric equivalents. But there was also a third column, called "Bakers' Percentage." I felt confused: the percentages of the ingredients added up to much more than 100 percent. For instance, the first component of the puff pastry, the water dough, included 20 percent cake flour, 80 percent bread flour, 10.2 percent butter, 50.7 percent water, and 1.8 percent salt. The fat dough, which would be folded with the water dough, contained 88.9 percent butter. This made no obvious sense. Chef Paul explained that the bakers' percentage is based on a formula that allows bakers easily to scale a recipe up or down, depending on how much they want to bake in a day. This

The fat dough, or roll-in (ingredients on left), is primarily butter with a little flour (bread and pastry); the water dough (ingredients on right) is mostly flour (bread and pastry), salt, and water with a little butter.

formula also makes it easy to fix mistakes—if you add too much salt, for instance, you can easily scale up the rest of the ingredients proportionally. He noted that the bakers' percentage is based on weight, either metric or standard American, and that each ingredient is listed as a percentage of the total weight of the flour, which is conceived of as the starting point. Thus the weight of the flour is always 100 percent. Suddenly the recipe became clear. The weight of the flour (or flours, as in our recipe) was a total of 40 ounces, which meant that the weight of each additional ingredient was divided by 40 ounces to arrive at the percentage in relation to the flour being used. That's why 20 grams of salt was 1.8 percent—of the flour, not of the total—and why 20 ounces of water was 50.7 percent. No wonder this component of the recipe was called the "water dough." From the bakers' percentage I now could see that water made up half of its total weight. Looking at a recipe this way yields a better understanding of the relationships among ingredients. Chef Paul conceded that the bakers' percentage can get confusing if you are making breads with sponges (starters), since you have to account for the weight of the flour used in the sponge as well. But since he focused on pastry doughs, he found the bakers' percentage simple and very useful.

But then he dismissed the arithmetic with a wave of his hand and suggested that we just watch him work and everything would come clear. As usual, he was right. First he sifted together some bread flour and cake flour, then set one-fifth of the total weight aside. To the remaining flour he cut

in butter that had been softened. The degree of softness is very important, Chef Paul said. The butter should be malleable but not greasy or beginning to melt. He accomplished this cutting in with the Hobart mixer, using the dough hook attachment on low speed, treating the fat as though he were making pie dough. When the mixture still contained visible lumps, he stopped the machine to show us how it should look. If the butter is mixed in too uniformly, he reiterated, then the layers won't form properly and the dough won't rise well.

Next Chef Paul dissolved a little salt in cold water and added it to the bowl, mixing for 3 to 5 minutes at medium speed. When the dough was mixed he turned it out onto a floured table, shaped it roughly into a rectangular block, and wrapped it in plastic wrap to relax in the refrigerator—at least 30 minutes and up to an hour. You can leave it longer, Chef Paul told us, but that will make your task more difficult, because the butter will become too hard to roll the dough out easily, so you'll need to let it soften a little at room temperature first.

While the water dough was resting, Chef Paul made the fat dough. Here the butter constituted a whopping 88.9 percent of the total weight of the flour. Fat dough is right! Using the paddle attachment, on low speed he blended until smooth the butter and the flour he had earlier set aside, a process that took around 2 minutes. The fat dough should not have any lumps. The main concern, however, is not to overmix, which can happen easily with professional mixers that heat up quickly. Chef Paul turned the fat dough out onto parchment paper and covered it with another piece of parchment. Then he rolled it out to a rectangle three-quarters of the size that the water dough rectangle would eventually be once it had been rolled out. This ratio was conceptually difficult for us to grasp, since the water dough hadn't yet been rolled out. But the fat dough had to be rolled out immediately so that it would firm up in the right shape—a matter of practice, Chef Paul assured us. After shaping the fat dough, Chef Paul wrapped it in plastic wrap and put it in the refrigerator. The idea, he explained, was—as with everything else—to temper the two doughs so that they are at the same consistency when combined. Tempering has to do with consistency, not just with temperature, he reminded us. In the case of puff pastry, if either component dough is too hard or too soft it will be impossible to create the distinct layers necessary for a successfully laminated dough.

While Chef Paul's doughs were chilling, we went to our stations to practice making our own laminated dough. We all felt tired and a little overwhelmed. For one thing, because of our late night at the restaurant most of us hadn't gotten enough sleep. More to the point, making puff pastry was the first procedure we'd encountered that relied heavily on practice and technique, and none of us felt particularly confident. The class was unusually quiet as we focused on the work at hand.

Lee and I managed to get our doughs into pretty good shape, though we felt a bit anxious about getting everything done within the allotted time. Chef Paul had a lot to demonstrate this morning, so our own labors were constantly interrupted as we ran over to

his table to watch him show us something new. The other students seemed uncharacteristically ruffled as well. At the demo table Lavinia fretted that her fat dough was too soft to fold into the water dough without melding them; Nick's dough kept sticking to the work surface, no matter how much flour he used. This anxious edge, Ray mentioned, was more like the atmosphere in cooking boot camp, where time pressure was always an issue. Our pastry class had been more relaxed up until now. True, we had to make sure that we didn't burn sugar when caramelizing it, or that we didn't overbeat cream and turn it into butter. But the pace had been slower. No longer! Only Lee appeared to be his usual cheerful self, eager to help everyone else out whenever he could.

Chef Paul asked someone to fetch his prepared doughs from the refrigerator. He floured the work surface lightly, using that professional Frisbee-like toss of the hand to scatter flour evenly over the work surface without any little piles. He rolled the dough out into a perfect rectangle about ¼ inch thick, large enough to cover two-thirds of a sheet pan. The butter—the fat dough—should be the same thickness, he said, and we had no doubt that he had rolled it out properly the first time. The edges of the rectangle must be straight, not wavy, Chef Paul continued, and it's important that the corners be square, not rounded. Otherwise the fat will not be properly trapped. These admonitions made us uneasy. Even though Chef Paul made the rolling look easy, we could sense that it demanded real skill.

He placed the firmed-up rectangle of fat dough onto half of the water dough rectangle, leaving 1 inch around the edges. He showed us the two-fold lock-in method, which sounded serious. After adding the fat dough and folding the water dough around it, he rolled it out into a rectangle (with perfectly square corners), brushed away the excess flour, wrapped the dough, and put it in the refrigerator to chill. Meanwhile, we students returned to our stations to try our hand at rolling out and combining the two doughs.

After his dough had firmed up, Chef Paul showed us how to place the rectangle on a floured surface with the closed (folded) end facing away from the baker. By keeping the three open ends at the front and sides you can keep track of the direction in which the dough is rolled. To my surprise, he rolled the dough out from side to side, rather than from front to back, until it extended to one and a half times the size of the sheet pan. Be careful not to roll the dough too thinly, he warned, or the layers will be lost. Chef Paul displayed the long strip of dough he had created. He proceeded to fold it into thirds—a technique, he explained, known as the three-fold method, which triples the number of layers and so is preferred for an airier pastry. Essentially, you fold the dough as you would a sheet of paper to put into a envelope. The four-fold, or book-fold, method would produce even more layers. For now, though, Chef Paul decided to stick to the three-fold method, which he recommended that we try. Chef Paul also suggested that, as beginners, we fold and roll the dough only five times,

since the layers become increasingly fragile with each subsequent fold. He didn't want us to risk compressing all of our carefully made layers.

Chef Paul wrapped the finished dough in plastic wrap to relax in the refrigerator for a half hour or so before baking, adding that it can be held for three to four days before use. He mentioned that the best puff pastry is prepared in a cool kitchen, which allows the butter to remain at the right temperature. No wonder puff pastry never took hold in the American South.

Just as we were processing all this information, Chef Paul told us that there was yet another way to lock in the butter, called the envelope lock-in method. For this method, the water dough is rolled into a square, not a rectangle. The fat dough, which has been rolled into a smaller square, is placed in the center, leaving four triangles around the edges. These four sides are then folded over the butter as though sealing an envelope, thereby locking in the fat. The rolling proceeds from there. No matter how you lock in the dough, Chef Paul emphasized, the important things to remember when making laminated doughs are that the water dough and the fat dough must be at the right temperature, the layers of fat must not be too thin or too thick, and the rolling and folding should be as uniform as possible. Otherwise, even if the pastry rises well, some spots will rise more than others and the finished product will be uneven (as we all soon discovered).

I asked Chef Paul how croissant and Danish pastry dough differ from regular puff

pastry. Though these doughs don't end up as crisp or as layered, they have a more tender texture. Chef Paul explained that croissant dough actually uses half the amount of butter as puff pastry, which surprised me, since it tastes so buttery. Croissant dough is folded in thirds only three times, not six, as is Danish pastry dough. But the main difference is that these doughs contain yeast and eggs. Chef

Paul reminded us that there is also something known as blitz puff pastry, which, as the name implies, you can make in a pinch if you're short of time, though it won't rise as high as the classic puff pastry. Blitz puff pastry dough must be rolled out evenly, to ½ inch thick. If it isn't rolled out thinly enough, it won't puff well, and it might not bake all the way through.

1. The first step in any folding method is called the lock-in. To begin, the fat dough is placed on half of the water dough. Then the water dough is folded over the fat dough, and the edges are sealed so that the butter is trapped inside the dough—if it leaks out, the steam won't leaven the layers. Immediately following the lock-in, Chef Paul turned the dough 90 degrees and rolled it out, making sure that all the edges were straight and the corners square.

2. Before each fold, the dough is turned 90 degrees, which allows the gluten strands to be worked in different directions to yield maximum rise. Each time the dough is turned and rolled out, it is folded into thirds (described on page 132). Chef Paul made a dimple mark in the dough to show which fold this was. Because the dough is usually folded and rolled six times, it's easy enough to forget which is the current fold; the dimples are an easy way to keep track. He put the dough on a sheet pan, wrapped it well, and left it in the refrigerator to rest and firm up a little.

3. The difference between laminated doughs and other pastries is that they are folded and rolled out, then folded and rolled out again. Some pastry doughs are given a type of fold known as a four-fold. Chef Paul explained its virtues: It quadruples the number of layers and can yield an astonishing 800 to 1,200 layers in the finished pastry! The four-fold method requires you to fold the short ends of the rectangle in to meet in the center. Then the entire sheet is folded in half, as if closing a book, giving this technique its other name: the book-fold method.

4. Chef Paul advised us to handle the dough as little as possible during the rolling and folding process so that it doesn't warm up, and to be sure to let it rest sufficiently between rollings. Finally, to reduce shrinkage, let the dough rest for 20 to 30 minutes before baking. When I saw how perfectly even his puff pastry was in a classic pastry like a napoleon, I was convinced of how critical the folding, rolling, and resting process is to the success of puff pastry.

The recipe for Classic Puff Pastry is on page 252. The recipe for Napoleons is on page 255.

BUTTERCREAM

Chef Paul told us to wrap up our puff pastry dough well. We would do the final shaping tomorrow. Today we still had to learn how to make perfect buttercreams.

I was beat. We all were, but for Chef Paul the morning seemed to have just begun. He was in his element, enjoying the bustle of the production kitchen, happy to be back in gear. Although he had risen at 4:30 a.m. to drive to the CIA in time for our 7:00 class, he showed no signs of flagging. We felt like sissies in his wake, but those laminated doughs had been daunting. Chef Paul chided us as we lingered by his worktable, reluctant to begin new labors. We must finish our buttercream before lunch, he decreed. Not a minute to waste!

I had never had much luck making buttercream at home—it often separated into fatty globules and wasn't the wonderfully smooth, lush frosting that I craved on layer cakes. But Chef Paul said that making buttercream was a snap, as long as we based it on an Italian meringue. This bit of information relieved me—I'd learned the Italian meringue technique in baking boot camp, so now I could let my mind rest while he explained the process to the rest of the class. But even through my less-than-attentive haze, I heard Chef Paul say that he was so expert that he didn't even need a thermometer to know when the sugar syrup had reached the soft ball stage. He just stuck his finger into the boiling syrup to test it! If you do it quickly enough, you won't get burned,

he assured us. Did anyone want to try? At first no one seemed game, but I was determined to show Chef Paul that I wasn't just a little woman. I announced that I'd try. Chef Paul dipped his right index finger and thumb into a glass of very cold water, then swooped down into the sugar syrup to retrieve a little. He immediately dipped his fingers back into the cold water and extracted them with a perfect soft ball of sugar in his hand. I took a deep breath, dipped my fingers into the cold water, and then plunged them into the syrup. I didn't get burned—it didn't even hurt! Chef Paul raised his eyebrows. Interestingly, the dynamics between us instantly changed. From that moment on, Chef Paul made an extra effort to share his expertise with me and evinced interest in my work.

Chef Paul drew our attention to the buttercream recipe, which in addition to 6½ ounces of butter called for Sweetex, an artificially sweetened shortening. Professional kitchens sometimes add shortening because it improves the product's shelf life, but Sweetex didn't sound at all appealing, so we were relieved that we didn't have to use it. We returned to our stations to make our own buttercreams. As we worked, Chef Paul made his rounds.

Ordinarily, we would have used the buttercream right away, and in fact we were eager to, but it was 11:00, time for lunch, and we knew what that meant—our protestations would be to no avail. Chef Paul said we could refrigerate the buttercream until we were ready to frost our cakes, at which point we'd warm it to room temperature and beat it

(continues on page 140)

1. Chef Paul told us that if we didn't want to feel so frantic, we could put the egg whites in the mixing bowl when we began heating the sugar syrup and mix them at lowest speed. Once the syrup was ready, we could turn the speed up to bring the whites quickly to soft peaks, and then add the syrup.

2. As the sugar syrup boiled, Lee and I carefully used a soft brush dipped in water to brush away any crystals that formed on the side of the pan. When the syrup reached 230° to 233°F (we tested it with an instant-read thermometer, not with our fingers), we began beating the egg whites to soft peaks. As soon as the syrup reached 240°F we transferred it quickly to a pitcher, then gradually streamed the syrup into the egg whites as the mixer continued to whip them on high speed.

$3.$ We continued beating the whites until they had cooled to room temperature, a good 15 minutes. Suddenly we heard a groan from Nick and Ray's station. They had added the syrup too quickly, causing the egg whites to collapse. Not to worry, Chef Paul reassured them: the whites will come back once the butter is beaten in. And sure enough, they did, like magic. Lee and I were glad for this bit of kitchen wisdom.

$4.$ Even though our egg whites were nice and billowy, when we began beating in the softened butter all at one go, the mixture looked broken beyond repair. But we followed Chef Paul's advice and kept whipping. The mixture came together and turned out perfectly. It was all I could do not to start spooning the buttercream into my mouth, but I contented myself with a few surreptitious swipes of the finger.

The recipe for Italian Buttercream, shown here, is on page 265.

again with the paddle attachment to make it fluffy and spreadable. This buttercream is very versatile, he added. It can be flavored with liqueurs or essences, or we could beat in some melted and cooled chocolate. Or we could make a rich hazelnut buttercream with brandy, vanilla extract, and praline paste. No matter the flavor, he continued, for best results we should always use European-style butter with a high fat content. With that advice ringing in our ears, we reluctantly put our buttercream in the refrigerator and traipsed upstairs to lunch.

The K-17 menu had changed again. Today's featured region was South America. I was impressed to see the famous Brazilian stew fcijoada on offer. This dish was far too heavy for 11 a.m., especially after puff pastry and buttercream, but I was curious to see how it had been prepared. Although toned down—without the difficult, if authentic, parts such as pigs' ears and tails—the CIA feijoada was very flavorful, and the braised collards on the side were a thrilling touch.

After lunch we cleaned up the kitchen, which was a little more time-consuming than usual because so much flour had scattered everywhere. No sooner had we wiped down the last table than it was time for our afternoon lecture, this one on how to pair wine with desserts.

DESSERT WINES

Our lecturer was a charming Englishman, Brian Smith, a professor in wine studies and liberal arts. Yet I sensed, for the first time, some nervousness among my classmates. Wine is funny in how it brings out people's insecurities. That morning we had accomplished some pretty amazing feats in the kitchen, but the imminent wine tasting threatened to strip us of our well-earned confidence. Brian cut through all of that. He was very friendly and accessible, and he wanted to make wines that way, too.

Brian explained that sweet wines contain residual sugar that hasn't fermented. Most of the great sweet wines are white, although vintners are now experimenting with sweet reds. The best sweet wines contain only natural sugars from the grapes, not sugar added by means of a sweetening agent. One way to achieve sweet wines is through controlled fermentation, in which the winemaker halts fermentation before all of the grape sugars have converted to alcohol. Many Rieslings and Gewürztraminers are made this way. Fermentation can also be halted by bringing the yeast down to around 38°F, which will stop its action; the wine is then separated from the yeast with a centrifuge. Brian added that sweet wines can also be made by adding grape juice that has not fermented, a process that German wine makers call *Süssreserve.* The addition of unfermented juice enhances the sweetness of wine that has undergone fermentation; because it is a natural product—the result of natural sugars in the wine grapes—it produces a good wine, one that does not taste artificially sweet. Even so, the best winemakers shun this sweetening practice.

Late-harvest wines are rich and sweet because the grapes have been left long on the vine—into October, sometimes even November. This lengthy ripening concentrates the sugars and allows higher levels of glycerol to develop. Late-harvest wines contain very high levels of residual sugar and can be intensely sweet, almost syrupy. Another method for creating ultra-sweet wines is known as raisining. For this process, grapes are picked and dried (essentially turned into raisins) before they are allowed to undergo fermentation. The texture of these wines is viscous, as in the late-harvest ones; their flavor is concentrated, with raisiny undertones.

Brian explained that sweet wines are so highly sought after that some winemakers are willing to take risks to create them. One of the most artful ways of producing sweet wines is to harness the devastating mold *Botrytis cinerea*, which can shrivel grapes on the vine and ruin an entire harvest. Skilled hands, however, can control the growth of the mold to yield the world's most revered sweet wines: Sauternes and Barsac in France, Tokaji in Hungary, Mosel in Germany. Some excellent sweet wines are also being made by this method in the Finger Lakes region of New York State. Brian told us that all of these regions share terrain that includes water near steep slopes, which encourages

mists to form, thereby keeping the grapes cool and damp—the perfect environment for the growth of mold. He explained that botrytis shrivels grapes by creating microscopic holes through which their water content evaporates. The result is a very ugly-looking grape, rusty in appearance; it is, however, wonderfully concentrated in sugars. Brian impressed us with the fact that a single bottle of Château d'Yquem, the most famous sweet wine, is made from the grapes of approximately eight vines. By contrast, a single vine typically yields three or four bottles of dry white wine.

Another type of exceptionally sweet wine is ice wine, for which the grapes are allowed to freeze on the vine, a process that concentrates their sugars. When the grapes are gently pressed, most of their water content remains frozen, but a small amount of highly concentrated sugar solution is pressed out. This juice is allowed to ferment. For a true ice wine, the grapes must be frozen naturally on the vine, not in a freezer. Vintners, especially in Europe, have some concern about global warming and how that will affect their ice wine production in the future.

We were eager to try the samples Brian had brought: six different wines from Germany, Italy, France, and California. We began with the least sweet of the bunch, a Dr. Loosen Erdener Treppchen Riesling Kabinett 2002 from Mosel-Saar-Ruwer, Germany, which contained only 7 percent alcohol. The wine was a pale straw green color, very minerally and flinty. As Brian nicely put it, this Riesling offered "a hint of a memory of

Dessert wines (from left to right) from least to most sweet: Dr. Loosen Erdener Treppchen Riesling Kabinett, Chiarlo Moscato d' Asti, Bonny Doon Vin du Glaciere, La Chapelle de La faurie, Quady Elysium.

sweetness." I liked the fact that it started out sweet on the tongue but ended up slightly sour, thanks to its high acidity. Brian explained that we discern sweetness on the receptors at the tip of our tongue. The acid receptors are on the sides, while bitterness is experienced at the back. As the wine washes from front to back over the different parts of the tongue, we experience various flavors and sensations. Acidity might not sound like

a good thing in a sweet wine, he continued, but it's quite important to the overall balance—key, in fact, so that the wine is not just cloying. He recommended serving this wine as an aperitif rather than for dessert.

We moved on to a Chiarlo Moscat d'Asti 2003 from Piemonte, Italy, also containing 7 percent alcohol. This wine, made from the white muscat grape, tickled our palates. Brian explained that it was frizzante, not spumante, which means that it was only lightly, not highly, sparkling. The wine carried undertones of lychee, white peaches, and tropical fruits. It felt clean on the palate, with good acidity. It wasn't at all overbearing.

We then tried a Baumard Clos Ste. Catherine 2001 from the Loire Valley in France. In contrast to the pale wines we had just tried, this one was bright, almost shockingly yellow. Brian explained that chenin blanc grapes were used for this wine, which was produced by both the late harvest and botrytis methods. In other words, the grapes had rotted and been left to dehydrate on the vine. At 12½ percent alcohol, it was much more alcoholic than the previous two, and its honey aroma was equally intense. Brian urged us always to check the aroma of wine both before and after swirling it in the glass. Even though the intense color and aroma promised incredible sweetness, this wine was dull.

Next came a Bonny Doon Vin du Glacière from 2001, an ice wine for which muscat grapes had been picked and then frozen rather than being frozen on the vine. Bonny Doon has to make ice wine this way because of its California location. The wine was sweet, without complexity. As a fan of ice wine, I wasn't wowed by their untraditional method, which would be impermissible in Germany or Austria, where production methods are strictly controlled. California has enough natural advantages without adding ice wine to its achievements, I thought.

Our fifth wine was the extremely sweet La Chapelle de Lafaurie-Peyraguey 1997, the second label of a famous château in the

Sauternes region of Bordeaux. The chateau turns grapes from its older vines into its first-label wines; grapes from the younger vines go into this second label, which has an alcohol content of 13½ percent. We tasted it and were not impressed. Brian was surprised— this was an excellent wine, he insisted. Then he tasted it and concurred: this bottle was out of condition, probably oxidized. He urged us to rinse our mouths well before trying the final wine, which provided the surprise of our tasting.

The Quady Elysium 2000 from Madera, California, is a big fortified red wine made from black muscat grapes. The grapes were fermented to 3 to 4 percent alcohol. Then, in a process known as mutage, grape brandy was added to halt the fermentation (the alcohol keeps the yeast from working). The alcohol also served to strengthen, or fortify, the wine. The Elysium had fresh grape aromas and flavors and a high percentage of natural sugar and alcohol. I simply loved it. Brian told us that the same company makes a wine from orange muscat grapes called Essencia, which contains a whopping 15 percent alcohol.

After guiding us through our tasting, Brian offered more details on sweet wines. Most Sauternes are made from the semillon grape, though sometimes sauvignon blanc is included. Both Sauternes and Barsac must be affected by botrytis in order to bear their appellation names. Some grapes, such as riesling, chenin blanc, sauvignon blanc, semillon, and furmint (for Tokaji) respond well to botrytis, which must settle on fully ripe grapes that have already developed their flavors. This process usually happens in late September or early October, when under the right climatic conditions the morning mist encourages the growth of the fungus; then the afternoon sun shrivels the grapes. I asked about the differences among Sauternes, Barsac, and Monbazillac. Brian explained that Barsac is virtually the same as Sauternes and is allowed to use the same appellation, while Monbazillac, although lively, is less complex.

Grape varietals for sweet wines include riesling, chenin blanc, and vidal. In Germany, riesling is used for ice wine, whereas in Ontario, Canada, the hybrid vidal grape is widespread. All of these varietals have a long growing season, which allows for a lot of photosynthesis and energy storage in the form of sugar. As the temperature drops, the acidity of the grape rises, which is why some winemakers prefer to harvest at nighttime—to capture the grape at its peak of balanced perfection.

We moved on to a discussion of how to pair wines with desserts. The rule of thumb, Brian told us, is that the wine must be sweeter than the food. Otherwise there's an equalizing effect, and nothing tastes as sweet as it should. Fruits, nuts, or light cheeses go best with sweet wines. Because too sweet a dessert is not good with dessert wine, when you want to highlight your wine don't serve your most sugary concoction.

Our lesson over, we examined the wine labels. All of our tension from the morning's labors had evaporated, and the afternoon imbibing had left us pleasantly relaxed. I discovered that I was also slightly groggy, so I went back to the inn to lie down—no energy to exercise today. But before I knew it, it was already time to drive back up the highway for dinner at Escoffier. This restaurant seemed fitting after the Francocentric approach of the day.

DINNER AT THE ESCOFFIER ROOM

I began with a lovely Pannequets de Saumon Fumé, Radis, et Basilic, otherwise known as Smoked Salmon Tartare with Radishes and Basil, followed by braised veal cheeks with tomato and olive that virtually melted in my mouth, the meat was so tender. For dessert we were excited to find Saint-Honoré on the menu—a glorified gâteau of pastry-cream-filled cream puffs. Here was our chance to see how well the baking and pastry students had executed their pâte à choux. The Saint-Honoré arrived gorgeous in its presentation, but the cream puffs were ever so slightly dry and should have been removed sooner from the oven. That didn't stop us from devouring them, of course.

We had learned from our previous CIA dinners that the service often depended on how far along in their training the waitstaff was. The waiters this evening were skilled and at ease, and Daniel speculated about how many of them would go on to work in restaurants. As holders of a degree from the most elite culinary school in America, they would be eminently hireable. That led us to the topic of celebrity chefs. We agreed that we preferred the closed fraternity of highly skilled chefs (such as Chef Paul) who did not feel the need to show off their talents on TV. We wondered what it would have been like to work under Chef Paul in the Essex House pastry kitchen. Challenging, no doubt!

At that point Lee confided that his parents had mixed feelings about his desire to open a restaurant. As he put it, the restaurant business is not all fame and fancy, as they show on television. There are hot flames, bad tempers, sharp knives, and hungry guests. And your life necessarily revolves around the restaurant. While others are enjoying themselves in the front of the house, there you are slaving away in the hot kitchen. A friend getting married? Sorry, you have to work. Valentine's Day? Same thing. Even New Year's Eve is nothing but work. On Mother's Day you'll cook for other people's mothers instead of being able to take care of your own. Lee's parents had hoped that he would become a doctor or a lawyer, one of the typically prestigious American professions. Yet they also understood that his true passion lay in food and in making others happy, which is really what Lee wanted to do.

Of course, Lee's was the voice of realism. Restaurant work is not all romance, but hard labor, and if you've ever caught sight of the scars and burn marks that parade up chefs' hands and arms, then you know that the kitchen is dangerous, too. Lee's words sobered us, and in the silence of the moment, we realized that the hour was already late. Once again we reluctantly said our goodnights, but this time our voices betrayed regret, for this was our second-to-last night together.

chapter 9

MOUSSE AND
BAVARIAN CREAM

I woke up feeling drained, less than eager to begin the day. With all its rigors, the day before had been the height of my boot camp experience. I had found my grail in the lesson on puff pastry, and had learned to make a spectacular buttercream besides. Today's lesson, on mousses and Bavarian creams, seemed anticlimactic. I loved working with dough; gelatin did not turn me on. So I was especially pleased to discover that Chef Paul felt the same way.

Chef Paul was particularly expansive this morning. He told us about his three sons, all of whom had attended the CIA. One was now the chef at Metrobis, a highly regarded restaurant in Simsbury, Connecticut (this son's wife wrote *Wife of a Chef,* of which Chef Paul disapproved). A second son was executive chef at the Marriott Marquis in New York City, the third a pastry chef at Commander's Palace in Las Vegas. Chef Paul was quite proud of his offspring and pleased that they had followed him into the kitchen. Then he went on—unexpectedly—to talk about celebrity chef Alain Ducasse's "attitude problem," as he put it. Ducasse apparently can't stand women in the kitchen, and Chef Paul let us know that he did not agree with this stance. I found this all tremendously interesting. From my perspective, Chef Paul had attitudes I associated with old-world French chefs, but here he was critiquing the chauvinism of the old guard. It was partly a matter of degree, I realized. In fact, Chef Paul was not entrenched in his ways—he had accepted me after only a few days, despite my initial dishevelment.

Chef Paul related an anecdote about meeting Alain Ducasse when he was opening his eponymous restaurant at the Essex House, where Chef Paul had worked for so many years. Ducasse had arrived at John F. Kennedy International Airport on a diplomatic passport from Monte Carlo, where his flagship restaurant is located. Charged with meeting Ducasse at the airport, Chef Paul discovered that Ducasse had already gone right from the plane to a waiting limousine. A real VIP, Chef Paul grumbled—he didn't like chefs who put on airs. Other gifted pastry chefs, such as Pierre Hermé and François Payard, were much more "mellow," Chef Paul noted approvingly. I got the sense that Chef Paul had never received his due of public acclaim. After all, he was the one who had introduced Silpat to the United States about fifteen years earlier. Silpat is a baker's dream—a nonstick mat that is spread on baking sheets. Unlike parchment, it is sturdy and can be used over and over again. Silpat is now also used in molds to allow very delicate baked goods to slip out without sticking. Among pastry chefs, it's a miracle material.

BAVARIAN CREAMS AND MOUSSES

Chef Paul began his lecture by stating that mousses and creams are an extremely important aspect of the pastry station, and that any chef worth his toque knows how to make them well. But then he confessed, "I'm not a gelatin freak." Like me, he didn't enjoy working with the viscid stuff. I liked him enormously for that frank admission.

I felt no surprise when Chef Paul reminded us that even when making mousses and creams, tempering is very important—if the components are not of the same consistency, they will not blend together well, and you'll end up with a mass of lumps. I suppose we must have looked a little bored: who among us hadn't already made a perfect chocolate mousse? Perhaps realizing that he had to impress us with the difficulty of the day's lesson, Chef Paul asserted that we should be grateful for this class, because regular students at the Culinary are not allowed to make Bavarian creams and mousses until they have worked with pastry for an entire year. The techniques are considered that difficult. Chef Paul went on to say that we could attend the Culinary Institute every day for three years and still learn something new—there is that much to master. He made us feel lucky, even privileged, to be exposed to mousses and Bavarian creams, considering that we were complete novices.

We began with a Bavarian cream, known in French as a *bavarois*. The Bavarian cream begins with a simple vanilla sauce, the crème anglaise we had learned to make on the first day of class. To this sauce gelatin is added for stability, then whipped cream is folded in to lighten the mixture. Exactly how this cream got its name is unknown, but our manual stated that a French chef working in Bavaria brought it to France—an explanation that seemed suspiciously Francophile to me. Chef Paul impressed upon us the importance of having our mise en place ready when attempting to make mousses and creams. I was beginning to see how everything built upon everything else. If I were to stay at the Culinary for more than a few days at a time, I was sure that all of these directives would become second nature. Of course a mise en place! Of course crème anglaise and pastry cream would always be chilling in the refrigerator so that I could make fanciful desserts at a moment's notice!

The mise en place for Bavarian cream included "bloomed gelatin," our recipe said— that is, gelatin that had already been softened in cold water, then heated gently over a water bath until dissolved. I asked Chef Paul about powdered gelatin versus sheet gelatin—the former is more common in the United States, while the latter is favored in Europe. He responded that it's fine to use either kind; the results will be the same. It's just important to know exactly how much gelatin is needed and not use too little or too much. One sheet of gelatin equals 2 grams of powdered gelatin, which means that for every ounce of powdered gelatin we would need to use 14 sheets. When Chef Paul realized that those numbers were meaningless to us, he explained that 1 ounce of gelatin is needed to firm 2 quarts of ingredients. This amount will make the end product nice and firm—perhaps firmer than those of us who aren't avowed gelatin freaks would like. One-half ounce of gelatin will yield a less firm product, but if the weather is warm that amount may not be enough to make it stable. As an aside, Chef Paul added that tropical fruits such as pineapples, papaya, kiwi, and mango have to be cooked first to de-activate certain enzymes they contain; other-wise these enzymes will prevent the gelatin from setting properly.

The mise en place also called for heavy cream that had been whipped to soft peaks, the already prepared vanilla sauce, and what-ever flavoring we desired. Chef Paul explained that the degree to which the cream is whipped has to do with tempering. If the peaks are too stiff, the cream won't fold easily into the vanilla sauce. He recommended adding flavoring to the vanilla sauce before setting it out for the mise en place so that there would be one less step to carry out later. Alternatively, he said, if we wanted the flavor of the cream to be more intense, we could soften the gelatin in the liquid flavor-ing instead of in cold water.

Not only ingredients, but equipment is part of the mise en place. So we needed to ready a whisk, a rubber spatula, and an ice bath for cooling the mixture quickly. Chef Paul then proceeded to demonstrate the Bavarian cream. First, he stirred the bloomed gelatin into the vanilla sauce. A good deal of skill is needed to add gelatin to the vanilla sauce, which has presumably been chilling in the refrigerator, so that it doesn't begin to set immediately. That's why tempering is so cru-cial. If the vanilla sauce is too cold, it will seize up; it should be at room temperature or even slightly warm. This ostensibly simple cream was, in fact, rather complicated.

After the gelatin has been added to the vanilla sauce, the mixture is placed over the ice bath and stirred constantly until it begins to thicken as it cools. At that point the cream should be removed from the ice and the whipped cream folded in. The mixture should be very smooth, without any lumps. This Bavarian cream may be poured into molds and served as is, or it can be used as a cake filling. Chef Paul poured some cream into individual molds and put it in the refrig-erator to firm up, which he said would take several hours.

Our next task was to make a mousse, which all of us considered elementary. The French word *mousse* means "foam." A gen-uine mousse is airy from the addition of beaten eggs or egg whites; it is not the kind of dense chocolate pudding all too often passed off as mousse in restaurants. Mousses belong in the pastry kitchen because, like Bavarian creams, they are frequently used as fillings for cakes or other desserts. When I first began making mousses in high school they were the height of elegance, but, like other fashionable foods in America, once they became ubiquitous they lost their cachet. In those early days, mousses were made with raw eggs, which contributed to their wonderfully light texture. But raw eggs fell out of favor with the rise in salmonella

poisoning. Now many mousse lovers heat the eggs lightly to kill any potential bacteria. Made in this way, mousses are completely food-safe.

Chef Paul explained that there are two methods for making mousse. The first is known as the sabayon method. At the mention of sabayon I perked up. I can still recall my first sabayon (an ethereal concoction of whipped egg yolks, sugar, and wine), eaten when I was twelve years old at a Montreal restaurant called La Vieille Porte when my family was visiting the World's Fair in that city. The restaurant seemed the height of ele-

gance, with red velvet banquettes and dark woodwork—or so I fuzzily picture it. But my memory is clear about the sabayon's pure lightness of being and the very adult taste of the sherry that flavored it.

To make a mousse by the sabayon method, sugar is mixed with egg yolks and any desired flavoring and then whipped over a hot water bath. The heat serves several purposes: it helps egg yolks whip to their maximum volume, it stabilizes the yolks, and, importantly, it kills any bacteria present. The lightly whipped egg mixture is transferred to a mixer, then beaten until it has

cooled to room temperature. Whipped cream and beaten egg whites, if desired, are folded in at this point.

For the cooked-sugar method, the egg yolks are beaten separately in a mixer until very pale yellow and airy. While the yolks are beating, the sugar is mixed with water and brought to the soft ball stage. This syrup is poured very slowly into the egg yolks, as we did when making Italian meringue, except in this case egg yolks, not egg whites, constitute the base. The mixture is beaten until it has cooled and achieved great volume. At that point the cream and bloomed gelatin, if being used, are folded in. For chocolate mousse made by either method, melted chocolate is added to the whipped egg yolk base before the cream is whipped in.

Chef Paul noted that for the cooked-sugar method, the best way to add the gelatin is to "liaison" it—in other words, to temper it with a little of the beaten egg yolks to make sure that it will blend evenly throughout. As he instructed us for the Bavarian cream, it's equally important when making gelatin-enriched mousse to have our molds ready so that the gelatin doesn't set up before the mousse has been molded.

Much as I dislike gelatin, I decided I should practice working with it. So, with Lee's agreement, I chose to make a gelatin-enhanced chocolate sabayon. We began by getting our mise en place ready, mindful of the fact that once the gelatin was added we would have no time to spare. First we sprinkled the gelatin over a mixture of cool water and brandy to bloom. Chef Paul had told us that when blooming gelatin, the ratio should

be 8 parts water (or other liquid) to 1 part gelatin. To boost the flavor of the sabayon we used half water and half brandy. While the gelatin was blooming I whipped some heavy cream and then put it into the refrigerator to hold. After 15 minutes, once the gelatin had softened, I heated it briefly over a hot water bath to melt. Meanwhile, Lee melted some semisweet chocolate over another hot water bath, while I separated the eggs. We weighed out the sugar and measured 3 ounces of sweet Marsala wine. That made me wonder why the recipe was called "Sabayon" instead of "Zabaglione," the Italian precursor to the French sabayon. Marsala is the hallmark flavor of the Italian dessert, while in France white wine is more often used. This recipe title struck me as another instance of the Francocentrism of the culinary world.

I methodically weighed out ⅛ ounce of vanilla extract, grumbling that Chef Paul expected us to weigh this small amount rather than use a measuring spoon or just eyeball it. The effort of walking over to the weighing station for such a piddling amount seemed unnecessary. Lee meanwhile set out molds for the finished sabayon. Finally, all of the components of our mise en place were ready, and it was time to start cooking.

Once my eggs and sugar had cooked to the requisite billowy texture, I removed the pan from the heat and continued to beat the yolks in the mixer until they had cooled to room temperature. Then Lee took over, and we finished our sabayon-style mousse, piping it into glasses and setting them into the refrigerator to firm (but not too much, I hoped) and chill.

1. Once again, the first step is a complete mise en place made by carefully weighing and organizing the ingredients. A mousse gets its texture from beaten eggs and whipped cream. Ours was to be a sabayon-style mousse flavored with chocolate, and we were also going to include some Marsala, both as we cooked the yolks and to bloom the gelatin. Hot water baths, whisks, bowls, and pastry bags completed our equipment mise en place.

2. In a pan over yet another hot water bath (it certainly helped to have a large kitchen arsenal at our disposal), I combined the Marsala with the egg yolks and some sugar and heated the mixture, all the while beating it vigorously by hand to make a sabayon base for the mousse. Chef Paul told us that any-where within the range of 145° to 180°F would be enough to kill the bacteria without overcooking the eggs. Little by little the egg yolks turned pale yellow and fluffy—they made me want to dive right in.

3. Working together, Lee and I scraped the melted chocolate into the sabayon mixture and beat it vigorously by hand. I carefully "liéed" the gelatin with the chocolate mixture, as Chef Paul had instructed, to make sure that it would get evenly dispersed. Then we gently folded the whipped cream into our chocolate sabayon mousse.

4. The mousse was done. We piped it immediately into the prepared molds and set them to chill in the refrigerator. We had a wonderful time licking the bowl. I hoped that the gelatin wouldn't make the mousse set up too firmly and destroy the soft texture I love.

The recipe for Chocolate Sabayon Mousse, shown here, is on page 264.

SHAPING PUFF PASTRY

Today's class didn't feel nearly as onerous as our lesson of the previous day, but neither had it been as thrilling. So I was pleased when Chef Paul said, "It's time to shape our puff pastry!" He would begin with a demonstration of napoleons, palmiers, fruit strips, pastry shells, and the dramatic pastry pithiviers, named after a town in France. For napoleons, Chef Paul said, you need a sheet of puff pastry, which must be rolled out quite thin, to ⅛ inch at most and preferably less, so that it will rise well and bake all the way through. After transferring the rolled-out sheet of pastry to the baking pan, Chef Paul covered it with a piece of parchment paper and then set a second sheet pan on top to keep it from rising unevenly. Once the pastry had attained its full volume in the oven, he would remove the second pan to allow the pastry to brown. I contemplated the amazing power of steam to lift pastry even under a heavy aluminum pan. Chef Paul placed the unbaked pastry in the refrigerator to rest for 15 to 20 minutes before baking.

Next he turned to shaping the palmiers. For these sweet, crisp pastries he dusted the work surface with confectioners' sugar instead of flour. I was surprised at how liberally he sprinkled it on. He rolled the dough out very thin into a rectangle, then brushed it lightly with water and covered it generously with confectioners' sugar. Next, he folded the two outer sides in toward the cen-

ter, using the four-fold lock-in method he had mentioned the previous day. He brushed the dough with water and again sprinkled the pastry heavily with confectioners' sugar so that the dough was thoroughly coated with sugar between all the folds. Then he folded the two sides in like a book. He made vertical slices less than ¼ inch thick along the length of the pastry. These slices he placed flat on the baking sheet, shaping them into the typical palmier (palm tree) shape. Chef Paul explained that when they were halfway done he would turn each palmier over to brown on the other side, resulting in a very crisp, beautifully caramelized pastry.

For fruit strips, Chef Paul showed us how to roll out the rectangle to the size of a sheet pan, 16 by 24 inches. He cut off strips from both of the long sides, then brushed the edges of the remaining rectangle with a wash made of beaten egg. He affixed the strips around the sides of the rectangle. With his fingers and a knife he crimped the edges to make a decorative pattern and ensure that the strips would adhere. Then he pricked the interior of the rectangle so that steam would be released—he didn't want the center to puff up as much as the outside edges. This way a kind of box or container would be formed to fill with fruit. After baking the pastry, he planned to fill the interior with a little pastry cream or whipped cream, top it with fresh fruit, and glaze it. Chef Paul told us that we could make one large fruit strip, as he had just demonstrated, or we could make smaller individual pastries by cutting the original sheet on the diagonal.

Chef Paul was clearly in his element, working efficiently and precisely, with never a ragged edge or an imperfect form to mar his production. Another appealing container, he enthused, is the pastry shell or case. To make that kind of case, you must begin with a perfect square. Easier said than done, I thought — this dough often had a mind of its own. Chef Paul showed how to fold the initial square into a triangle. Then you must notch the triangle on two sides in order to create a hollowed-out center when it is unfolded. The remaining side of the triangle is folded back across the notched sides, and ta-da—there's your container! It did look like sleight of hand. Chef Paul brushed this pastry shell with egg wash to give it a nice sheen, cautioning us never to overbake puff pastry, or it will turn bitter. He recommended putting the pastry into the oven at 380°F, then reducing the temperature to 365°F once the pastry has puffed up and begun to brown. No fair, cried Daniel—how many home ovens are calibrated that precisely? All right, Chef Paul conceded with a smile, put the pastry in at 375°F or even 400°F. The idea is to give the pastry a lift with a blast of hot air, then reduce the temperature so that the pastry doesn't brown too quickly before baking through.

After this demonstration, Chef Paul sent us back to our stations to play with our dough. Lee tackled a fruit strip, while I decided to go all out and make a pithiviers. This pastry appealed to me not only for its spectacular presentation, but also because it contains my favorite flavor, almond. And I liked the idea of putting to use the pastry

cream and the frangipane filling that we had already made. All the components were at hand: puff pastry dough, already rolled, folded, and chilled; pastry cream; and frangipane filling. Unfortunately, I hadn't had time to bring the frangipane to room temperature. The filling was very hard, too hard to work with, so I scooped some out of the bowl and agitated it with the paddle attachment on low speed until it had softened slightly. Then I mixed it with a little pastry cream to make it less dense.

I divided the dough in half, then rolled out one-half to a 12-inch square. With a sharp knife I cut a circle out of that square, temporarily setting aside the scraps of dough (both Chef Kate and Chef Paul had taught us that in a good kitchen nothing ever goes to waste). I mounded the frangipane filling high in the center of the circle, leaving a 1-inch border all around. Then I moistened the border with water and brushed it with egg wash. Next I rolled out the second piece of dough into another 12-inch square and cut an identical circle from it, which I carefully draped over the domed filling, pressing it down firmly all the way around to enclose it (the egg wash helped it to adhere). I now had a covered mound with a round border encircling it. This border looked a little ragged, so I placed a bowl over the filling and cut around it to give the border a cleaner look.

The next step was to decorate the pastry. A classic pithiviers has a spiral pattern on the dome, which not only looks decorative but also helps the pastry to bake all the way through. Beginning in the center of the dome,

I sliced halfway through the pastry in spiral cuts that radiated all the way around. This work was painstaking but pleasurable—it felt like art, not drudgery. For a final touch I cross-hatched the border to open up the pastry and make it look dramatic on baking. I had been concentrating so much on each tiny detail that I hadn't yet looked at the whole pastry. When I did, I was a little disappointed to discover that it wasn't perfectly even all the way around. Still, it looked good for a first attempt; perfection would come with practice. With my fingers and the blunt edge of a knife I made a crimping pattern around the edges, as Chef Paul had done on the fruit strip. I was eager to bake the pithiviers right away, but (as usual) there wasn't time before lunch. Chef Paul suggested that I keep it in the refrigerator to bake the next day, our last day of class. Then I could bring a fresh pastry home and impress everyone. It was a little hard to forgo immediate satisfaction, but the thought of bringing home a trophy appealed to me. I followed his advice.

I didn't have much appetite for lunch but felt that I should taste another South American specialty, so I opted for what I hoped would be a lighter choice, the Potato Tortilla. I honestly couldn't tell what made this tortilla South American, apart from the fact that it was made with potatoes, native to South America. I also had a taste of Bori-Bori, a Paraguayan beef and dumpling soup, and a salad of surprisingly beautiful greens with a terrific fire-roasted tomato vinaigrette. So much for my lack of appetite! Over lunch we discussed what we were getting out of the class. We all agreed that our ability to understand how recipes work was vastly improved,

and that we had a new respect for the intrinsic properties of ingredients. All of us were glad that we'd tried our hand at puff pastry, but my fellow campers were not as enthralled with it as I. They wanted faster results, without so much fuss. Usually I do, too. And yet I'd glimpsed the more exquisite rewards of patience in Chef Paul's world.

AFTERNOON LECTURE
COFFEE AND TEA TASTING

The afternoon was given over to another lecture and tasting, this one on coffee and tea, taught by Jerry Fischetti, an associate professor in business management. For the first time, our class was held outside of the Colavita Center, in the private room adjoining the Apple Pie Bakery. It was a tight fit for so many of us, but we were charmed by the décor. The room, meant to recall a wine cellar, was lined with corks, and a chair rail around the sides displayed wine labels. Our instruction today was limited to nonalcoholic beverages, though. Jerry had set each place at the long table with a paper placemat, on which eleven circles were filled with different kinds of tea leaves. The range of colors and textures was gorgeous, from the pale green Jasmine Yin Hao to the deep, nearly black Oolong Iron Goddess of Mercy and the vivid red Ruby Sippers Blood Orange and Pear. All of these evocative names came from the company Serendipiteas. Jerry handed

Tea varieties include (clockwise from top) Oolong: Iron Goddess of Mercy; Green: Fiji, Jasmine, I of Newton; Tisane: Ruby Sippers, Chamomile, Par Amour; Black: Chocolate Chai, Chai, Irish Breakfast, Earl Gray

each of us a booklet produced by the CIA that spelled out everything we needed to know about coffee and tea. He suggested that we not bother to take notes on his comments but simply read the manual later. He wanted us to concentrate on the sensual experience at hand, the tasting of the coffees and teas.

Jerry brewed the teas in sequence, from the subtlest to the spiciest, ending with the fruit and herbal tisanes. As we waited for each variety to steep (each had its own optimal brewing time), Jerry talked about the best way to serve it—green teas in cast-iron pots, black teas in porcelain. He discussed other types of tea, too, such as the earthy Black Pu-erh, a compressed brick tea from China. Black tea, he continued, is 100 percent fermented, while oolong is fermented from 15 percent (a light oolong) to as much as 75 percent (a strong one). Green and

white teas do not generally undergo fermentation. Scented tea is layered with blossoms, bits of dried fruit, and the like, which are removed before packaging save for a few decorative pieces. Pekoe tea, Jerry told us, is not a type of tea but a term used to designate leaf quality. There are several grades, including tippy golden flowery orange pekoe (the top grade), orange pekoe (a whole leaf with no tip), all the way down to pekoe fanning and pekoe dust, the lowest grades. This system leads to such odd acronyms as SFTGFOP: who would have guessed that these letters stand for special fine tippy golden flowery orange pekoe? As we tasted the teas, we nibbled on miniature cookies from the bakery. Unlike at a wine tasting, it was not bad form to tease our palates with other flavors. So we enjoyed tiny checkerboard cookies and buttery shortbreads.

Then we moved on to coffee. Again Jerry had prepared several varieties for us to taste, made from both robusta and arabica beans. He told us that robusta beans contain twice as much caffeine as arabica. Jerry made each batch in a coffee press, explaining that the beans' essential oils come out in café pressé, while they don't in drip or percolated coffee. Since the oils remain in the press pot, they can increase your cholesterol level, so that might be a consideration for some people, he added. I really liked the dark, rich Costa Rican coffee from the La Minita plantation, which I hadn't tasted before. Jerry discussed issues of harvest and sustainability, then moved on to coffee service, his strong suit—before coming to the Culinary he had served as a food and beverage manager in various places. Jerry was so enthusiastic about his subject, and so full of answers to all of our questions, that we ended up staying until 4:00, even though the class was supposed to end at 3:15.

My head was buzzing, whether from the caffeine or simply the glut of the day's information, I wasn't sure. I went for a walk to clear my mind. It was March, the raw time of year that nevertheless hints of spring with its scent of thawing earth. I tried to concentrate on all we had learned this week but found it impossible—there were too many thoughts floating around my head. So I just walked in circles around the campus, breathing in the fresh air. I had brought clothes to change into for dinner, so after my walk I went to the student center to shower. I still had a little time to kill, and so I stopped in at the library to leaf through its vast collection of food magazines. I was looking forward to dinner. Our class had really bonded, and I anticipated our gathering as much as a night out with old friends. We would be having this, our last meal, at American Bounty, my favorite CIA restaurant.

DINNER AT THE
AMERICAN BOUNTY RESTAURANT

The maître d' seated us promptly at 6:30. Because our group was smaller than at the baking boot camp, we weren't given the private dining room, a fact that pleased me since it had been so difficult to converse around that wide table. Tonight we sat at two tables and just laughed and laughed. We ordered extra bottles of wine, each of us vying to pay rather than complaining that more ample amounts of wine weren't included in our package. The hours passed, and before we knew it, it was 9:00, then 10:00, yet still we didn't want to leave. We had captured something special. We had opened up to each other, revealing not so much about our daily lives as about our aspirations and fears. Daniel commented that our conversations reminded him of his college days when he would sit for long hours doing nothing but talking with good friends.

What is the chemistry for this kind of group? I wondered. What are the ingredients, and how do they come together to produce such an extraordinary result? And how much tempering of one's own personality is involved? At one point Ray seemed to express the magic formula obliquely when he said that "pastry camp seems to have completed my transition from a cook who prepares food to one who just wants to spend time in the kitchen making things." Our conversations weren't just pro forma, and our little community didn't just reflect rote social technique. We had developed passion, and that's what set us apart. I wanted to find a

deeper connection between our kitchen activity and our group dynamics. Was it because we had come to this class with the belief that making pastry was a precise and difficult process and so were less upset by failure than the baking boot camp crew had been? Had this circumstance allowed us to open up more to each other? Whatever the reason, this boot camp had brought us together in an extraordinary way.

The Hilde Potter Dining Room in the American Bounty Restaurant

chapter 10

QUICK AND ELEGANT DESSERTS

Our course manual stated that one of the lessons for today was on chocolate, but Chef Paul said that since we'd already had a chocolate lecture we could jump right into tempering and making chocolate cake decorations ourselves. Today's class would focus instead on putting together all of the various components we'd made during the week—the sponge cakes, the mousses and fillings, the buttercream, and now the chocolate decorations. Plating desserts is extremely important, Chef Paul emphasized, because the dessert must look appetizing and beautiful. He added that if there was time this morning, we would also try our hand at making soufflés and crêpes.

DECORATIVE CHOCOLATE SHAPES

We began by tempering the chocolate. Lee and I decided to try the block method that Chef Patricia had demonstrated, which seemed easier than the table method. We melted some bittersweet chocolate over hot water, testing it until the temperature reached 115°F. Then we dropped in a block of chocolate (roughly 25 percent of the weight of the melted chocolate) and stirred until the temperature had cooled to 90°F. We repeated the procedure over a second water bath with white chocolate, this time cooling the mixture down to 85°F, as Chef Patricia had taught us. We took a piece of parchment paper and spread it with the white chocolate. We let it dry slightly, then spread dark chocolate over the white, swirling them together to create a beautiful marbled effect. When the

chocolate was sufficiently firm we cut out decorative shapes with a sharp knife. I could hear Ray from across the room. "I'm not artistic!" he sputtered, frustrated at the fussy work. Chef Paul just laughed and decided to show us all how to make a less intricate decoration. He inflated some small balloons and dipped them into the tempered chocolate. When the chocolate hardened, he popped the balloons, and there were beautiful little chocolate cups to fill with ice cream or mousse or fresh berries. We oohed and ahhed over that trick.

DESSERT SAUCES

Next it was time to make dessert sauces to garnish our mousses and Bavarian creams. If it had been summer, we would have made our own sauces from scratch by straining fruits through a chinois to purée them. But no fresh fruits were on hand, so we worked with the concentrated purées in the pantry, combining them with water and sugar in a saucepan and bringing the mixture to a boil. In a small bowl we made a slurry of cornstarch and cold water, then whisked it in. When the sauces had thickened, we removed them from the heat, transferred them to bowls, and strained them until absolutely smooth. Lee's raspberry sauce turned out a brilliant red; my blackberry sauce was deep purple, very lush.

Next we tackled lemon butter sauce. For this preparation we simply put lemon juice, sugar, and a vanilla bean in water, brought the mixture to a boil, and then cooked it down until it had reduced to a third of its original volume. We cooled the sauce to 98°F and then whisked in room-temperature cubed butter until a smooth emulsion had

Pithiviers, page 253

formed. This sauce needs to be kept warm or else it will separate, Chef Paul advised. He told us that any type of citrus juice could be substituted for the lemon.

These tasks provided a sense of accomplishment, but all I wanted was to get my pithiviers into the oven! I was relieved to find that it hadn't disappeared from the refrigerator overnight. I brushed the dough all over with egg wash and put it in to bake at 375°F. After 40 minutes I took a peek. What a thrill—the pastry was perfectly browned, just gorgeous! The spirals were a little lopsided, it's true, but the pithiviers looked impressive. I turned the heat up to 450°F, sprinkled the pastry all over with confectioner's sugar, and returned it to the oven to caramelize.

DECORATING CAKES

It was time to decorate our cakes. By now the chocolate decorations had firmed up, and our cakes were ready to fill and ice. We had already whipped the refrigerated buttercream to a good spreading consistency. Using toothpicks inserted around the circumference of the cake as a guide, I sliced my sponge cake with a serrated knife into three equal layers. The bottom layer I placed on a decorative cardboard cake plate and brushed it generously with the simple syrup we had made earlier in the week. As the cake sat, it would soak up the syrup and become nice and moist. I topped this layer with some buttercream, then set the next layer on top of it and repeated the process, spreading the cake with syrup and topping it with more buttercream. I placed the final layer baked side down so that the top of the cake would be flat, and so that the syrup would soak in more easily.

I used a spatula to smooth buttercream over the top and sides of the cake and to build up the edges at the top. At that moment Chef Paul materialized with a pastry turntable and set my cake on it. He proceeded to show me how to make a very smooth and professional-looking top by spinning the turntable while holding a long spatula at a slight angle. Then I experimented with a decorating comb to make ridges in the buttercream. My final touch was to decorate the top and sides of the cake with various chocolate pieces, some laid flat and others standing on end, in what I hoped appeared as an avant-garde pattern. Lee, meanwhile, was experimenting with the pastry tube, piping buttercream from different tips. Chef Paul interceded here, too, showing Lee an easy way to fill the pastry tube. I had always made a small mess trying to fill the pastry tube by reaching down into it with a frosting-laden spatula or spoon and ending up with frosting all over my hand, sometimes my arm. Chef Paul simply held the bag with the tip facing down, placed his hand on the tip, and pushed it up to reveal the inside of the bag, in effect turning the bag nearly inside out. That way it could easily be filled without having to reach deep into its interior. When the bag was full, he retracted his hand and squeezed the top of the bag to release any air. Lee and I marveled at his ease.

Buttercream Torte, page 194

SOUFFLÉS

"Time for one last project!" Chef Paul called out.

Now that I had a gorgeous pithiviers and a splendid layer cake to boot, I had had enough, but Lee was eager for more. And Chef Paul insisted that he couldn't let us go until we had tried making soufflés! My weariness must have gotten in the way, because even though the soufflés I make at home always turn out perfectly, this one did not. I didn't like the recipe, which was predicated on pastry cream rather than just a little flour or cornstarch to bind. Chef Paul had said that we could use any leftover pastry cream for dessert soufflés but recommended making a new batch that would be firmer.

Chocolate Soufflé, page 235

For a quart of milk, this recipe replaced the 2½ ounces of cornstarch in the original with 6 ounces of flour and ½ ounce of cornstarch, and it substituted 12 egg yolks for the 7 in the original.

Lee and I mixed this new pastry cream with 2 more egg yolks and a tablespoon of flavoring—he chose Grand Marnier. Then we beat 6 egg whites with 6 ounces of sugar to make a soft French-style meringue, which we folded into the pastry cream. Chef Paul cautioned us not to overwhip the meringue, or it wouldn't expand in the oven, which, as we all knew, is the very point of a soufflé. We spooned the mixture into individual ramekins that Lee had buttered and sugared to keep the soufflés from sticking, and set them in the oven for 20 minutes. The result sorely disappointed us. Not only was the soufflé not ethereal enough (all of those stabilizers really did make the pastry cream bind), but it didn't have enough flavor, tasting mainly of starch.

It was time for our last lunch. Today's theme was Mexico, and aware that no one would be preparing me such meals to order again anytime soon, I treated myself to Pork with Red Chili Sauce, Fried Corn Bread, Creamed Pinto Beans, and Flour Tortillas, with a serving of Pozole Verde soup on the side. My classmates and I were subdued over our meal—whether from exhaustion or sadness that the week had come to an end, I wasn't sure. We made our way slowly back to the Colavita Center, where we scrubbed counters and stoves in an effort to leave the kitchen spotless for the next recruits.

PASTRY BOOT CAMP GRADUATION

Then came graduation. As before, we had champagne, and we toasted Chef Paul as we had toasted Chef Kate in the baking boot camp. But this time we also toasted one another and affirmed our friendship. This time we lingered, shared e-mail addresses, and promised to stay in touch. There was a round of hugs, and then another, and then another still. We were only slightly embarrassed to find that we had tears in our eyes and were actually finding it difficult to say farewell.

And so we left, burdened with baked goods but uplifted by this coming together, this tempering of personal ingredients that we had brought to the camp. What had we learned? We now thought about composing recipes and putting ingredients together in particular ways. We had also learned patience and a willingness to play with recipes until we got them just right. Yet despite all that its name implied, boot camp was neither prescriptive nor limiting. Rather, it had liberated us in that we now understood methods and ingredients and could work freely with them. This liberation was a little surprising. As Carrie wrote to me afterward: "The experience was transformative in a few ways: The people I met and got to know ended up inspiring me in many ways, to try and get everything I can out of life, to love and serve others, to strive to be the best person I can be, and to follow my heart and my passions." I couldn't have said it better myself.

chapter 11

WHAT WE BAKED

Quick Breads and Cakes

SMOKED PROVOLONE AND THYME MUFFINS

For variations in flavor you can substitute other cheeses for the smoked provolone, such as smoked mozzarella, aged cheddar, Monterey Jack (plain or peppered), or smoked Gouda. You can also try using other herbs such as chives, basil, oregano, or marjoram to come up with your own signature muffins. These muffins may be made ahead of time, then refreshed by briefly reheating them in a 250°F oven. They may also be frozen for up to 8 weeks. To serve, thaw at room temperature, then reheat in a warm oven.

MAKES 12 MUFFINS

2 cups all-purpose flour

1 cup grated smoked provolone cheese

1 tablespoon baking powder

1 tablespoon chopped fresh thyme (or 2 teaspoons dried)

½ teaspoon salt

Freshly ground black pepper to taste

Pinch of cayenne pepper

1 whole egg

2 tablespoons Coleman's dry mustard

1½ cups milk

¼ cup (½ stick) unsalted butter, melted and cooled

Dash Tabasco or to taste

1. Preheat the oven to 350°F. Spray or brush muffin tins lightly with oil or line with muffin papers.

2. Stir together the flour, cheese, baking powder, thyme, salt, and peppers in a large mixing bowl. Make a well in the center of the dry ingredients and add the egg and dry mustard. Blend well with a fork. Add the milk, butter, and Tabasco and mix just until all ingredients are combined. Do not overmix.

3. Spoon the batter into the muffin tins, filling them three-quarters full. Bake for 20 to 25 minutes, or until the tops spring back when lightly pressed with a fingertip.

4. Cool the muffins in the tin for about 10 minutes, then turn them out of the pan. Serve while still warm.

ZUCCHINI BREAD

Ever wonder what to do with that bumper crop of zucchini? This moist quick bread, almost like a cake, is one solution. It's healthy, too, with its whole wheat flour and vegetable oil in place of butter.

MAKES 2 LOAVES

2¼ cups all-purpose flour

½ teaspoon baking powder

¾ teaspoon baking soda

1 teaspoon salt

1 teaspoon ground cinnamon

1 teaspoon ground nutmeg

¾ cup sugar

¾ cup packed light brown sugar

1 cup vegetable oil

3 eggs

2 cups grated zucchini

¼ cup whole wheat flour

1 cup coarsely chopped pecans

1. Preheat the oven to 350°F. Grease and flour two 9-inch loaf pans.

2. Sift together 2 cups of the all-purpose flour with the baking powder, baking soda, salt, cinnamon, and nutmeg. Combine the sugar, brown sugar, oil, and eggs and mix on medium speed using a paddle attachment until blended, about 2 minutes. Add the sifted dry ingredients and mix until just combined, about 30 seconds.

3. Toss the grated zucchini with the remaining all-purpose flour and the whole wheat flour. Blend the zucchini and the pecans into the batter.

4. Divide the batter evenly between the two pans. Bake for about 1 hour 25 minutes, or until a tester inserted in the center comes out clean and the loaves spring back when lightly pressed.

BOSTON BROWN BREAD

Boston brown bread was the traditional New England Saturday-night accompaniment to baked beans. Unlike most American breads, it is steamed rather than baked. This bread has a rich molasses and cornmeal flavor and is wonderfully moist. I like it best served warm with plenty of butter, though it is also perfect for sopping up gravy from pot roasts and stews.

MAKES 1 LOAF

- ½ cup all-purpose flour
- ½ cup whole wheat flour
- ½ cup rye flour
- ½ cup cornmeal
- ¾ teaspoon baking soda
- ½ teaspoon salt
- 1 egg
- ½ cup dark molasses
- 1½ cups buttermilk

1. Preheat the oven to 375°F. Generously spray a 9-inch loaf pan or a 1-pound coffee can with cooking spray.

2. Sift the flours, cornmeal, baking soda, and salt into a bowl. In a separate bowl, beat together the egg, molasses, and buttermilk. Make a well in the center of the dry ingredients, pour in the wet ingredients, and mix just until the batter is smooth. Pour the batter into the prepared pan or coffee can.

3. Cover the loaf pan tightly with foil, then place it in a larger baking pan (the sides of the larger pan should reach above the loaf pan). Pour enough boiling water into the large baking pan to come halfway up the sides of the loaf pan. (To make the bread in a coffee can, place the filled can in a stock pot or similar large pot with ovenproof handles. Add enough boiling water to cover about two-thirds of the coffee can.) Tightly cover the larger pan with foil. Bake undisturbed for 2½ hours, or until a skewer inserted into the center of the bread comes out clean.

4. When the bread is done, remove the loaf pan or coffee can from the larger pan and remove the foil. Let the bread cool in the pan for 10 minutes, then loosen the edges, turn the loaf out onto a wire rack, and cool slightly. Serve while still warm.

Baker's Note: For a variation, add 1 cup of raisins to the batter and steam in a greased 1-quart pudding mold.

DATE NUT BREAD

I love this bread lightly toasted and spread with cream cheese. These rich, moist loaves keep very well.

MAKES 2 LOAVES

4 cups pastry flour
2 teaspoons baking powder
¾ teaspoon baking soda
1 teaspoon salt
½ cup (1 stick) unsalted butter, softened
1 cup packed light brown sugar
2 eggs
2 cups chopped pitted dates
1 cup chopped toasted pecans
1¾ cups water, divided

1. Preheat the oven to 350°F. Grease and flour two 9-inch loaf pans.

2. Sift together the flour, baking powder, baking soda, and salt and set aside. By hand with a wooden spoon or with an electric mixer using the paddle attachment, cream the butter and sugar together until very smooth and light, about 3 minutes. Add the eggs one at a time, mixing until smooth and scraping down the bowl between each addition.

3. Stir the flour mixture into the creamed butter mixture until it is evenly blended, scraping down the bowl as needed. Add the dates, pecans, and half of the water and stir until smooth. Add the remaining water and stir until smooth.

4. Divide the batter evenly between the prepared loaf pans, filling them about three-quarters full. Gently tap the filled pans to release any air bubbles. Bake until a skewer inserted into the center of the loaf comes out clean and the tops are golden brown, 50 to 60 minutes.

5. Cool the date bread for about 10 minutes before removing from the pans. Transfer them to a rack to finish cooling before slicing and serving or wrapping to store. They can be held at room temperature for up to 3 days or frozen for up to 6 weeks.

PUMPKIN BREAD

This recipe captures the essence of autumn. I like to bake pumpkin bread throughout the winter—it delivers the same heady aroma and flavor as pumpkin pie without the overload of butter and cream.

MAKES 2 LOAVES

½ cup raisins

1½ cups all-purpose flour

1¼ cups whole wheat flour

½ teaspoon salt

1 teaspoon baking powder

¾ teaspoon baking soda

½ teaspoon ground cinnamon

¼ teaspoon ground nutmeg

⅛ teaspoon ground cloves

1 cup puréed cooked pumpkin (fresh, canned, or frozen)

¾ cup sugar

2 eggs

½ cup vegetable oil

1. Preheat the oven to 375°F. Plump the raisins by pouring the boiling water over them, letting them rest for about 10 minutes, then draining. Grease and flour two 9-inch loaf pans.

2. Sift together the all-purpose flour, whole wheat flour, salt, baking powder, baking soda, cinnamon, nutmeg, and cloves. In another bowl combine the raisins, pumpkin, sugar, eggs, and oil and mix well. Stir the dry ingredients into the pumpkin mixture all at once, and mix just until the dry ingredients are blended into the batter.

3. Transfer the batter into the prepared loaf pans and bake for 50 to 55 minutes. Let the breads cool in the pans for 10 to 15 minutes. Ease them out of the pans and continue cooling on a rack.

Baker's Note: For a variation, add ½ cup of chopped walnuts when mixing the batter.

SERVING SUGGESTIONS: This is a good bread to serve with a main-course salad, or on its own at breakfast with a cream cheese spread.

BANANA NUT BREAD

Bananas didn't become a breakfast staple in the United States until the 1920s, when export companies began a marketing campaign to convince Americans to eat these vitamin-laden tropical fruits. Not surprisingly, recipes designed to use up overripe fruit soon followed. Banana bread, with its moist, cakelike texture, is by now an American classic.

MAKES 1 LOAF

- ½ cup whole walnuts or pecans
- 2 cups all-purpose flour
- ¼ teaspoon salt
- 1 teaspoon baking powder
- ½ cup (1 stick) unsalted butter, softened
- ½ cup sugar
- ⅓ cup honey
- 1 tablespoon grated orange rind
- 3 very ripe bananas, peeled and lightly mashed
- 2 eggs
- 2 teaspoons vanilla

1 Preheat the oven to 350°F. Grease and flour a 9-inch loaf pan. Toast the nuts in a skillet over high heat, stirring frequently, until the nuts give off a good aroma and are just starting to brown. Immediately transfer the nuts to a bowl and cool completely. Chop the nuts by hand using a chef's knife, or place them in a mini food processor and pulse it off and on just until they are coarsely chopped.

2 Sift together the flour, salt, and baking powder. In another bowl cream the butter and sugar together until light and fluffy. Add the honey, grated orange rind, and bananas and mix until well combined. Add the eggs, one at a time, to the banana mixture, beating well after each addition. Add the vanilla and mix until blended. Add the dry ingredients to the banana mixture all at once. Stir until they are just blended into the batter. Fold the nuts into the batter, then pour the batter into the prepared loaf pan.

3 Bake for 65 to 70 minutes, or until the bread begins to shrink from the edge of the pan and the center of the loaf springs back when lightly pressed. Remove the bread from the oven and let it rest for 10 to 15 minutes, then ease the bread out of the pan and continue cooling on a rack.

Baker's Note: To give an extra dimension of texture and flavor to the finished bread, prepare the following topping: rub together ½ cup sugar, ⅓ cup softened butter, 3 tablespoons peanut butter, and ¾ cup flour to a mealy consistency. Sprinkle this topping evenly over the batter right before baking, then bake as directed.

SERVING SUGGESTIONS: Serve as part of a basket of bread at a brunch or lunch. Or feature it lightly toasted and topped with cream cheese or peanut butter as an open-faced breakfast sandwich.

CHIPOTLE SKILLET CORNBREAD

This savory cornbread is dense with nuggets of corn. The addition of chopped red and green peppers makes it colorful and festive, while chipotle peppers lend an appealing smokiness. This bread is just right for a southwestern-style meal.

MAKES 8 SERVINGS

2 teaspoons unsalted butter
1 cup all-purpose flour
1 cup yellow cornmeal
¼ cup sugar
2 teaspoons baking powder
½ teaspoon salt
½ cup corn kernels
1 cup milk
1 egg
¼ cup vegetable oil
2 tablespoons chipotle peppers in adobo sauce
¼ cup diced red pepper
¼ cup diced green pepper

1. Preheat the oven to 400°F. Lightly grease a 9-inch cast iron skillet with the butter and place the skillet in the oven to preheat.

2. In a large mixing bowl, place the flour, cornmeal, sugar, baking powder, and salt and stir until all the ingredients are thoroughly mixed. In a separate bowl, combine the corn kernels, milk, egg, oil, and peppers. Stir with a fork until well blended. Make a well in the center of the dry ingredients, pour in the corn mixture, and mix until evenly moistened; the batter will be lumpy, but all the ingredients should be thoroughly incorporated.

3. Pour the batter into the heated skillet and bake for 25 to 30 minutes, until a toothpick inserted into the cornbread comes out clean. Allow the cornbread to cool for 10 to 15 minutes before cutting it into 8 wedges.

Variation

CHIPOTLE CORN STICKS Corn stick pans are made from cast iron, so they should be preheated to get a crispy crunchy corn stick. Place the corn stick pan in the oven while it preheats. When the batter is mixed, remove the pan from the oven and brush liberally with oil. Pour in enough batter to fill each indentation about half full. Bake until the edges are crisp and golden, 12 to 15 minutes.

COUNTRY-STYLE CORNBREAD

For a crisp crust, bake cornbread in a cast-iron skillet (a 9-inch one is perfect for this recipe) or a corn stick pan. Place the skillet or pan in the oven to heat while you mix the batter, then brush liberally with oil just before pouring it.

MAKES 12 SERVINGS

1¼ cups bread flour
¾ cup yellow cornmeal
¼ cup sugar
2 teaspoons baking powder
¼ teaspoon baking soda
½ teaspoon salt
2 eggs
1½ cups buttermilk
2 tablespoons melted butter or corn oil
¼ teaspoon vanilla

1. Preheat the oven to 400°F. Spray a 9-inch square baking pan with cooking spray or preheat a cast iron skillet in the oven. (See Chipotle Skillet Cornbread recipe, page 179, for information about corn stick pans.)

2. Combine the flour, cornmeal, sugar, baking powder, baking soda, and salt in a bowl and mix thoroughly. Combine the eggs, buttermilk, butter or oil, and vanilla in a separate bowl and mix thoroughly. Make a well in the center of the flour mixture, pour in the egg mixture, and stir by hand just until the batter is moistened.

3. Pour the batter into the pan and bake until a knife inserted in the center comes out clean and the top of the cornbread springs back lightly to the touch, 25 to 30 minutes. Allow the cornbread to cool slightly before cutting.

BISCUITS

The secret to making good biscuits is to mix the dough only until the ingredients just hold together—it will still look shaggy and rough. Roll the dough out gently, being careful not to use too heavy a hand. The process of folding and chilling ensures a wonderfully light and flaky texture.

MAKES 12 BISCUITS

1⅓ cups pastry flour

1 cup bread flour

2 teaspoons sugar

1 tablespoon baking powder

¼ teaspoon baking soda

¾ teaspoon salt

¼ cup (½ stick) unsalted butter, cubed

¾ cup buttermilk

1 egg, lightly beaten

Egg wash of 1 egg whisked with 1 tablespoon water

1. Preheat the oven to 425°F. Line a baking sheet with parchment paper or grease lightly.

2. Combine the pastry and bread flours, sugar, baking powder, baking soda, and salt in a medium-sized mixing bowl. Add the cubed butter and rub into the flour mixture with your fingertips until the mixture resembles coarse grains, about 2 minutes. Add the buttermilk and the beaten egg and mix with a wooden spoon to form a shaggy mass.

3. Roll the dough out on a lightly floured surface to a ½-inch thickness. Fold dough into thirds, place onto a sheet pan, and refrigerate for 10 minutes. Turn the dough 90 degrees, roll ½ inch thick, and fold into fourths. Chill the dough for 10 minutes. Turn dough 90 degrees, roll ½ inch thick, and fold into fourths. Chill the dough for 10 more minutes.

4. Roll dough out ½ inch thick and cut with a 2½-inch round biscuit cutter, cutting biscuits as close together as possible. Gather any dough scraps, gently pressing them together, and cut more biscuits. These biscuits will not be as tender and flaky as the first cuts but they will be just as tasty.

5. Place the biscuits 1 inch apart on the prepared baking sheet. Brush biscuit tops with the egg wash and bake until golden brown, 10 to 12 minutes.

Angel Biscuits and Cheddar Jalapeño Biscuits (pages 183 and 184)

ANGEL BISCUITS

Adding yeast to the dough makes these biscuits lighter and more tender than traditional baking powder biscuits; the buttermilk lends a pleasing tang.

MAKES 10 TO 12 BISCUITS

> 1⅛ teaspoons (½ envelope) active dry yeast
>
> ¼ cup warm water
>
> 2½ cups all-purpose flour
>
> 1½ teaspoons baking powder
>
> ½ teaspoon baking soda
>
> 2 tablespoons sugar
>
> ½ teaspoon salt
>
> 1 cup buttermilk
>
> ½ cup melted shortening
>
> Egg wash of 1 egg white whisked with 1 tablespoon water

1. Preheat the oven to 425°F. Lightly oil a baking sheet.

2. Stir together the yeast and warm water in a small bowl and let stand for 5 minutes, or until the yeast foams. Combine the flour, baking powder, baking soda, sugar, and salt in a second bowl and stir to distribute all of the ingredients evenly.

3. Add the buttermilk and melted shortening to the yeast mixture. Make a well in the center of the dry ingredients and pour in the yeast and buttermilk mixture. Quickly stir the ingredients just until the dough begins to form a heavy, shaggy mass. Do not overmix.

4. Turn the dough out onto a well-floured surface and pat it into a square, then roll it out to about ½ inch thick with a rolling pin. Cut into 2-inch circles using a biscuit cutter. Place the biscuits about 1 inch apart on a greased cookie sheet. Allow to rise slightly in a warm place, about 30 minutes. Brush the tops of each biscuit lightly with the egg wash.

5. Bake until the tops of the biscuits are light brown, 15 to 18 minutes. Remove the biscuits from the oven and cool slightly. Serve the biscuits while they are still warm.

CHEDDAR JALAPEÑO BISCUITS

Of all the biscuits we made in boot camp, these were my favorite. They literally melt in your mouth. If you don't want to take the time to cut out individual biscuits, you can quickly cut the dough into triangles, like scones.

MAKES 12 BISCUITS

1½ cups bread flour

1¼ cups all-purpose flour

2 teaspoons sugar

2 teaspoons baking powder

¼ teaspoon baking soda

1 teaspoon salt

½ cup (1 stick) cold unsalted butter, cubed

1½ cups grated cheddar cheese

¾ cup whole milk

1 egg, lightly beaten

1 tablespoon jalapeño, minced

Egg wash of 1 egg whisked with 1 tablespoon water

1. Preheat the oven to 425°F. In a medium bowl combine the bread flour, all-purpose flour, sugar, baking powder, baking soda, and salt. With a pastry blender, fork, or two knives, cut the butter into the flour until the mixture is the consistency of coarse cornmeal; set aside.

2. In a small bowl, combine the cheese, milk, 1 egg, and jalapeño. Add this cheese mixture to the flour mixture and stir just until the dough starts to pull away from the sides of the bowl. Do not overmix.

3. Scrape the dough from the bowl onto a lightly floured surface and knead lightly 8 to 12 times, gently pressing the dough together as you knead. Roll out or use your fingertips to press down the dough to a 1-inch thickness; using a 2-inch round cutter, cut the dough into biscuits. Gather scraps together, reroll, and cut additional biscuits.

4. Place the biscuits on an ungreased baking sheet approximately 1 inch apart and lightly brush the tops with the egg wash. Bake until golden brown, 12 to 15 minutes.

See photograph on page 182.

CREAM SCONES

For the most delicate texture, make sure the cream is very cold. The baking time for these scones is longer than you might expect because the scones are still frozen when they go to the oven. Coarse sugar adds a nice finish, but you can use granulated sugar if the coarse grains are unavailable. Serve with sweet butter or split them and fill with whipped cream and berries.

MAKES 10 SCONES

> 3¾ cups bread flour
> ½ cup sugar
> 1 tablespoon baking powder
> ½ teaspoon salt
> 2 cups heavy cream, cold
> 2 tablespoons milk
> 3 tablespoons coarse sugar for topping

1. Cut two 10-inch circles of parchment paper. Use one to line a 10-inch round cake pan. Reserve the second piece.

2. Sift the flour, sugar, baking powder, and salt together into a mixing bowl. Make a well in the center of the flour mixture.

3. Add the cream to the flour mixture and stir by hand just until the batter is evenly moistened.

4. Place the dough in the lined cake pan and press into an even layer. Cover the dough with the second parchment paper circle. Freeze the dough until very firm, at least 12 hours.

5. Preheat the oven to 350°F. Prepare a baking sheet by spraying it lightly with cooking spray or lining with parchment paper.

6. Thaw the dough for 5 minutes at room temperature, then turn it out of the cake pan onto a cutting board. Cut the dough into 10 equal wedges and place the individual wedges on the baking sheet about 2 inches apart. Brush the scones with milk and sprinkle with the sugar.

7. Bake the scones until golden brown, 30 to 40 minutes. Cool the scones on the pans for a few minutes, then transfer to cooling racks. Serve scones warm or at room temperature.

GLAZED CHOCOLATE CHERRY SCONES

Dried cherries add a hint of tartness to these tender scones. You can also add chunks of semi-sweet chocolate, or try substituting dried blueberries or cranberries for the cherries.

MAKES 10 SCONES

3¾ cups bread flour
½ cup sugar
1 tablespoon baking powder
½ teaspoon salt
1 cup dried unsweetened cherries
½ cup chopped bittersweet chocolate
2 cups heavy cream, cold
2 tablespoons milk
1 cup confectioners' sugar, sifted

1. Line a round cake pan with a circle of parchment paper, and cut a second circle the same size.

2. Sift the flour, sugar, baking powder, and salt together into a mixing bowl. Add the dried cherries and chocolate and toss them with the dry ingredients until evenly distributed. Make a well in the center of the flour mixture. Add the cream to the flour mixture and stir by hand just until the batter is evenly moistened.

3. Place the dough in the lined cake pan and press into an even layer. Cover the dough with the second parchment paper circle. Freeze the dough until very firm, at least 12 hours.

4. Preheat the oven to 350°F. Prepare a baking sheet by spraying it lightly with cooking spray or lining with parchment paper. Thaw the dough for 5 minutes at room temperature, then turn it out of the cake pan onto a cutting board. Cut the dough into 10 equal wedges and place the individual wedges on the baking sheet about 2 inches apart.

5. Bake the scones until golden brown, 30 to 40 minutes. Cool the scones on the pans for a few minutes, then transfer to cooling racks. Mix the milk and confectioners' sugar together to make a glaze and spoon over the scones while they are still warm. Serve scones warm or at room temperature.

See What We Learned: Scones, page 52.

HAM AND CHEDDAR SCONES

Freezing the dough before cutting it into wedges not only makes it easy to work with but also means that you can serve fresh scones at a moment's notice. These golden scones, studded with ham and scallions, make a zesty alternative to dinner rolls.

MAKES 10 SCONES

3¾ cups bread flour

¼ cup sugar

1 tablespoon baking powder

½ teaspoon salt

1 cup diced ham

½ cup diced cheddar cheese

½ cup sliced scallions

2 cups heavy cream, cold

1. Cut two 10-inch circles of parchment paper. Use one to line a 10-inch round cake pan. Reserve the second piece.

2. Sift the flour, sugar, baking powder, and salt together into a mixing bowl. Add the ham, cheese, and scallions and toss with the dry ingredients until evenly distributed. Make a well in the center of the flour mixture, add the cream, and stir by hand just until the batter is evenly moistened.

3. Place the dough in the lined cake pan and press into an even layer. Cover the dough with the second parchment paper circle. Freeze the dough until very firm, at least 12 hours.

4. Preheat the oven to 350°F. Prepare a baking sheet by spraying it lightly with cooking spray or lining with parchment paper. Thaw the dough for 5 minutes at room temperature, then turn it out of the cake pan onto a cutting board. Cut the dough into 10 equal wedges and place the individual wedges on the baking sheet about 2 inches apart.

5. Bake the scones until golden brown, 30 to 40 minutes. Cool the scones on the pans for a few minutes then transfer to cooling racks. Serve scones warm or at room temperature.

APPLE SOUR CREAM COFFEE CAKE

The type of apple you choose will determine the flavor and texture of the finished coffee cake. Tart apples such as McIntosh or Granny Smith are fine choices, but for a mellower taste, try a Northern Spy or Cortland. This cake freezes well. If you wish, bake it in a foil cake pan, and once it has cooled, wrap tightly and seal. Label the package with the contents and the date it was prepared. To serve, thaw the coffee cake at room temperature for an hour, then warm gently in a 250°F oven, unwrapped, for about 15 minutes.

MAKES 1 CAKE (8 SERVINGS)

3 cups all-purpose flour
3 teaspoons ground cinnamon
2 teaspoons baking powder
½ teaspoon baking soda
½ teaspoon salt
3 cups peeled, sliced apples
¾ cup (1½ sticks) unsalted butter, softened
1¼ cups sugar
3 eggs
½ cup sour cream

1. Preheat the oven to 325°F. Grease and flour one 9-inch square baking dish.

2. Sift together the flour, 2 teaspoons of the cinnamon, the baking powder, baking soda, and salt. Set aside. Finely chop half of the apples and leave the other half sliced.

3. Cream the butter and 1 cup of the sugar together on medium speed until very light and fluffy, 3 to 5 minutes. Add the eggs one at a time, beating well to combine after each addition. Scrape the sides and bottom of the bowl to combine the ingredients thoroughly. Add the chopped apples and sour cream and stir until combined.

4. Stir in the sifted dry ingredients. Add the sliced apples and fold them into the batter gently, just until the slices are coated. Pour the batter into the prepared pan, spreading it into an even layer.

5. Stir together the remaining sugar and cinnamon and sprinkle evenly over the surface of the batter. Bake 45 to 50 minutes in a preheated oven, or until tester comes out clean and the edges shrink from the sides of the pan.

GINGER CAKE

The batter is a very light taffy color as it is mixed, but the finished cake will be quite dark.

MAKES ONE 9-INCH LOAF (10 SERVINGS)

1½ cups all-purpose flour

2 teaspoons powdered ginger

1 teaspoon baking powder

½ teaspoon baking soda

1 teaspoon salt

½ cup (1 stick) unsalted butter, softened

1 cup sugar

½ cup molasses

½ cup buttermilk

3 eggs

1. Grease a 9-inch loaf pan. Preheat the oven to 350°F.

2. Sift together the flour, ginger, baking powder, baking soda, and salt and set aside.

3. Cream together the butter and sugar until very light. Add the molasses and buttermilk and continue beating until the mixture is quite smooth. Add the eggs one at a time, beating until blended after each addition. Add the sifted dry ingredients and stir until the batter is very smooth.

4. Spread the batter into the prepared pan and bake for 35 minutes, or until the center springs back when lightly pressed with a fingertip. The edges will shrink away from the sides of the pan. Cool the cake thoroughly before unmolding from the pan.

SERVING SUGGESTION: Serve with Lemon Butter Sauce (page 259) and Chantilly Cream (page 266).

CRANBERRY QUICK BREAD

Cranberries have been commercially farmed in Massachusetts since the early nineteenth century. They appear in the markets in the fall, just in time for Thanksgiving baking. I always buy extra and freeze them for use throughout the year.

MAKES 2 LOAVES (20 SERVINGS)

1 cup (2 sticks) unsalted butter, softened

1½ cups sugar

5 eggs

3 tablespoons orange zest

5 cups all-purpose flour

1 tablespoon baking powder

½ teaspoon baking soda

¾ teaspoon salt

1½ cups milk

3½ cups cranberries

1. Preheat the oven to 350°F. Grease two 9-inch loaf pans. Cream the butter and sugar together until light and fluffy. Gradually add the eggs and orange zest, scraping down the bowl between additions.

2. Combine the flour, baking powder, baking soda, and salt. Set aside ¼ cup of the flour mixture. Add the remaining dry ingredients to the creamed mixture in thirds, alternating with milk, and blend until thoroughly incorporated. Dust the cranberries with the reserved flour mixture and fold into the batter.

3. Divide the batter between the loaf pans. Bake for 60 to 75 minutes or until a skewer inserted in the center of the bread comes out clean.

VANILLA SPONGE CAKE

Sponge cake, also known as génoise or pan di Spagna, is a sweet, delicate cake that is also relatively healthy, since it is made from egg foams with very little added fat. Sponge cakes are often liberally brushed with sugar syrup to moisten them. For a rich dessert, fill them with Chocolate Sabayon Mousse (page 264) or whipped soft ganache. Or simply layer the cakes with lightly sweetened whipped cream and sliced strawberries or other fresh fruits. Top with a final layer of whipped cream and garnish with a few perfect berries.

MAKES TWO 8-INCH LAYERS

2 cups cake flour

6 tablespoons (¾ stick) unsalted butter plus extra for greasing

1 tablespoon vanilla extract

1¼ cups sugar

5 large eggs

5 large egg yolks

1. Preheat the oven to 375°F. Lightly butter two 8-inch cake pans and line with parchment paper.

2. Sift the flour twice and set aside. Melt the butter in a saucepan over low heat. Remove from the heat, add the vanilla extract, and stir to combine. Set aside to cool.

3. Combine the sugar, eggs, and egg yolks in a bowl (use the bowl of a stand mixer if you have one) and set the bowl over a pan of barely simmering water. Whisking constantly with a wire whisk, heat until the mixture is warm to the touch or reaches 110°F on an instant-read thermometer.

4. Remove the bowl from the heat. Whip the eggs on medium speed until the foam is three times the original volume and no longer increasing in volume, about 5 minutes.

5. Fold the flour into the egg mixture using a rubber spatula. Blend a small amount of the batter into the melted butter and then fold into the remaining batter.

6. Fill the prepared cake pans about two-thirds full. Bake until the cake begins to shrink away from the sides of the pan and a tester inserted in the center of the cake comes out clean, about 30 minutes.

7. Let the layers cool in the pans for a few minutes before turning out onto wire racks. Let cool completely before finishing with frosting and filling.

See What We Learned: Foamed Batters, page 114.

Variation

CHOCOLATE SPONGE CAKE Replace ½ cup of the cake flour with cocoa powder. Sift the cake flour and cocoa powder together twice. Proceed as directed.

ANGEL FOOD CAKE

In order to reach a lofty height, angel food cake needs to cling to the sides of the pan, both as it bakes and while it cools. This is why the pan is ungreased and the cake is cooled upside down. Some angel food cake pans have little "feet" on the rim to hold the cake above the tabletop or counter. If your pan has no feet, place the inverted pan on a bottle with a long, relatively thin neck.

MAKES ONE 9-INCH TUBE CAKE (8 SERVINGS)

1 cup cake flour
1¼ cups sugar, divided
½ teaspoon salt
12 egg whites
2 tablespoons water
1 teaspoon cream of tartar
1 teaspoon vanilla extract

1. Preheat the oven to 350°F. Sift the flour, ¼ cup of the sugar, and the salt twice onto parchment or waxed paper and set aside.

2. In a stand mixer fitted with the whisk attachment, whip the egg whites and water on low speed until foamy, 2 minutes. Add the cream of tartar and continue to whip until the egg whites form soft peaks, 2 minutes. Add the vanilla extract, then gradually add the remaining 1 cup sugar while whipping. Continue until the egg whites are glossy and form medium peaks, 3 to 4 minutes.

3. With a rubber spatula or wide spoon, gently fold the sifted flour and sugar mixture into the egg whites. Spoon the batter into an ungreased 10-inch angel food cake pan, run a butter knife through the batter once to ensure that there are no air pockets, and smooth the top. Bake until golden brown on top, 40 to 45 minutes.

4. Turn the cake pan upside down and let it cool completely before turning out the cake. Use a spatula or thin knife to release the cake from the sides of the pan and turn out carefully.

POUND CAKE

This cake is good served on its own or with a simple accompaniment, such as Raspberry Sauce (page 258) or Chantilly Cream (page 266).

MAKES 1 LOAF CAKE (8 SERVINGS)

All-purpose flour for dusting

1½ cups cake flour, sifted

1 teaspoon baking powder

½ teaspoon baking soda

½ cup (1 stick) unsalted butter, at room temperature

¾ cup granulated sugar

½ teaspoon salt

½ cup sour cream

2 large eggs

1 teaspoon vanilla extract

1. Preheat the oven to 350°F. Lightly grease and flour an 8½-inch loaf pan. Sift the cake flour, baking powder, and baking soda into a bowl and set aside.

2. In a stand mixer fitted with the paddle attachment, cream together the butter, granulated sugar, and salt on medium speed, scraping down the bowl with a rubber spatula as needed, until the mixture is smooth and light in texture, 4 to 5 minutes.

3. In a separate bowl, blend the sour cream, eggs, and vanilla extract. Add the egg mixture to the butter mixture in 3 additions, alternating with the sifted dry ingredients. After the last addition of the egg mixture, mix on low speed until just blended, scraping down the bowl as needed, 1 minute.

4. Pour the batter into the prepared pan and spread into an even layer. Bake until a skewer inserted near the center of the cake comes out clean, 50 to 55 minutes.

5. Remove the cake from the oven and cool completely in the pan on a wire rack. Release the sides of the cake from the pan with a narrow spatula and unmold. Slice and serve at room temperature.

BUTTERCREAM TORTE

Straight edges and a level top give layer cakes a professional look. To keep a serving plate clean of frosting, tuck strips of parchment or waxed paper underneath the edges of the cake before you start to work.

MAKES 1 TORTE (8 SERVINGS)

1 Vanilla Sponge Cake (page 192)

1 cup Simple Syrup (page 260), use as needed

4 cups Italian Buttercream (page 265)

Chocolate curls, cigarettes, disks, or shavings for decoration

Chopped pistachios for decoration

1. Set the cake on a flat, stable surface. Use a ruler to divide the cake into three equal layers and insert toothpicks into the sides of the cake in four or five spots around its circumference to guide your eye and knife as you cut.

2. Working from one side to the other, cut horizontally through the cake with a serrated knife, using a gentle back-and-forth sawing motion. Rest the hand not holding the knife flat on the top of the cake to help you keep the knife level and the layers evenly thick. Brush away loose crumbs from each layer using a pastry brush.

3. Place the first layer of cake directly on a serving plate, turntable, or cake stand and brush lightly with a little of the simple syrup to moisten the cake.

4. Spread ¾ cup of the buttercream on the first layer. Leave a rim around the edge of the cake unfilled to allow for the filling to spread after the next layer is placed on it. Top with the second layer and brush with a little of the simple syrup and spread with another ¾ cup of the butttercream. Place the third layer on the cake and brush with some simple syrup. Carefully straighten up the layers.

5. Brush away loose crumbs from the tops and sides of the cake. Spread a little of the buttercream evenly but thinly over the tops and sides of the cake. This coating needn't completely cover the cake; its function is to glue any loose crumbs onto the cake and hold them in place. Let the coating set up for about 1 hour in the refrigerator.

6. Once the crumb coat is set, spoon a generous amount of icing onto the cake's top. Using a back-and-forth stroke with a level palette knife, spread the icing in an even layer that extends over the top edge of the cake.

7. To apply the buttercream to the sides of the cake, scoop up some of the buttercream with a palette knife and hold the knife vertically to spread icing on the sides; use a generous amount so that you create a layer thick enough to completely coat the cake. Use as many strokes as necessary, turning the cake to apply an even coat and scooping up more icing as you work. Once you have applied the icing all the way around the cake, hold your palette knife straight up and down with the blade at a 45-degree angle to the side of the cake. Turn the cake against the knife to smooth out the icing. The excess will rise above the top of the cake. After the edge is smooth, hold your palette knife horizontally and parallel to the top of the cake and smooth the excess from the edge toward the center of the cake. This makes a sharp edge all around the cake and a very level top. Use the a knife blade to "mark" the cake into 8 slices.

8. Any remaining icing can be piped in rosettes on the top. Garnish with chocolate cigarettes and cutouts and gently press the chopped pistachios around the bottom edge of the cake.

See photo on page 166.

CARAMEL CHOCOLATE MOUSSE CAKE

Molded cakes consist of layers of cake and a filling that is soft enough to pour during assembly. Chill or freeze the filled cake so it can be easily sliced.

MAKES 1 TORTE (8 SERVINGS)

1 Chocolate Sponge Cake (page 192)
1 cup Simple Syrup (page 260), use as needed
2 cups Chocolate Bavarian Mousse (page 263)
2 cups Caramel Mousse (page 264)
2 cups Soft Ganache (page 267), whipped
Chocolate curls, cigarettes, disks, or shavings for decoration
Cocoa powder for decoration

1. Line a springform cake pan with plastic wrap. Leave a 2- or 3-inch overhang of plastic wrap to be sure the top of the cake doesn't stick to the mold as you remove the springform.

2. Set the cake on a flat, stable surface. Use a ruler to divide the cake into three equal layers and insert toothpicks into the sides of the cake in four or five spots around its circumference to guide your eye and knife as you cut. Working from one side to the other, cut horizontally through the cake with a serrated knife, using a gentle back-and-forth sawing motion. Rest the hand not holding the knife flat on the top of the cake to help you keep the knife level and the layers evenly thick. Brush away loose crumbs from each layer using a pastry brush.

3. Put the first layer of cake into the lined mold (trim the cake if necessary so that it fits snugly into the mold). Brush with a little simple syrup. Add the Chocolate Bavarian Mousse and spread it into an even layer. Add another layer of cake and brush with syrup. Top with the Caramel Mousse and spread it into an even layer. Add the third layer of cake and brush with syrup. Cover the mold tightly with plastic wrap. Refrigerate or freeze the cake until it is firm, at least 3 hours for most cakes.

4. Unmold the torte from the pan by releasing the hinge and carefully removing it from the cake. Remove the plastic wrap and transfer the cake to a serving plate, turntable, or cake stand.

5. Scoop up some of the whipped soft ganache with a palette knife and hold the knife vertically to spread icing on the sides; use a generous amount so that you create a layer thick enough to completely coat the cake. Use as many strokes as necessary, turning the cake to apply an even coat and scooping up more icing as you work. Once you have applied the icing all the way around the cake, hold your palette knife straight up and down with the blade at a 45-degree angle to the side of the cake. Turn the cake against the knife to smooth out the icing. The excess will rise above the top of the cake. After the edge is smooth, hold your palette knife horizontally and parallel to the top of the cake and smooth the excess from the edge toward the center of the cake.

6. Refrigerate the cake until the ganache is firm. Just before serving, top the cake with the shaved chocolate or chocolate curls and dust with the cocoa powder. Cut into pieces and serve.

Yeast Breads

BAGUETTES

A great baguette is usually about 3 inches in width with a crisp crust and a chewy interior. Despite these loaves' universal appeal, it was not until the twentieth century that the word "baguette" came into English usage.

MAKES 2 LOAVES

1¾ cups room-temperature water (68°–76°F)

1 teaspoon active dry yeast

4 cups bread flour plus extra as needed

2 teaspoons salt

Cornmeal for dusting

1. Combine the water and yeast in a bowl and stir until the yeast is completely dissolved. Add the flour and salt and mix with the dough hook on low speed just to incorporate. Increase the speed to medium and knead until the dough is smooth and elastic, 10 to 12 minutes.

2. Transfer the dough to a lightly oiled bowl, turn to coat, cover with plastic wrap or a damp towel, and let rise in a warm place until nearly doubled in size, about 30 minutes. Fold the dough gently, then let rise for another 45 minutes.

3. Fold the dough over on itself, pressing gently to release the gas. Transfer the dough to a lightly floured work surface, cut into 2 equal pieces, and round each piece into a smooth ball, pinching the seams together at the bottom of the ball. Cover the dough and let rest, seam sides down, until relaxed, about 30 minutes.

4. Prepare a baking sheet by scattering it with cornmeal. To shape the baguettes, on a lightly floured surface press each ball of dough into a rectangle. Holding the short edges of the rectangle, lift and stretch the dough until the rectangle is about 8 inches long. Roll the dough into a cylinder, pressing the seam closed with the edge of your palm. Transfer the dough, seam side down, to the prepared baking sheet. Cover the loaves and let rise until increased in volume by three-quarters, about 1 hour.

5. Preheat the oven to 425°F. Score each loaf in several places by making diagonal slashes just through the outer layer of dough with a very thin blade. Just before baking the bread, brush or mist each baguette lightly with water. Brush or mist the bread 1 or 2 more times during the first 5 minutes of baking. Bake until the loaves are golden and sound hollow when tapped on the bottom, about 30 minutes. Remove the loaves from the oven and let cool on wire racks before serving.

PARKER HOUSE ROLLS

These tender rolls are an American classic, first served at Boston's Parker House Hotel in the 1850s. Sometimes called "pocketbook rolls" for their distinctive shape with a crease down the center, these small breads are perfect for an elegant dinner party. This dough is very forgiving. You can prepare it the day before, then bake the rolls just before serving. They're also delicious the next day for breakfast, toasted and spread with jam.

MAKES ABOUT 2 DOZEN ROLLS

¾ cup milk

⅓ cup warm water

2¼ teaspoons (1 envelope) active dry yeast

2 tablespoons sugar

3 tablespoons unsalted butter, softened

2 eggs, lightly beaten

2½ to 3 cups bread flour

1 teaspoon salt

½ cup melted unsalted butter (or more as needed)

Egg wash of 1 egg whisked with 2 tablespoons milk

1. Scald the milk by bringing it just to a boil over medium heat, then allow the milk to cool to room temperature. Combine the warm water, yeast, and sugar in a large bowl and stir well. Let this mixture sit for 2 to 3 minutes or until it is quite frothy. Add the cooled milk, 3 tablespoons softened butter, eggs, 1½ cups of the flour, and the salt. Stir well for several minutes until the dough begins to form long elastic strands. Add more flour gradually until the dough is too heavy to stir.

2. Turn the dough out onto a lightly floured work surface and knead for about 10 minutes, adding only enough flour to prevent the dough from sticking. The dough should be moist, smooth, and springy. Place the dough in a large, lightly oiled bowl, cover with a clean cloth, and place in a warm, draft-free spot to rise for 1 to 2 hours or until double in volume. While the dough is rising, lightly grease two 9-by-11-inch baking pans.

3. Punch the dough down and flatten to about 1 inch thick. Cut rectangles of dough about 1 inch by 2 inches. Press the dull side of a table knife in the center of each rectangle to make a crease. Brush the rolls with a thin coating of melted butter, and fold them in half so that the butter is on the inside. Place the rolls in the prepared pans. They should be close, but not touching one another. Cover the shaped rolls and let them rise until nearly doubled.

4. Preheat the oven to 350°F. Brush the rolls lightly with egg wash and bake for 15 to 20 minutes or until golden brown and baked through. Let the rolls cool slightly before serving.

Baker's Note: This dough can be allowed to rise very slowly in a cool spot, or overnight in the refrigerator. Let the dough return to room temperature before final shaping and baking. If desired, scatter some sesame or poppy seeds on the rolls after they have been brushed with egg wash.

FOCACCIA

Begin making this dough the day before you plan to bake the focaccia. The biga, or starter, improves both texture and taste.

MAKES 2 LOAVES

2 cups water, 68°–76°F, divided
1 teaspoon instant dry yeast, divided
4½ to 5 cups bread flour, divided
½ cup extra-virgin olive oil, divided
2¼ teaspoons salt

GARNISHES (OPTIONAL)
2 plum tomatoes, thinly sliced
2 tablespoons fresh herbs
4 garlic cloves, sliced and sautéed
¼ cup grated parmesan cheese
1 medium onion, thinly sliced and sautéed
1 teaspoon coarse sea salt

1. To prepare the biga, combine ¾ cup of the water and ¼ teaspoon of the yeast and stir until the yeast is completely dissolved. Add 1½ cups of the flour and stir until thoroughly combined. Cover and let rise for 8 to 10 hours, until the biga has risen and begun to recede; it should still be bubbly and airy. It will have the consistency of very loose bread dough.

2. Combine the remaining yeast with ¼ cup of the water and stir until dissolved in the bowl of an electric mixer. Add the remaining 1 cup water, the biga, 3 cups of the flour, and 3 tablespoons of the olive oil and mix on low speed for 2 minutes. Add the salt and continue to mix for 2 minutes. Increase the speed to medium and mix for 30 seconds, adding some of the remaining flour if necessary. The dough should be very loose.

3. Transfer the dough to a lightly oiled bowl, cover, and let rise in a warm place until the dough has almost doubled in size, about 45 minutes. Fold the dough gently over on itself two or three times, cover, and let rise a second time until almost doubled in size, about 45 minutes.

4. Preheat oven to 400°F. Prepare a baking sheet by generously coating with 1 tablespoon of the remaining olive oil. Divide the dough into two equal pieces. Shape the dough lightly into 2 round pieces. Cover and let rest 15 to 20 minutes.

5. Using your fingertips, gently press each round of dough down and outward to shape into a circle 8 inches in diameter and about 1 inch thick. Brush the dough lightly with olive oil. Cover and let rise until the dough springs back slowly to the touch but does not collapse, 30 to 45 minutes.

6. Using your fingertips, gently dimple the loaves, spreading the circle to 10 inches in diameter. Drizzle each loaf with 2 tablespoons olive oil. Scatter with the optional toppings at this point if desired.

7. Bake focaccias until they have a golden brown crust and sound hollow when thumped on the bottom, 20 to 25 minutes. Brush lightly with olive oil, then cool completely on racks.

CIABATTA

This recipe makes a bread with a deep, complex flavor by using a poolish, a head start for the yeast. A poolish requires advance planning, since it takes 8 to 10 hours to develop. However, you can skip this step if you want to make ciabatta in a single day. Simply stir together all of the water and all of the yeast until the yeast is dissolved, then add all of the flour and the salt. Mix and knead as directed for the final dough. Rising and baking times will remain the same.

MAKES 2 LOAVES

> 5 cups bread flour, divided
>
> 2 cups room-temperature water (68°–76°F), divided
>
> ¾ teaspoon active dry yeast, divided
>
> 2 teaspoons salt
>
> Cornmeal for dusting

1. To prepare the poolish, combine 1½ cups of the flour, 1 cup water, and ¼ teaspoon of the yeast in the bowl of a stand mixer fitted with the dough hook and mix on low speed until thoroughly combined, 3 minutes. Transfer to a bowl, cover, and let rise in a warm place until it has risen and begun to recede but is still bubbly and airy, 8 to 10 hours.

2. Combine the remaining 3½ cups flour and ½ teaspoon yeast in the bowl of a stand mixer fitted with the dough hook. Add the remaining 1 cup water, the poolish, and salt and mix on low speed for 3 minutes. Increase the speed to medium and knead until the dough is blended but not too elastic, 3 minutes more. The dough should be wet and slack.

3. Transfer the dough to a lightly oiled bowl, turn to coat, cover with plastic wrap or a damp towel, and let rise until nearly doubled in size, about 30 minutes. When you press the dough with a fingertip, the indentation should not fill in again rapidly. Fold the dough over on itself by lifting the edges up and over the center and pressing gently to release the gas. (The dough should feel like jelly.) Allow the dough to relax in the bowl for another 15 minutes.

4. Turn the dough out onto a well-floured work surface and dust the top of the dough with additional flour. Using your palms, gently stretch the dough into an 8-by-9-inch rectangle that is an even 1 inch thick. Avoid tearing or puncturing the dough with your fingertips. Using a floured bench scraper, cut the dough into two 3-by-4-inch rectangles. Cover the dough and let rest again for 15 to 20 minutes.

5. Gently free the dough from the table with a bench scraper, trying not to stretch or tear it. Carefully flip the dough pieces onto a floured, clean, flat-weave kitchen towel. Gently stretch each piece into a 10-by-4½-inch rectangle. Let the dough rise in a warm place, covered, until the dough springs back slowly to the touch but does not collapse, 30 to 45 minutes.

6. Preheat the oven to 425°F. Prepare 2 baking sheets by scattering them with cornmeal. Flour the top of the dough lightly. Carefully flip the dough onto the baking sheets. Bake until each ciabatta has a golden brown crust and sounds hollow when thumped on the bottom, 25 to 30 minutes. Let cool completely on wire racks.

See What We Learned: Wet Doughs, page 84.

CHALLAH

MAKES 1 LARGE OR 2 SMALL LOAVES

2 teaspoons active dry yeast

1 cup room-temperature water (68°–76°F)

3½ to 4 cups bread flour

6 large egg yolks

¼ cup vegetable oil plus extra as needed

¼ cup sugar

2½ teaspoons salt

Egg wash of 1 large egg whisked with 2 tablespoons cold milk or water

1. Combine the yeast and water in the bowl of a stand mixer fitted with the dough hook. Add 3½ cups of the flour, the egg yolks, oil, sugar, and salt and mix thoroughly on low speed for 4 minutes. Increase the speed to medium and knead for 4 minutes; add additional flour if the dough is too soft. The dough should be slightly soft but not sticky.

2. Transfer the dough to a lightly oiled bowl, turn to coat, cover with plastic wrap or a damp towel, and let rise until nearly doubled in size, about 1 hour.

3. Fold the dough over on itself and cover loosely with a cloth. Let the dough rest until relaxed, 15 to 20 minutes. To make a large loaf, divide the dough into three equal pieces; to make two smaller loaves, divide the dough into six equal pieces. Working with one piece of dough at a time, place each piece on a lightly floured surface and press gently with your fingertips to stretch into a rectangle, using as little flour as possible to keep the dough from sticking. Fold the long top edge of the dough to the center of the rectangle, pressing lightly with

your fingertips to tighten the outer layer of the dough. Continue to roll the dough and use the heel of your hand to seal the dough into a cylinder shape; keep the seam straight.

4. Roll each piece of the dough into a tapered cylinder 12 inches long. Increase the pressure of your hands as you work outward from the center. Lay three ropes of dough parallel to one another. Begin braiding in the center of the strands. Place the left strand over the center strand, and then the right strand over the new center strand. Repeat this process until you have reached the end and braided as much of the dough as possible. Pinch the ends together tightly. Turn the braid around so that the unbraided strands are facing you. Repeat the braiding sequence until you have again reached the end of the dough. Pinch the ends together tightly and place the dough seam side down on a baking sheet. (Repeat to make a second loaf.)

5. Brush the dough lightly with egg wash and allow to rise a second time until it springs back slowly to the touch but does not collapse, 1 hour. Do not cover the dough; the egg wash will make it stick to the covering and disturb the crust.

6. Preheat the oven to 350°F. Very gently brush the dough with egg wash again before baking. (If the first layer of egg wash is dry before you apply a second coat, the challah will be shinier after it is baked.) Bake until the challah is a dark golden brown, shiny, and very lightweight, 25 to 30 minutes. Let cool completely on wire racks.

See What We Learned: Braided Loaves, page 64.

RAISIN CINNAMON SWIRL BREAD

This comforting loaf will fill your kitchen with the warm smell of cinnamon as it bakes. If you don't like raisins, you can omit them, or substitute ½ cup chopped walnuts for a little crunch.

MAKES 2 LOAVES

1½ teaspoons active dry yeast

1½ cups whole milk, warmed to 110°F

4½ cups bread flour

¼ cup (½ stick) unsalted butter, softened

¼ cup sugar

1 egg, lightly beaten

2 teaspoons salt

⅔ cup packed raisins

4 teaspoons ground cinnamon, divided

Egg wash of 1 egg whisked with 2 tablespoons cold milk or water

¼ cup packed brown sugar

1. Place the yeast and warm milk in the bowl of a mixer and stir to dissolve completely. Let the yeast proof until foamy, about 5 minutes. Add the flour, butter, sugar, egg, and salt. Mix the ingredients together on low speed using the dough hook just until the dough begins to come together (it will look rather rough), about 2 minutes.

2. Increase the speed to medium-high and mix until the dough is smooth, an additional 4 minutes. Transfer the dough to a lightly floured work surface, add the raisins and 2 teaspoons of the cinnamon. Knead just long enough to distribute the raisins through the dough, 5 or 6 times.

3. Shape the dough into a ball and place it in a lightly greased bowl. Cover with plastic wrap and let the dough rise in a warm place until doubled in size, about 2 hours. Fold the dough gently over on itself in three or four places, turn it out onto a lightly floured work surface, and cut it into 2 equal pieces. Cover the dough and let it rest until relaxed, about 15 minutes.

4. Lightly grease two 9-inch loaf pans. Working with one piece of dough at a time, roll the dough into a rectangle 8 by 12 inches and ½ inch thick. Dust the dough and rolling pin lightly with flour if necessary to prevent the dough from sticking. Brush lightly with egg wash. Mix the brown sugar with the remaining 2 teaspoons cinnamon and sprinkle half of this mixture evenly over the dough. Roll the dough into a cylinder starting with the long side of the dough. Pinch the dough together to seal the seams and tuck the ends under. Place the loaf seam side down into a loaf pan. Brush lightly with egg wash. Repeat with the second piece of dough to make another loaf.

5. Cover the loaves and let them rise in a warm place until they nearly fill the pans and spring back slowly to the touch without collapsing, 1½ to 2 hours.

6. Preheat the oven to 375°F. Gently brush the bread again with egg wash. Bake the loaves until the crust is brown and the sides spring back when pressed, 25 to 30 minutes. Remove the bread from the pans and cool completely on a rack before slicing and serving.

BRIOCHE À TÊTE

This rich French bread is traditionally baked in a fluted mold. You can bake a single large one for dramatic effect or make several smaller ones, as in the recipe below. If you're unable to find brioche molds, you can use muffin tins instead. For the best texture, let the dough rise slowly in the refrigerator overnight. If it becomes too warm as you shape the individual loaves, return it to the refrigerator to firm up.

MAKES 12 BRIOCHES

> 2¼ teaspoons (1 envelope) active dry yeast
>
> ¼ cup whole milk, warmed to 110°F
>
> 2 cups bread flour
>
> 2 eggs, lightly beaten
>
> 1 tablespoon salt
>
> ¾ cup (1½ sticks) unsalted butter, diced and softened
>
> Egg wash of 2 egg yolks whisked with 2 tablespoons heavy cream

1. Place the yeast and milk in the bowl of a mixer and stir to dissolve completely. Let the yeast proof until foamy, about 5 minutes. Add the flour, eggs, and salt. Mix the ingredients together on low speed using the dough hook just until the dough begins to come together as a rather rough and crumbly dough, about 4 minutes. Gradually add all the butter. Increase the speed to medium-high and mix until the dough is extremely smooth and satiny, an additional 15 minutes. Scrape the bowl down from time to time to blend the dough evenly. Transfer the dough to a clean bowl, cover tightly, and refrigerate overnight.

2. Fold the dough gently over on itself in three or four places, turn the dough out onto a lightly floured work surface, and cut it into 12 equal pieces. Place the pieces on a baking sheet and let them rest in the refrigerator until relaxed, about 15 minutes.

3. To shape brioches à tête, remove the dough from the refrigerator and preshape each piece by rolling it into a 3-inch-long cylinder. Coat the edge of your palm with flour, then roll the dough back and forth about 1 inch from one end of the cylinder to create a head (tête) that is still attached to the cylinder; it should look like a bowling pin. Transfer the brioche, tête up, to a prepared mold. Hold the tête with the fingertips of one hand and push it down into the larger portion of the dough so that the tête sits up on the surface of the brioche. Brush lightly with egg wash. Repeat until all the brioches are shaped. (If the dough starts to get warm and sticky as you work, return it to the refrigerator until it is cool and easy to handle again.) Cover the shaped brioches with a clean, damp towel and let rise until they are nearly doubled in size, 1 to 2 hours.

4. Preheat the oven to 400°F. Lightly brush the brioches again with egg wash and bake until golden brown, about 20 minutes. Cool slightly in the pan and then unmold and cool completely on a wire rack before serving.

STICKY BUNS WITH PECANS

If you and your family love sticky buns, you can double or even triple the recipes for the cinnamon smear and pan smear and store them for later use. Keep them in airtight containers in the refrigerator for up to 2 weeks. Our recipe produces oversized buns with plenty of sticky caramel, but you can make smaller versions if you prefer. You will need to reduce the overall baking time somewhat.

MAKES 12 STICKY BUNS

2¼ teaspoons active dry yeast

¾ cup milk, warmed to 110°F

3½ to 4 cups bread flour

¼ cup sugar

¼ cup (½ stick) unsalted butter, softened

2 eggs, lightly beaten

1 teaspoon salt

2 cups Pan Smear (page 210)

Egg wash of 1 egg whisked with 2 tablespoons cream or milk

1 cup Cinnamon Smear (page 210)

1. Place the yeast and warm milk in the bowl of a mixer and stir to dissolve completely. Let the yeast proof until foamy, about 5 minutes. Add the flour, sugar, butter, eggs, and salt. Mix the ingredients together on low speed using the dough hook just until the dough begins to come together, about 2 minutes; it will look rather rough. Increase the speed to medium-high and mix until the dough is smooth, an additional 5 minutes.

2. Shape the dough into a ball and place it in a lightly greased bowl. Cover with plastic wrap and let the dough rise in a warm place until doubled in size, about 2 hours. Fold the dough gently over on itself in three or four places. Cover again and let rise until doubled a second time, about 1 hour.

3. Preheat the oven to 400°F. Prepare two 9-inch square baking pans by pouring 1 cup pan smear into each of them. Roll the dough into a rectangle that is 8 by 14 inches and about ¼ inch thick. Dust the dough and rolling pin lightly with flour if necessary to prevent the dough from sticking. Lightly brush a 1-inch-wide strip of egg wash along the long side of the dough closest to you. Spread the cinnamon smear evenly over the remaining dough. Roll the dough up to form a log, starting with the edge opposite the egg-washed strip. Pinch the dough together to seal the seam. Slice into 12 even pieces. Place 6 rolls in each of the prepared pans. Cover the rolls and let them rise until they have nearly doubled, about 30 minutes. Brush lightly with egg wash.

4. Bake the rolls until they are baked through and the crust is golden brown, 25 to 30 minutes. As soon as you remove the pans from the oven, turn each pan over onto a plate. Lift the pan away and let the rolls cool before serving them. If the sticky buns cool down and are hard to get out of the pan, you can warm the bottom of the pan to loosen them.

Pan Smear

If you prepare the pan smear in advance, be sure to recombine it by stirring with a wooden spoon before adding it to your baking pan.

MAKES 2 CUPS

1 cup light brown sugar
¾ cup dark corn syrup
1 cup heavy cream
½ cup pecans, toasted and chopped

Combine all of the ingredients in a saucepan and heat to thread stage (220°F), stirring frequently to prevent scorching. Cool to room temperature before using.

Cinnamon Smear

MAKES 1 CUP

½ cup bread flour
⅓ cup sugar
2 teaspoons ground cinnamon
3 tablespoons unsalted butter
3 egg whites

1. Mix together the flour, sugar, and cinnamon in the bowl of a mixer. Add the butter to the flour mixture. Using the paddle attachment, mix on medium speed for 1 minute, or until it looks like coarse meal and there are no visible chunks of butter.

2. With the mixer on medium speed, add the egg whites in two additions. Continue to mix until fully combined, scraping down the bowl as necessary.

Cookies

CHOCOLATE CHUNK COOKIES

Chocolate and cherries are a match made in heaven. To make these cookies large and dramatic—which is how I like to serve them—use a heaping 2 tablespoons of dough for each one.

MAKES 24 COOKIES

3 cups all-purpose flour

¾ teaspoon baking soda

½ teaspoon salt

1 cup (2 sticks) unsalted butter, at room temperature

1 cup granulated sugar

¾ cup tightly packed light brown sugar

2 large eggs, at room temperature

1 teaspoon vanilla extract

2 cups bittersweet chocolate chunks or chips

1 cup tart unsweetened dried cherries, optional

1. Preheat the oven to 375°F. Lightly spray cookie sheets with cooking spray or line them with parchment paper. Sift the flour, baking soda, and salt into a bowl and set aside.

2. In a stand mixer fitted with the paddle attachment, cream together the butter and sugars on medium speed until light in texture and smooth, about 2 minutes.

3. Add the eggs one at a time and the vanilla extract and blend until incorporated.

4. On low speed or by hand with a wooden spoon, mix in the sifted dry ingredients, the chocolate chunks, and the dried cherries, if using. Scrape down the bowl as needed to blend evenly.

5. Use one of the following options to shape the cookies: Use 2 serving spoons to drop the dough onto the prepared baking sheets, spacing them about 2 inches apart. If desired, slightly flatten the cookies before baking. Or roll the dough into logs, chill until firm, then slice and place on prepared baking sheets.

6. Bake until the cookies are cracked on top but still slightly moist, rotating the pans as necessary to bake evenly, about 14 minutes.

7. Transfer the cookies to wire racks and let cool completely.

See What We Learned: Creamed Batters, page 26.

MUDSLIDE COOKIES

These are the ultimate chocolate cookies—dense and moist. After the cookies have been shaped they can be placed in the freezer to firm up, then transferred directly to the oven to ensure a fudgy interior. Even if you don't freeze the mudslides first, be careful not to overbake them.

MAKES 24 COOKIES

¼ cup (½ stick) unsalted butter

3 ounces unsweetened chocolate

10 ounces bittersweet chocolate

½ cup cake flour

1 teaspoon baking powder

¼ teaspoon salt

1 teaspoon instant coffee

1 tablespoon water

½ teaspoon vanilla

4 eggs

1⅓ cups sugar

1. Preheat the oven to 350°F and line two sheet pans with parchment paper. Melt the butter with the unsweetened and bittersweet chocolates in a metal bowl over barely simmering water and reserve. In a small bowl, sift together the flour, baking powder, and salt and set aside. In a separate small bowl, mix the instant coffee and water, add the vanilla, and reserve.

2. Beat the eggs, sugar, and coffee mixture with a whip attachment on high speed until light and thick, 6 to 8 minutes. Reduce the speed and add the chocolate mixture. Blend on medium speed until evenly mixed, 1 to 2 minutes. On low speed, add the dry ingredients until just blended, 1 minute. If necessary, refrigerate the dough until firm enough to hold its shape, 15 to 30 minutes.

3. Using a ¼ cup measure, scoop the dough onto the sheet pans lined with parchment. Bake cookies until they are cracked on top but still appear moist, about 14 minutes. Be sure not to overbake. Cool slightly on sheet pans and transfer to wire racks to cool completely. Store in an airtight container.

Oatmeal Raisin Cookies (left, page 215), Mudslide Cookies (center), and Peanut Butter Cookies (right, page 214)

PEANUT BUTTER COOKIES

In the 1890s, John Harvey Kellogg of cornflakes fame touted peanut butter as a healthy substitute for regular butter. By the turn of the twentieth century the classic American PB&J sandwich and peanut butter cookies had been born. The addition of chopped peanuts gives these cookies a satisfying crunch.

MAKES 24 COOKIES

2½ cups pastry flour
1 teaspoon salt
½ teaspoon baking soda
½ teaspoon baking powder
1 cup packed light brown sugar
1 cup sugar
1 cup (2 sticks) unsalted butter, softened
1¼ cups peanut butter
2 eggs
1 cup chopped roasted peanuts

1. Sift the flour, salt, baking soda, and baking powder together. Set aside. Cream the sugars and butter on high speed for 3 minutes, or until light and fluffy, scraping down the bowl as needed. Add the peanut butter and blend until just combined, about 1 minute. Add the eggs one at a time, and continue to scrape down the bowl. Add the flour mixture and peanuts. Mix just long enough to combine the ingredients.

2. Divide the dough in half and roll into logs that are approximately 20 inches long. Wrap each log in a half sheet of parchment and then in plastic wrap, label, and freeze.

3. Preheat the oven to 350°F. Cut the logs into pieces about 1 inch thick and place the cookies onto parchment-lined sheet pans. Bake until golden brown but still soft in the middle, about 20 minutes. Allow the cookies to cool to room temperature before serving.

See photo on page 213.

BUTTER COOKIES

Don't be distressed if these crisp little cookies settle as they bake and lose some of their distinctive rosette shape. Just sandwich any misshapen ones together with a little chocolate ganache or jam.

MAKES 24 COOKIES

1 cup plus 2 tablespoons unsalted butter, softened
¾ cup confectioners' sugar, sifted
¾ teaspoon vanilla
⅛ teaspoon lemon zest
1 egg
2⅔ cups cake flour, sifted

1. Preheat the oven to 375°F. Cream together the butter, sugar, vanilla, and lemon zest on medium speed with an electric mixer using the paddle attachment for 3 to 4 minutes, or until the mixture is light, fluffy, and smooth. Do not overmix. Add the egg and continue to mix, scraping down the sides of the bowl as necessary. Add the cake flour and mix together just until blended.

2. Pipe into rosettes 1¾ inches in diameter by 1 inch high using a No. 8 star tip. Bake until light golden brown, 11 to 12 minutes.

OATMEAL-RAISIN COOKIES

"Old-fashioned" oats are made from oats that have been steamed slightly to soften before being flattened between rollers. Quick-cooking oats are also steamed, but they are cut into three or four pieces before being rolled. Either old-fashioned or quick-cooking rolled oats can be used in cookie recipes, with no significant change in texture. But steel-cut oats should not be used, since they have not been precooked.

MAKES 24 COOKIES

1½ cups all-purpose flour

½ teaspoon baking powder

½ teaspoon ground cinnamon

1 teaspoon salt

1 cup (2 sticks) unsalted butter, softened

1 cup packed light brown sugar

1 cup sugar

2 teaspoons vanilla

2 eggs

3 cups rolled oats

¾ cup dark raisins

1. Preheat the oven to 375°F. Lightly spray cookie sheets with cooking spray or line them with parchment paper. Sift the flour, baking powder, cinnamon, and salt into a bowl and set aside.

2. In a stand mixer fitted with the paddle attachment, cream together the butter, sugars, and vanilla on medium speed until smooth and light in texture, 2 minutes. Add the eggs one at a time, beating well after each addition. On low speed, mix in the flour mixture, oats, and raisins until just combined. Scrape down the bowl as needed to blend evenly. Chill the dough for 10 minutes.

3. Divide the dough into 2 equal pieces and roll each piece in waxed or parchment paper to make a 12-inch-long log about 2 inches in diameter. Refrigerate until firm enough to cut, about 30 minutes. Slice each log into 12 pieces and place the slices on cookie sheets in even rows, spacing the cookies about 2 inches apart. Bake the cookies in batches until they are cracked on top but still slightly moist, rotating the pans as necessary to bake evenly, 14 to 15 minutes. Transfer to wire racks and let cool completely.

See photo on page 213.

CHOCOLATE BROWNIE CHEESECAKE

MAKES ONE 9-INCH CAKE (10 SERVINGS)

¾ cup all-purpose flour

¾ cup cocoa powder

½ teaspoon salt

⅛ teaspoon baking powder

⅛ teaspoon baking soda

1⅔ cups granulated sugar, divided

¾ cup (1½ sticks) unsalted butter, melted

5 eggs

1 pound cream cheese, at room temperature

1 teaspoon vanilla

1. Preheat the oven to 350°F. Lightly butter and flour a 9-inch springform pan.

2. Sift together the flour, cocoa powder, salt, baking powder, and baking soda. Set aside.

3. Combine 1⅓ cups of the sugar and the melted butter in a bowl and mix thoroughly with a wooden spoon or whisk. Add 4 of the eggs, mixing thoroughly. Fold in the dry ingredients, mixing just long enough to make a smooth batter. Pour the batter into the prepared pan, reserving ½ cup for marbling the top.

4. Beat together the remaining ⅓ cup of sugar and the cream cheese with an electric mixer until very smooth and light. Add the vanilla and the remaining egg and mix until evenly combined. Pour this batter into the center of the brownie batter, keeping it away from the sides of the pan.

5. With a teaspoon, carefully spoon the remaining brownie batter around the top of the cake. Run a butter knife through the pools of brownie batter for a marbled effect.

6. Bake until the edges of the cheesecake begin to shrink from the sides of the pan and the center is set but still moist, 30 to 40 minutes. If the top is browning too quickly, cover the cake loosely with foil. Cool completely on a rack in the pan and chill for at least 3 hours before cutting into pieces.

FUDGE BROWNIES

Brownies can be made either cake style or fudge style, depending on the texture you want. I'm definitely in the fudge camp! For that rich, fudgy consistency, be sure to remove the pan from the oven when the center of the brownies still appears slightly wet. Otherwise the brownies will end up too dry.

MAKES 9 BROWNIES

> ¾ cup (1½ sticks) unsalted butter
>
> 4 ounces unsweetened chocolate, chopped
>
> 2 eggs
>
> 1⅓ cups sugar
>
> 2 teaspoons vanilla
>
> ¼ teaspoon salt
>
> ¼ cup cake flour, sifted
>
> ¾ cup coarsely chopped toasted walnuts

1. Preheat the oven to 350°F. Lightly spray a 9-inch square baking pan with cooking spray or line it with parchment paper, leaving an overhang on 2 sides to help remove the brownies from the pan. Melt the butter and chocolate in a saucepan over low heat or in a bowl in the microwave in 15- to 20-second intervals, stirring and blending gently with a spoon.

2. In a stand mixer fitted with the whisk attachment, whip the eggs, sugar, vanilla, and salt together on high speed, scraping down the bowl with a rubber spatula as needed, until thick and light in color, 4 to 5 minutes.

3. While stirring, pour some of the egg mixture into the melted chocolate mixture to lighten it, then pour the chocolate into the remaining egg mixture and blend on medium speed, scraping down the bowl as needed. Mix in the flour and nuts on low speed until just blended. The batter will be very wet. Pour the batter into the prepared pan and spread evenly.

4. Bake until a skewer inserted into the center of the brownies comes out with a few moist crumbs still clinging to it, 30 to 40 minutes. Allow the brownies to cool completely in the pan on a wire rack. Use the parchment overhang to help unmold the brownie bar, then cut into 3-inch-square pieces.

Variation

GLAZED BROWNIES Brownies may be glazed with Chocolate Glaze (page 267) after removing them from the pan, but before they are cut into squares (line the pan with parchment paper to facilitate removing them uncut). After glazing, the brownies should be refrigerated for approximately 30 minutes to allow the glaze to set before cutting them into individual bars.

Pies and Tarts

FLAKY PIE DOUGH

Pie doughs may be difficult to roll out for several reasons. They may be too warm, or perhaps a little too much water has been added to the dough, or the weather is humid. Marble pastry boards and rolling pins, which stay cooler than the surrounding air, help to keep pastry dough cool and easy to handle. Another trick for working with pie dough is to roll out the dough between two pieces of parchment or waxed paper.

MAKES ENOUGH FOR ONE 9-INCH PIE

SINGLE-CRUST PIE

1⅓ cups all-purpose flour plus extra for dusting

½ teaspoon salt

½ cup (1 stick) cold unsalted butter, lard, or vegetable shortening, diced (or a combination of butter and shortening equal to ½ cup)

¼ cup ice water, or as needed

DOUBLE-CRUST PIE

2⅔ cups all-purpose flour plus extra for dusting

1 teaspoon salt

1 cup (2 sticks) cold unsalted butter, lard, or vegetable shortening, diced (or a combination of butter and shortening equal to 1 cup)

½ cup ice water, or as needed

1. Stir together the flour and salt with a fork to blend. Cut the fat into the flour using a food processor, pastry blender, or 2 knives. (For pies with liquid fillings such as custard, or cooked fruit fillings that are thickened with cornstarch or tapioca, the bits of fat should be evenly small, and the mixture should resemble a coarse meal. This will result in a mealy pie crust, which is less likely to become soggy as the pie bakes. For pies to be filled with fruit or another nonliquid filling, leave some bits of fat in larger pieces, about the size of a small pea, for a crisp and flaky texture in the baked crust.)

2. Drizzle a few tablespoons of ice water over the surface of the flour mixture and quickly rub the water into the flour. Continue to add the water, a tablespoon or so at a time, just until it holds together when you press a handful of it into a ball. The dough should be evenly moist, not wet, and shaggy or rough in appearance.

3. Turn the dough out onto a lightly floured work surface. Gather and press the dough into a ball. For a double-crust pie, divide the dough into 2 roughly equal pieces. Pat each ball into an even disk, wrap well, and let chill in the refrigerator for 20 minutes.

4. Working with a single disk at a time, unwrap the dough, place it on a lightly floured

(continued)

work surface, and scatter a little flour over the top. Alternatively, place the dough between sheets of parchment or waxed paper. Roll out the dough for the bottom crust of a pie into an even round about 13 inches in diameter (for a 9-inch pie pan). It should be about ⅛ inch thick.

5. Fold the dough in half or roll it loosely around the rolling pin, and gently lift and position it over the pan. Unfold or unroll the dough and ease it into the pan without stretching, making sure that the pan sides and the rim are evenly covered. Press the dough gently against the sides and bottom. Trim the overhang to 1 inch. For a single-crust pie, tuck the dough overhang under itself and flute the edges. Fill and bake the pie according to recipe directions. For a double-crust pie, roll out the second piece of dough into an 11-inch round (for a 9-inch pie pan), then cut vents in it. Fill and finish the pie according to recipe directions.

6. If necessary, bake the crust blind as follows: Preheat the oven to 400°F. Prick the dough evenly over the bottom and sides. Line the crust with a piece of waxed or parchment paper and fill with dry beans or pie weights. Bake just until the edges of the dough appear dry but have not taken on any color—6 to 7 minutes. Remove the beans and paper, return the crust to the oven, and bake an additional 5 minutes, or until the bottom of the crust appears dry as well. Fill as directed in the recipe.

CHERRY PIE

For the deepest cherry flavor in this pie, use the sour cherries (also called tart or pie cherries) that come on the market briefly in midsummer. Sour cherries are smaller and rounder than sweet ones, with a brighter red color. They have a short season and don't keep well once picked. If you can't find fresh sour cherries, look for those that have been frozen or canned, but be sure to check the label to see whether they've been sweetened and adjust the sugar accordingly. Or replace the sour cherries with sweet cherries—just cut back a little on the amount of sugar.

MAKES ONE DOUBLE-CRUST 9-INCH PIE

- 1 recipe double-crust Flaky Pie Dough (page 219)
- 2 tablespoons minute tapioca
- 2 tablespoons cornstarch
- 1 cup sugar
- ½ teaspoon ground cinnamon
- ¼ teaspoon freshly grated nutmeg
- ¼ teaspoon salt
- 1¼ pounds (about 3 cups) pitted fresh, thawed frozen, jarred, or canned sour cherries, juice reserved if using jarred or canned
- 1 teaspoon freshly squeezed lemon juice
- 2 tablespoons unsalted butter
- Egg wash (1 large egg whisked with 2 tablespoons milk or water) for brushing

1. Roll out the pie dough rounds and use one round to line a 9-inch pie pan as directed on page 220. Keep the dough-lined pan and other round chilled while you prepare the filling.

2. To make the cherry filling, blend the tapioca and cornstarch with about ¼ cup of the water. (Add just enough water for a thick, soupy consistency.) Set aside.

3. Stir together the sugar, cinnamon, nutmeg, and salt in a saucepan. Add 1 cup of the reserved cherry juice or water and the lemon juice and bring to a boil over high heat. Gradually add the tapioca mixture while whisking constantly, and return to a boil. Add the cherries and simmer for another minute. Remove the pan from the heat and stir in the butter. Transfer the filling to a shallow bowl or pan and cool in the refrigerator until completely chilled, about 30 minutes; stir the filling occasionally to cool more quickly.

4. Preheat the oven to 425°F. Pour the cherry filling into the dough-lined pan, mounding it slightly. Using a paring knife or pastry wheel, cut the other dough round into 14 to 16 strips about ½ inch wide. Brush the rim of the pie shell with egg wash. Lay half of the strips over the filling, parallel to each other and spaced about ½ inch apart. Fold every other strip in half, back on itself. Lay down another strip so that it is next to the fold. Unfold the folded strips to weave the strips, add another perpendicular strip, then unfold the strips.

5. Continue folding back alternate strips and weaving a lattice, working from the center to the edge of the pie, then rotate the pie 180 degrees and repeat the process on the second side. Trim the excess dough so that the edges of the dough are almost even with the edges of the pan and crimp the edges to seal. Brush the lattice evenly and lightly with egg wash.

6. Place the pie on a baking sheet and transfer to the oven. Bake just until the crust is lightly browned and the filling is heated through, 30 to 40 minutes. Let the pie rest for at least 20 minutes before cutting into wedges. Serve warm or at room temperature.

See What We Learned: Lattice Tops, page 48.

TART DOUGH

When fat is combined with flour to make dough, it surrounds (in effect, greases) the proteins in the flour and keeps them from joining into long, stretchy strands of gluten. The shorter the strands, the more tender the baked good.

MAKES ENOUGH FOR EIGHT 3-INCH TARTLETS OR ONE 9-INCH TART

½ cup (1 stick) unsalted butter, softened
¼ cup sugar
½ teaspoon vanilla
1 egg yolk
1½ cups cake flour, sifted

1. In a stand mixer fitted with the paddle attachment, cream together the butter, sugar, and vanilla on medium speed, scraping down the bowl as needed, until smooth and light in color, about 2 minutes. Add the egg yolk and blend until smooth, 1 to 2 minutes more. Add the flour all at once, mixing on low speed or by hand with a wooden spoon until just blended, about 30 seconds. The dough will be very crumbly when you remove it from the mixer. Use a gentle touch to press the dough into a disk, being careful not to work it so much that the pastry becomes tough. Wrap the dough tightly and refrigerate for 20 minutes before rolling.

2. When you are ready to roll out the dough, place it on a lightly floured work surface or between sheets of parchment or waxed paper. Scatter a little flour over the top of the dough and roll it out into an even round about 2 inches larger in diameter than your tart pan. To transfer the dough to the tart pan, fold the dough in half or roll it loosely around the rolling pin, and gently lift and position it over the pan. Unfold or unroll the dough and ease it into the pan. Trim the overhang cleanly by rolling over the edge with a rolling pin. Gently use your fingertips to press the dough against the sides and bottom of the pan. Fill and finish the tart according to recipe directions.

APPLE PIE

This is one of the most versatile recipes we made at boot camp. In the summer, pears, peaches, plums, or apricots can be substituted for the apples, with excellent results. You can also add plumped raisins, currants, or nuts to vary the texture and flavor. It's also fun to play around with the crust. For decorative effect, roll out the dough and cut it into lattice strips, or roll out the pastry scraps, cut out leaf shapes, and place them on top of a vented crust. For a homier treatment, make a deep dish pie with a single crust. Simply pour the filling into a lightly greased 2½-inch-deep pie plate or a 9-inch square baking pan. Top with half a recipe of pie crust, and bake as directed. Spoon the warm pie directly from the baking dish, along with all of its juices.

MAKES ONE 9-INCH PIE (8 SERVINGS)

¾ cup packed light brown sugar

¼ cup all-purpose flour

¾ teaspoon ground cinnamon

¼ teaspoon ground nutmeg

6 to 7 apples, peeled, cored, and thinly sliced (about 7 cups)

2 tablespoons freshly squeezed lemon juice

Double-crust Flaky Pie Dough (page 219)

3 tablespoons unsalted butter, cut into small pieces

Egg wash of 1 egg yolk whisked with 1 teaspoon milk or water

1. Preheat the oven to 425°F. Position a rack in the middle of the oven.

2. Stir together the sugar, flour, cinnamon, and nutmeg in a large bowl with a fork. Add the apples to the bowl, sprinkle them with the lemon juice, and toss to coat all the slices evenly with the spice mixture.

3. Divide the dough in half and roll out the first half to fit the pie plate. Mound the apples in the pie shell, making the center higher than the sides. Dot the top evenly with the butter.

4. Roll out the second half of the dough for the top crust and cut two or three vents. Lay the top crust over the apple filling and crimp the edges. Brush the top crust lightly with egg wash.

5. Set the pie in the middle of the oven and place a sheet pan underneath to catch drips. Bake the pie for 15 minutes at 425°F, turning the pan to encourage even browning. Reduce the oven temperature to 350°F and bake until the top crust is golden brown and the apples feel tender when pierced through the steam vents with a knife, 40 to 45 minutes more. Remove the pie from the oven and cool it on a rack. Serve warm.

LEMON MERINGUE PIE

The secret to making a meringue topping that doesn't weep is to spread it on while the filling is still warm. That way it is less likely to break down from contact with a cool surface. Better yet, take the time to make a Swiss meringue, which is more stable.

MAKES ONE 9-INCH PIE (8 SERVINGS)

2 cups water, divided

1 cup sugar, divided

5 tablespoons lemon juice

1 tablespoon lemon zest

½ teaspoon salt

⅓ cup cornstarch

3 egg yolks

2 tablespoons unsalted butter

Single-crust Flaky Pie Dough (page 219), baked blind

Swiss Meringue (recipe follows)

1. To make the filling, combine 1½ cups of the water, ½ cup of the sugar, the lemon juice, zest, and salt in a medium saucepan. Bring to a boil over medium-high heat. Combine the remaining ½ cup sugar and the cornstarch in a medium bowl. In a separate bowl whisk together the egg yolks and the remaining ½ cup water. Add this egg mixture to the sugar mixture. Mix until well blended and reserve.

2. When the lemon juice mixture comes to a boil, add about half of it to the egg yolk mixture while whisking constantly. Return the egg yolk mixture to the remaining lemon juice mixture in the pan and boil for 1 minute, whisking constantly. Add the butter and continue to stir

until blended. Pour the lemon filling into the prebaked pie shell, spreading evenly to fill the pie crust.

3. Evenly distribute the meringue over the top of the warm filling. Make sure the meringue touches the edges of the crust to prevent shrinking and weeping. Brown the meringue, if desired, by broiling for a few minutes.

Swiss Meringue

Warming egg whites and sugar before you beat them into a meringue dissolves the sugar completely for a smooth texture and keeps the foam slightly more stable. In a Swiss meringue, the eggs and sugar are warmed together before beating.

MAKES ABOUT 4 CUPS

4 egg whites

1 cup sugar

Put the egg whites and sugar in the clean, grease-free bowl of a stand mixer fitted with the whisk attachment and stir together until the sugar is blended into the whites. Place the bowl over a saucepan of simmering water and stir frequently until the mixture reaches 110° to 120°F. Transfer the bowl to the mixer and beat on high speed until the meringue is thick and glossy and has the desired peak (soft, medium, or stiff) according to its intended use.

Baker's Note: You may prefer to use pasteurized egg whites in this recipe to eliminate any food safety concerns.

CITRUS TART WITH CHOCOLATE CRUST

This luscious tart takes advantage of several basic recipes in the baker's repertoire—tart dough, pastry cream, sponge cake, and simple syrup—making it a perfect vehicle for experimentation. Try adding different flavorings to the pastry cream and simple syrup, such as almond and Grand Marnier, or chocolate and brandy.

MAKES ONE 9-INCH TART (8 SERVINGS)

Chocolate Tart Dough (recipe follows)
1½ cups Pastry Cream (page 261)
1 layer Vanilla Sponge Cake (page 192)
6 tablespoons Simple Syrup, flavored (page 260)
1 cup apricot jam, warmed and strained
3 medium navel oranges, cut into segments
1 grapefruit, cut into segments
Apricot Glaze (page 260), as needed
½ cup pistachios, toasted and coarsely ground

1. Roll out the tart dough ⅛ inch thick and line a 9-inch tart shell. Trim any excess. Bake the shell blind (see page 220). Remove from the oven and cool completely on a rack before assembling the tart.

2. Fill the tart shell with pastry cream. Top the pastry cream with the sponge cake layer and brush with simple syrup. Spread the moistened sponge cake with apricot jam.

3. Arrange citrus fruit slices in concentric circles to cover the sponge cake completely.

4. Brush the fruit with apricot glaze. Garnish the outer rim of the tart with pistachios.

Chocolate Tart Dough

MAKES ONE 9-INCH PIE OR TART (8 SERVINGS)

1 cup sugar
⅔ cup unsalted butter, softened
2 eggs
2 tablespoons milk
3 cups all-purpose flour
½ cup sifted unsweetened cocoa powder

1. Cream the sugar and butter by hand or with the paddle attachment of a stand mixer until smooth and light, about 2 minutes. Gradually add the eggs and milk and beat until smooth, scraping the bowl as necessary, another 2 to 3 minutes. Add the flour and cocoa powder and mix just until incorporated (do not overmix).

2. Gather the dough into a ball and wrap it in plastic wrap. Chill in the refrigerator for 15 to 20 minutes to firm the dough slightly. Roll out the dough on a floured work surface, adding just enough flour to the board and the rolling pin to keep it from sticking.

LEMON SHAKER TART

Though it has a double crust, this unusual pie is more like a tart. It was a favorite recipe of the nineteenth-century Ohio Shakers, who were known for their baked goods. For best results, begin making this pie two or three days ahead of serving so that the lemons have plenty of time to mellow. Since the rinds are eaten, it's important to use lemons grown organically, without chemical pesticides or fertilizers. This pie is wonderfully tart and refreshing.

MAKES ONE 9-INCH TART (8 SERVINGS)

> 2¾ cups very thinly sliced organic lemons (about 3), seeds removed
>
> 2 cups sugar
>
> Double-crust Flaky Pie Dough (page 219), rolled out and kept chilled
>
> 5 eggs, lightly beaten
>
> Egg wash of 1 egg whisked with 1 teaspoon water

1. Combine the lemon slices with the sugar and toss to combine evenly. Cover the bowl and allow the mixture to rest at room temperature for at least 24 and up to 36 hours.

2. Preheat the oven to 450°F. Roll out the dough and ease it into a 9-inch tart pan with a removable bottom, covering the sides and rim of the pan evenly and making an even overhang on all sides. Trim the overhang to ¼ inch and gently press the dough into the sides of the pan.

3. Using a slotted spoon, transfer the lemon slices into the tart pan, allowing as much of the syrup to drain back into the bowl as possible. Add the eggs to the syrup left in the bowl and beat well. Pour the egg-syrup mixture over the lemons. Brush the rim of the dough lightly with the egg wash. Do not allow it to form pools in any depressions in the crust.

4. Roll out the second piece of dough for the top crust. Center the crust over the filling. Press the top and bottom crusts together around the edges, trim the overhang to ½ inch, and then crimp or flute the edges. Cut vents in the top crust. Brush the top lightly with the egg wash.

5. Bake the tart for 15 minutes. Lower the oven temperature to 350°F and continue to bake until a knife inserted through one of the vents comes out clean, another 30 minutes. Chill for at least 2 hours before unmolding. Serve chilled or at room temperature. The tart can be stored in the refrigerator for up to 2 days.

Baker's Note: Cutting the lemon slices very thin is critical to the success of this pie. Use a mandoline or a Japanese-style slicer for the right thinness. As you slice the lemon into rounds, you'll expose the seeds. Use the tip of a paring knife to remove them.

RUSTIC PEACH GALETTE

This freeform tart is one of my favorite ways to use peaches when they're in season, since they play the starring role. The ladyfinger crumbs absorb some of the peach juices to keep the crust crisp. You'll need about half of a 3- or 4-ounce package of ladyfingers for this recipe. Allow the cookies to dry unwrapped at room temperature for 2 or 3 hours before crumbling them with your hands or grinding them in a food processor.

MAKES ONE 8-INCH TART (8 SERVINGS)

Single-crust Flaky Pie Dough (page 219)

4 medium peaches

2 tablespoons freshly squeezed lemon juice

2 tablespoons granulated sugar

1 teaspoon ground cinnamon

¼ teaspoon ground nutmeg

½ cup crumbled ladyfingers

Egg wash of 1 egg whisked with 2 tablespoons milk or water

2 tablespoons coarse sugar

1. Roll the pie dough into a 10-inch round. Keep it chilled while you prepare the peaches.

2. Preheat the oven to 400°F. Use a paring knife to cut and pull away the skin from the peaches; if the skin is very firmly attached, score the skin in an X on the blossom (bottom) end of the fruit, lower the peaches into rapidly boiling water for 30 seconds, then transfer to a bowl of ice water to stop the cooking. The skin will pull away easily. Remove the pits. Cut into slices ¼ inch thick and toss with the lemon juice, granulated sugar, cinnamon, and nutmeg.

3. Transfer the dough to a parchment-paper-lined baking sheet. Sprinkle with the ladyfinger crumbs, leaving a 2-inch border free of crumbs. Pile the peaches on top of the cake crumbs, leaving the border unfilled. Brush a 1-inch perimeter of the dough lightly with egg wash. Fold the dough edges in toward the center, over the fruit, pinching and folding it to seal the edge and create a pleated border. Brush the pleated edge of the galette lightly with egg wash and sprinkle with the coarse sugar.

4. Bake until the pastry is golden brown and the peaches hot and juicy, about 25 minutes. Remove the tart from the oven and cool on the pan on a wire rack for at least 20 minutes before slicing. Serve warm or at room temperature.

Baker's Note: You can substitute apples, sour cherries, apricots, or pears for the peaches.

CRANBERRY-PECAN PIE

When my family moved to Texas when I was in high school, I discovered pecan pie. I spent my first few months in our new kitchen baking my way through dozens of pecan pie recipes to find the perfect one. My quest hasn't yet ended, but this pie comes close to perfection. The use of light corn syrup instead of dark allows the flavor of the pecans to come through.

MAKES ONE 9-INCH PIE (8 SERVINGS)

1 cup toasted pecan halves

½ cup fresh or frozen cranberries

Single-crust Flaky Pie Dough (page 219), baked blind

½ cup packed light brown sugar

2 tablespoons all-purpose flour

¾ cup light corn syrup

3 eggs, lightly beaten

¼ cup (½ stick) unsalted butter, melted and cooled

2 teaspoons vanilla

¼ teaspoon salt

1. Preheat the oven to 400°F. Spread the nuts and cranberries in an even layer over the bottom of the pie shell. Stir the brown sugar and flour together in a mixing bowl until well blended. Add the corn syrup, eggs, butter, vanilla, and salt and blend well. Pour the mixture over the nuts, disturbing the nuts as little as possible.

2. Place the pie on a baking sheet and bake until the center is softly set, 30 to 35 minutes. Let the pie rest for at least 20 minutes before slicing. Serve warm or at room temperature.

Desserts

ANGEL FOOD SUMMER PUDDING

Summer puddings are a favorite English dessert made by soaking cake slices in flavored syrup and layering them with poached or fresh fruits. Although these puddings are not cooked, they resemble traditional steamed puddings because of the way they are molded. To make a single large pudding instead of individual ones, use a clear glass bowl or footed trifle dish. Since the pudding can be served directly from the dish, there is no need to line it first with plastic wrap.

MAKES 6 SERVINGS

2 cups stemmed and quartered strawberries

2 cups blackberries

2 cups raspberries

½ cup sugar

2 tablespoons freshly squeezed lemon juice

2 tablespoons framboise or other raspberry liqueur (optional)

2 tablespoons honey, or to taste

Angel Food Cake (page 193)

Chantilly Cream (page 266)

Mixed Berry Compote (page 258)

1. Combine the berries with the sugar and lemon juice in a saucepan and simmer over low heat for 5 minutes. Remove the berries from the heat and stir in the framboise, if using, and honey. Use a slotted spoon to lift the berries out of the syrup and set aside.

2. Slice the angel food cake into ½-inch-thick slices and add the slices to the berry syrup, turning to coat evenly. Line six coffee cups or 10-ounce soufflé dishes with plastic wrap. Line the bottom and sides of the dishes completely with slices of the cake, reserving six slices for the tops. Spoon the berries into the center, filling the mold. Lay another slice of cake on top of the berries. Fold the plastic wrap over the puddings and press down gently. Chill the puddings for at least 3 hours, or up to overnight.

3. Unmold the puddings and unwrap. Serve on dessert plates with Chantilly Cream and Mixed Berry Compote.

Baker's Note: This dessert can also be made using a prepared angel food cake, and frozen berries can be used if fresh berries are unavailable. Serve with peach ice cream instead of Chantilly Cream.

BREAD AND BUTTER PUDDING

This comforting bread pudding will be as good as the bread you use for the base—a loaf rich in butter and eggs will yield the tastiest results. Be sure to remove the pudding from the oven when the center is still moist, since it will continue to firm up as it cools.

MAKES 6 SERVINGS

¼ cup raisins

⅓ cup rum

8 slices enriched bread, such as challah or brioche, cut into 1-inch cubes

3 tablespoons unsalted butter, melted and kept warm

2 cups whole milk

3 eggs, lightly beaten

1 egg yolk, lightly beaten

⅓ cup sugar

½ teaspoon vanilla

¼ teaspoon ground cinnamon

1. Preheat the oven to 350°F. Combine the raisins with the rum and warm in a small saucepan over low heat. Remove from the heat and allow the raisins to plump for about 10 minutes. Drain and reserve.

2. Meanwhile, drizzle the bread cubes with the melted butter, spread on a baking sheet, and toast in the oven, stirring once or twice, until golden brown, 10 to 12 minutes.

3. Combine the milk, eggs, egg yolk, sugar, vanilla, and cinnamon and stir until the sugar has fully dissolved. Grease a 2-quart shallow casserole, 8-inch square baking dish, or individual ¾-cup ceramic ramekins with butter and place in a larger rectangular baking dish. Add the bread cubes and raisins to the ramekins or dish and ladle the milk mixture over the bread, reserving about ¾ cup. Refrigerate the bread pudding(s) and the reserved milk mixture for about 30 minutes while the bread absorbs the liquid.

4. Spoon the remaining milk mixture onto the soaked bread. Place the baking pan in the oven, and pour hot water into the pan to come two-thirds of the way up the side of the ramekins or dish. Bake until the custard is set but still jiggles in the middle when gently shaken, about 30 minutes for small ramekins and 50 minutes for a larger baking dish. Let stand for 15 minutes after removing from the oven. The pudding may be served warm or chilled.

PUMPKIN BREAD PUDDING

I like to serve this bread pudding with vanilla sauce flavored with brandy or bourbon. For a deeper flavor, I sometimes replace the sugar with ¾ cup maple syrup.

MAKES 8 SERVINGS

2 cups milk

4 whole eggs

1 cup sugar

7 slices whole-grain bread, diced

1½ cups puréed cooked pumpkin (fresh or canned)

½ cup raisins

½ teaspoon ground cinnamon

⅛ teaspoon ground cloves

⅛ teaspoon ground nutmeg

⅛ teaspoon ground allspice

1. Preheat the oven to 300°F. Lightly butter a 2-quart casserole or baking dish.

2. Beat together the milk, eggs, and sugar until thoroughly blended. Add the bread cubes to the milk mixture and stir to moisten evenly. Let rest about 15 minutes. Stir in the pumpkin, raisins, cinnamon, cloves, nutmeg, and allspice. Pour the batter into the casserole and cover with foil or parchment paper.

3. Place the casserole inside a larger baking pan on a kitchen towel, and add enough hot water to the baking pan to come up to the level of the bread pudding, to make a water bath. Bake about 45 minutes, removing the cover during the last 15 minutes of baking time. The pudding should be completely set and the top lightly browned.

CHOCOLATE SOUFFLÉ

MAKES 4 SERVINGS

Softened butter for greasing molds

5 tablespoons granulated sugar (divided use) plus more for dusting

4 ounces bittersweet chocolate, chopped

2 tablespoons unsalted butter

1½ cups Pastry Cream (page 261)

5 large egg whites

Confectioners' sugar for dusting

1. Preheat the oven to 400°F. Lightly grease four 6-ounce soufflé molds with the butter. Dust with granulated sugar to coat the butter evenly, emptying out any excess. Wipe the rims clean.

2. Melt the chocolate with 2 tablespoons butter over very low heat or in a microwave on low power. Stir until blended. Add the melted chocolate-butter mixture to the pastry cream and stir until the mixture is smooth and light.

3. Whip the egg whites to medium peaks with a handheld mixer. Add one-third of the whipped whites to the pastry cream and gently fold in just until incorporated. Add the remaining egg whites and fold in just until incorporated. Divide evenly among the prepared soufflé molds on a baking sheet and bake undisturbed until the soufflés appear set but soft, 18–20 minutes.

4. Sift a little confectioners' sugar over the top of each soufflé and serve at once.

See photo on page 168.

ORANGE SOUFFLÉ

To produce the lightest, airiest soufflé, whip the egg whites to medium, not stiff, peaks before folding them into the pastry cream base. And be sure to use a light touch when folding. It's better to leave a few patches of whipped egg white than to deflate the mixture (and all of your careful work) by overfolding.

MAKES 4 SERVINGS

Softened butter for greasing molds

5 tablespoons sugar, divided, plus extra for dusting molds

2 egg yolks

2 tablespoons all-purpose flour

⅛ teaspoon salt

¾ cup milk

½ teaspoon vanilla

2 tablespoons orange juice concentrate, thawed

½ teaspoon grated orange zest

5 egg whites

Confectioners' sugar for dusting

1. Preheat the oven to 400°F. Lightly grease four 6-ounce soufflé molds with butter. Dust with sugar to coat the butter evenly, emptying out any excess. Wipe the rims clean.

2. In a bowl, blend 2 tablespoons sugar, the egg yolks, flour, and salt. Set aside.

3. Heat the milk and remaining 3 tablespoons sugar in a small saucepan over medium-high heat. Bring to a boil and remove from the heat. Whisk in the vanilla and let cool slightly.

4. Gradually add the warm milk to the egg yolk mixture, whisking constantly. Return the mixture to the saucepan over medium heat. Whisk constantly until the mixture thickens and comes to a boil, about 3 minutes, to make a pastry cream. Remove from the heat. Transfer the pastry cream to a bowl and place over a pan of cold water. Whisk until the pastry cream is cool, about 5 minutes. Add the orange juice concentrate and zest to the pastry cream. Set aside.

5. Whip the egg whites to medium peaks. Add one-third of the whipped whites to the pastry cream and gently fold in just until incorporated. Add the remaining egg whites and fold in just until incorporated. Divide evenly among the prepared soufflé molds on a baking sheet and bake undisturbed until the tops are golden brown and the soufflés appear set but soft, 18 to 20 minutes. Sift a little confectioners' sugar over the top of each soufflé and serve at once.

Variations

ALMOND SOUFFLÉ Use finely chopped toasted almonds in place of the sugar coating for the molds. Replace the orange juice concentrate and zest with ½ teaspoon almond extract and 1 tablespoon amaretto.

COFFEE SOUFFLÉ Omit the orange juice concentrate and zest and add 2 teaspoons instant coffee or espresso powder to the milk mixture.

CRÈME BRÛLÉE

Crème brûlée means "burnt cream" in French, but in fact the cream isn't burnt at all; the custard is simply topped with a "burnt" coating of sugar. The trick is to cook the sugar quickly into a glasslike crust without overcooking the custard below.

MAKES 6 SERVINGS

2½ cups heavy cream
¾ cup granulated sugar, divided
⅛ teaspoon salt
½ vanilla bean
5 egg yolks, lightly beaten
6 tablespoons superfine sugar

1. Preheat the oven to 325°F. Lightly coat six 6-ounce ramekins or custard cups with cooking spray and set them on a kitchen towel in a deep baking pan.

2. Combine the cream, ½ cup granulated sugar, and the salt in a nonreactive saucepan over medium heat. Split the vanilla bean in half lengthwise and scrape out the seeds. Add the seeds and the pod to the milk mixture. Bring the mixture to a simmer, stirring until the sugar dissolves. Remove the pan from the heat and let the mixture steep for at least 30 minutes. Strain into a clean pan and return to a simmer.

3. Meanwhile, blend the egg yolks with the remaining ¼ cup granulated sugar. Gradually add about one-third of the hot cream to the yolks, whisking constantly. Add the remaining hot cream and stir. Strain the custard through a fine-mesh sieve into a clean container. Carefully ladle or pour the custard into the prepared ramekins, filling them three-quarters full.

4. Place the baking pan on a pulled-out oven rack. Add enough boiling water to come halfway up the sides of the ramekins. Carefully slide in the rack and bake the custards until the edges have set and a nickel-sized spot in the center jiggles slightly when a custard is shaken, 20 to 25 minutes.

5. Remove the ramekins from the water bath. Let the custards cool on a rack for 30 minutes, wrap individually, and refrigerate for at least 3 hours or up to 3 days before finishing with the brûlée layer.

6. To finish, evenly coat the top of each custard with 1 tablespoon superfine sugar. Use a kitchen blowtorch or the broiler to evenly melt and caramelize the sugar. Serve immediately.

CRÈME CARAMEL

*This gorgeous baked custard is smooth and
creamy. When caramelizing the sugar, add a
small amount of lemon juice or corn syrup to
help prevent sugar crystals from forming, so that
the caramel does not become grainy.*

MAKES 6 SERVINGS

¾ cup sugar, divided
¼ teaspoon fresh lemon juice
1¼ cups whole milk
1¼ cups heavy cream
2 eggs
1 egg yolk
1 teaspoon vanilla

1. Preheat the oven to 325°F. Lightly grease
the bottom and sides of four ½-cup ramekins
and set them on a kitchen towel in a deep baking pan.

2. Combine 6 tablespoons of the sugar and the
lemon juice in a small, heavy skillet. Cook over
medium heat, stirring gently with a wooden
spoon, until the sugar melts, about 1 minute.
Continue to cook without stirring until the
sugar turns a deep golden brown, about 2 minutes. Immediately remove from the heat and
divide the caramel evenly among the ramekins.

3. Combine the milk, cream, and 3 tablespoons of the sugar in a small saucepan and
bring to a boil over high heat, stirring constantly. Remove from the heat.

4. In a bowl, whisk the remaining 3 tablespoons sugar with the eggs, egg yolk, and
vanilla. While whisking constantly, slowly pour
a small amount of the hot milk mixture into
the egg yolk mixture. Stir the tempered egg
mixture into the pan with the remaining hot
milk mixture. Divide the custard evenly among
the ramekins. Place the baking pan with the
ramekins in the oven and pour hot water into
the pan to come two-thirds of the way up the
sides of the ramekins.

5. Bake until the custards are set but still jiggle in the middle when gently shaken, about 35
minutes. Refrigerate for at least 12 hours or up
to 2 days before serving. To serve, run a thin
knife under hot water and run the knife around
the edge of the custard. Unmold the custard
onto a small plate. The caramel in the bottom
of the cup will form a sauce.

POTS DE CRÈME

Pots de crème are a delicate custard whose name (literally, "pots of cream") comes from the lidded cups they were traditionally baked in to keep a skin from forming on the custard. Here, the traditional lid is replaced with a sheet of parchment paper or aluminum foil draped loosely over the custards as they bake, trapping just a bit of steam for a lightly set, smooth custard. Make sure that the paper or foil rests on the rims of the cups without touching the custard itself so that the surface isn't marred.

MAKES 6 SERVINGS

1 cup whole or low-fat milk
1 cup heavy cream
¾ cup sugar, divided
3 ounces bittersweet chocolate, melted
1 egg
2 egg yolks
1 teaspoon vanilla

1. Preheat the oven to 325°F. Lightly coat six 6-ounce ramekins or custard cups with cooking spray and set them on a kitchen towel in a deep baking pan.

2. Combine the milk and cream with ¼ cup of the sugar in a nonreactive saucepan and bring to a simmer over medium heat. Remove from the heat and keep warm. Place ¼ cup of the sugar in a heavy saucepan and cook over medium heat until the sugar liquefies and turns a deep golden brown, 4 to 5 minutes. Add the hot cream mixture to the caramel in 3 addi-tions, bringing to a boil after each addition and stirring to dissolve, about 5 minutes total. Add the melted chocolate. Strain the cream mixture into a clean saucepan and return to a simmer.

3. While the cream mixture heats, blend the egg and egg yolks with the remaining ¼ cup sugar in a heatproof bowl. Temper the eggs by gradually adding about one-third of the hot cream mixture, whisking constantly. Add the eggs to the remaining cream mixture and stir. Add the vanilla to the custard mixture, stir, and strain into the prepared ramekins, filling them three-quarters full.

4. Place the baking pan on a pulled-out oven rack. Add enough boiling water to come halfway up the sides of the ramekins. Cover the pan loosely with parchment paper or aluminum foil and bake until the pots de crème are very glossy on top and jiggle only slightly when shaken, 20 to 25 minutes. Remove the ramekins from the water bath. Let the pots de crème cool on a rack for 30 minutes, wrap individually, and refrigerate for at least 3 hours or up to 3 days before serving in the ramekins.

MIXED BERRY COBBLER

Cobblers belong to the large family of fruit-based desserts that are enjoyed throughout the United States. Different parts of the country prefer their own interpretations of the dish. Some cobblers, like this one, feature a cakelike batter, while others include either a pastry crust or a biscuit topping. Serve cobblers with ice cream or whipped cream.

MAKES 12 SERVINGS

Butter for greasing molds

1½ cups all-purpose flour

2 teaspoons baking soda

1 teaspoon cream of tartar

1 teaspoon salt

½ cup (1 stick) unsalted butter, softened

1 cup sugar, divided

1 egg, lightly beaten

½ cup buttermilk

3 pints raspberries, blackberries, or blueberries, or a mixture

1. Preheat the oven to 350°F. Butter a 9-inch baking dish or 6 individual molds. Sift the flour, baking soda, cream of tartar, and salt into a bowl; set aside.

2. In a stand mixer fitted with the paddle attachment, cream together the butter and ¾ cup of the sugar on low speed until light in texture, about 2 minutes, or mix by hand in a large mixing bowl. Beat in the egg, mixing until smooth, about 2 minutes. Incorporate the flour mixture into the butter by adding the flour alternately with the buttermilk, beginning and ending with the flour mixture.

3. Arrange the berries in the baking dish. Add the remaining ¼ cup sugar and mix lightly. Spoon the batter over the berries. Bake until the crust is golden brown and a toothpick inserted into the crust comes out clean, 40 to 50 minutes. Remove the cobbler from the oven and let cool on a wire rack for 10 minutes before slicing. Serve warm.

SPICED BERRY AND PEAR CRISP

This autumnal dessert is a nice twist on the more usual apple crisp. Unlike cobblers, which are made with a biscuit topping, crisps have a sweet, crumbly upper layer, made here with a combination of oats and nuts. Crisps are best when served quite warm, though not piping hot. You can bake this dessert in advance, then reheat it gently in a 275°F oven for 15 minutes. Serve with a dollop of lightly whipped cream or a scoop of vanilla or ginger ice cream.

MAKES 6 TO 8 SERVINGS

3 cups mixed berries

4 medium pears (Bartlett or Comice), peeled, cored, and diced

½ cup packed brown sugar

1 tablespoon freshly squeezed lemon juice

1 teaspoon grated lemon zest

¾ teaspoon ground cinnamon, divided

¼ teaspoon ground nutmeg

¼ teaspoon ginger

½ cup all-purpose flour

½ cup rolled oats

½ cup toasted chopped nuts (almonds, walnuts, or pecans)

½ cup sugar

½ teaspoon salt

¼ cup (½ stick) unsalted butter, diced

1 egg, lightly beaten

1. Preheat the oven to 375°F. Lightly butter a deep 2-quart baking dish or 6 individual gratin dishes.

2. Combine the berries, pears, brown sugar, lemon juice, lemon zest, ¼ teaspoon of the cinnamon, the nutmeg, and ginger in the baking dish. Spread into an even layer.

3. Combine the flour, oats, nuts, sugar, salt, and the remaining ½ teaspoon cinnamon in a food processor. Pulse the machine on and off a few times to combine. Add the diced butter to the oatmeal mixture and process just until the mixture looks crumbly.

4. Spread the oatmeal mixture evenly over the filling and bake in a preheated oven until the top is golden brown and the fruit is tender, about 1 hour.

Baker's Note: Other fruits may be used, including apples, peaches, and nectarines, alone or in combination with fresh berries, nuts, and raisins or other dried fruits. You can replace half of the flour with coconut for the topping. The fruit filling can be prepared in advance and held up to 3 hours at room temperature before topping and baking.

To reduce the overall calories and fat in this dish, cut the butter back to 1 or 2 tablespoons, or omit it entirely. Use only the egg white instead of the whole egg, and cut the nuts back to half the amount suggested in the ingredient list.

Pastries

APPLE-FILLED TURNOVERS

This recipe makes full-size turnovers, but you can make miniature versions if you like. Whether large or small, the pastries should not be overfilled, or the filling will ooze out as they bake. To make the turnovers more festive, mix confectioners' sugar and water with a few drops of lemon juice or vanilla, and drizzle this icing over them. The unbaked pastries may be frozen for up to 3 months.

MAKES 12 PASTRIES

> 1½ pounds Blitz Puff Pastry (page 248)
> Egg wash of 1 egg whisked with 2 tablespoons cream or milk
> 1½ cups Apple Filling (recipe follows)
> 1 cup Apricot Glaze (page 260), warm

1. Preheat the oven to 375°F. Roll the puff pastry into a rectangle 12 by 16 inches. Dust the dough and rolling pin lightly with flour if necessary to prevent the dough from sticking. Cut the dough into twelve 4-inch squares. Place the squares on a baking sheet and let them chill in the refrigerator until firm, about 10 minutes.

2. To assemble the turnovers, take the puff pastry dough from the refrigerator. Brush the edges lightly with egg wash. Place 2 tablespoons of the filling at the center of each square. Fold one corner of the dough over the filling and line it up with the opposite corner of the dough to make a triangle. Press the edges firmly together to seal the filling inside the dough. Chill for 10 minutes before baking.

3. Brush the turnovers lightly with egg wash. Cut a small opening in the center of each turnover with a very sharp paring knife or a razor blade. Bake the turnovers until golden brown, about 20 minutes. Transfer to cooling racks and brush with Apricot Glaze while they are still hot. Cool completely before serving.

Apple Filling

Use this filling for the turnovers above. You can also use it as a filling for various shapes of Danish pastries.

MAKES 2 CUPS

> 4 cups sliced Granny Smith apples, peeled and cored
>
> 6 tablespoons sugar
>
> 3 tablespoons canola oil, divided
>
> ¼ cup applejack or apple-flavored brandy
>
> ¼ cup apple juice
>
> 3 tablespoons currants
>
> ¾ teaspoon orange zest
>
> ¼ teaspoon vanilla
>
> ¼ teaspoon ground cinnamon
>
> ⅛ teaspoon ground nutmeg

1. Toss the sliced apples with the sugar and set aside.

2. Heat a sauté pan over medium-high heat and add 1 tablespoon of the oil. Add the sugared apples to the pan, working in batches and adding more canola oil as needed to keep the apples in a single layer. Sauté until the apples are golden on both sides, about 4 minutes. Transfer the apples to a bowl. Add the applejack or brandy, apple juice, currants, orange zest, vanilla, cinnamon, and nutmeg to the pan, stir to release the sugar from the pan, and simmer until slightly reduced and thickened, 1 or 2 minutes. Stir the filling gently until the currants are evenly distributed.

3. Cool the filling over an ice bath, stirring from time to time. Once the filling has reached room temperature, it is ready to use or store in a covered container in the refrigerator for up to 5 days. Warm the filling over low heat or in the microwave if necessary.

BEAR CLAWS

These popular pastries get their name from their resemblance to bear paws with claws extended. If you make the Blitz Puff Pastry and Almond Filling a few days ahead and store them in the refrigerator, you can easily have fresh pastries for brunch.

MAKES 12 PASTRIES

> 2 pounds Blitz Puff Pastry (recipe follows)
> 2 cups Almond Filling (recipe follows)
> Egg wash of 1 egg whisked with 2 tablespoons cream or milk
> 2 cups sliced almonds
> 1 cup Apricot Glaze (page 260), warm
> Powdered sugar, optional

1. Preheat the oven to 425°F. Cut the dough in half. Working with one piece of dough at a time (keep the second piece in the refrigerator), roll out each piece of dough ⅛ inch thick and into a rectangle 6½ by 24 inches. Turn the dough so that the longest edge is lengthwise on the work surface.

2. Pipe half of the almond filling lengthwise in a line just below the center of the dough. Lightly brush the puff pastry below the filling with egg wash.

3. Fold the top edge of the dough over the filling and line it up with the bottom edge of the dough. Press the excess dough together firmly to form a seal around the filling. If the dough has become soft, refrigerate it for 10 minutes or until it becomes firm again.

4. Cut vertically through the unfilled dough at ½-inch intervals using a knife or bench scraper, making sure not to cut through the seal around the filling. This will form the toes in the bear claws. Brush the dough lightly with egg wash and sprinkle it with sliced almonds. Cut the dough into 3½-inch lengths and place the bear claws on parchment-lined sheet trays. Pull the dough over the exposed filling on each end and press the upper edges together behind the filled part of the bear claw to separate the toes. Refrigerate for 15 to 20 minutes. Repeat with the second piece of dough.

5. Bake until golden brown, about 20 minutes. Brush the pastries with the Apricot Glaze while they are still hot. Let the bear claws cool completely before serving. Dust with powdered sugar if desired.

Almond Filling

MAKES 2 CUPS

> ½ cup almond paste
> 2 tablespoons dark rum
> 2½ cups cake crumbs or crumbled ladyfingers
> 6 egg whites (more as needed)

Mix the almond paste and rum on medium speed using the paddle attachment until thoroughly combined and smooth, 1 to 2 minutes. Add the cake crumbs and mix until just combined, about 1 minute. Add the egg whites slowly and mix until the filling reaches piping consistency, about 1 minute. Add an additional egg white if necessary. The filling is ready to use now or store in a covered container in the refrigerator for up to 2 days. To make the filling easier to pipe, let the filling warm at room temperature for about 15 minutes before using, and stir well by hand or in a mixer until spreadable.

Blitz Puff Pastry

Blitz puff pastry is nearly as flaky and buttery as the classic puff pastry, but you can put it together quickly. For larger batches, you can use a stand mixer with a dough hook to blend the dough. Divide the dough into smaller pieces before wrapping and freezing to have your own pastry on hand to make sweet and savory treats.

MAKES 2½ POUNDS

2 cups (4 sticks) unsalted butter
3½ cups all-purpose flour
1¾ teaspoons salt
1 cup cold water

1. Cut the butter into ¼-inch cubes. Refrigerate until chilled and firm.

2. Combine the flour and salt in a large mixing bowl. Add the butter and toss with your fingertips until the butter is coated with flour. Add all but about 2 tablespoons of the cold water. Mix with a pastry blender or a table fork until an evenly moist but still rough dough forms. Add additional water if necessary if the dough is not moist enough to hold together when pressed into a ball.

3. Cover the dough tightly with plastic wrap. Cool in the refrigerator until the butter is firm but not brittle, about 20 minutes.

4. Turn the dough out onto a lightly floured work surface. Roll it into a rectangle approximately 12 by 30 inches; the dough should be about ½ inch thick.

5. Fold the dough in thirds like a letter (this is the first of four 3-folds). Turn the dough 90 degrees so that the long end is once again parallel to the edge of your work surface. Roll the dough out to a rectangle as described above and fold once more (this is the second of four 3-folds). Wrap the dough tightly in plastic wrap and chill for 30 minutes in the refrigerator. Continue rolling and folding the dough for the third and fourth 3-folds as described above, chilling the dough in between folds for 30 minutes each time.

6. After completing the final 3-fold, wrap the dough in plastic wrap and allow it to firm under refrigeration for at least 1 hour before using. The dough will last up to 1 week in the refrigerator or it may be frozen for up to 2 months.

CHERRY CHEESE DANISH

For professional-looking pastries, bake these flaky Danishes with the cheese filling, then add the cherry filling after removing them from the oven. That way the cherries will not darken in color and the pastry will look wonderfully fresh.

MAKES 12 PASTRIES

> 1½ pounds Blitz Puff Pastry (page 248)
> Egg wash of 1 egg whisked with 2 tablespoons cream or milk
> ¾ cup Cream Cheese Filling (recipe follows)
> ¾ cup Apricot Glaze (page 260), warmed
> ¾ cup filling from Cherry Pie (page 220), warmed

1. Line a baking sheet with parchment paper. Roll the puff pastry dough into a rectangle 12 by 16 inches. Dust the dough and rolling pin lightly with flour if necessary to prevent the dough from sticking. Cut the dough into twelve 4-inch squares. Place the squares on a baking sheet and let them chill in the refrigerator until firm, about 10 minutes.

2. To make a basket, fold squares of dough in half to make a triangle. Position the triangle so that the point of the triangle is away from you. Use a sharp knife to make a cut parallel to the two shorter sides of the triangle. These cuts should come to within ¼ inch of the point, but should not cut entirely through it. These two cuts make the rim for the basket.

3. Open out the triangle and brush very lightly with egg wash. Fold one basket rim over to line up with the opposite side. Repeat with the second rim. Add 1 tablespoon cheese filling to each basket. Transfer to the baking sheet and chill while the oven preheats.

4. Preheat the oven to 425°F. Bake the baskets until golden brown, about 20 minutes. Transfer to cooling racks and brush with Apricot Glaze while they are still hot. Spoon 1 tablespoon cherry filling into each basket. Cool completely before serving.

Cream Cheese Filling

Cornstarch helps the filling to bind as it bakes. You can store this filling in a zip-close plastic bag. When you are ready to fill your Danish or other pastries, simply cut away one corner of the bag and use it as a disposable pastry bag.

MAKES 2 CUPS

> 8 ounces cream cheese
> 6 tablespoons sugar
> 1⅔ cups cornstarch
> ¾ teaspoon lemon zest
> ¾ teaspoon orange zest
> 1 teaspoon vanilla
> 2 eggs

By hand with a wooden spoon or with an electric mixer using the paddle attachment, cream the cheese, sugar, cornstarch, lemon zest, orange zest, and vanilla together until very smooth and light. Add the eggs one at a time, mixing until smooth and scraping down the bowl between each addition. Scrape down the bowl to blend evenly. The filling can be used immediately or stored in a covered container in the refrigerator for up to 2 days.

CROISSANTS

MAKES 16 CROISSANTS

WATER DOUGH

2¼ teaspoons (1 envelope) active dry yeast

¼ cup water (68° to 72°F)

3 cups bread flour

2 teaspoons salt

3 tablespoons sugar

1¼ cups milk

3 tablespoons unsalted butter, softened

FAT DOUGH

1¼ cups (2½ sticks) chilled unsalted butter

Egg wash of 1 egg whisked with 2 tablespoons milk or water

1. To make the water dough, blend the yeast with the water in a small bowl and let rest until a foam forms on top, about 5 minutes. Combine the flour, salt, and sugar in the bowl of an electric mixer using a dough hook attachment. Add the milk, soft butter, and yeast mixture to the flour and mix with the dough hook on low speed until just incorporated.

2. Place the dough on a lightly floured surface, cover, and allow to rise for 2 hours at room temperature. Fold the dough over onto itself, transfer it to a parchment-lined sheet pan, and spread it out in an even layer. Wrap tightly with plastic wrap and refrigerate until cool, at least 30 minutes and up to overnight.

3. To make the fat dough, use a rolling pin to pound out the chilled butter until it is pliable. Shape into a rectangle that is about half the size of the rectangle of water dough. Wrap the butter and return it to the refrigerator to chill slightly.

4. Place the fat dough onto half of the chilled water dough. Fold the water dough over the fat dough and press down on the edges with your fingertips to completely enclose it. Turn the dough 90 degrees and roll out to a rectangle, about ½ inch thick. Fold the dough into thirds (a 3-fold), mark the dough, cover, and refrigerate until firm, about 30 minutes. Repeat for a total of 3 or 4 foldings and rollings, chilling it each time.

5. Remove the dough from the refrigerator. Roll the dough out to an 8-by-16-inch rectangle. Cut the dough into 4-inch squares and then cut the squares into triangles; you should have 16 triangles. Roll them up from the broad end of the triangle to the tip. Place them on lined baking sheets about 2 inches apart, curving the edges. Cover the croissants and let them rise in a warm spot until they are nearly doubled in size, about 1 hour.

6. Preheat the oven to 375°F. Brush the tops of the croissants with a little egg wash and bake until golden and baked through, about 15 minutes. Cool the croissants on a rack and serve.

Variations

PAIN AU CHOCOLAT Cut good-quality eating chocolate (bittersweet or semisweet) into 16 sticks about 2 inches long and ¼ inch thick. Place one piece of chocolate along the long edge of the croissant dough triangle before you roll it up. (The chocolate is easiest to cut if it is at room temperature. If it shatters, simply stack up the pieces to make a filling of the same approximate dimensions.) Brush with egg wash, sprinkle with coarse sugar if desired, and bake as directed above.

HAM AND CHEESE CROISSANTS Cut 16 pieces of thinly sliced country-cured ham and 16 pieces of aged cheddar or Gruyère. Cut the croissant dough into 2-by-4-inch rectangles rather than triangles. Top the croissant dough with a slice of ham and a slice of cheese. Fold in the narrow edges of the dough and roll the dough up to make a cylinder shape (this will keep the ham and cheese inside the croissant as it bakes). Brush with egg wash, sprinkle with sesame seeds, and bake as directed above.

Pain au Chocolat (bottom),
Croissants (middle), and
Ham and Cheese Croissants (top)

CLASSIC PUFF PASTRY

MAKES 4 POUNDS

> 4½ cups bread flour
>
> 1⅓ cups cake flour
>
> ⅓ cup softened unsalted butter
>
> 2 teaspoons salt
>
> 1⅓ cups cold water
>
> 3 cups (6 sticks) unsalted butter, cut into large
> cubes

1. Combine the bread and cake flours in a mixing bowl. Remove and reserve 1 cup of this flour mixture.

2. Add the ⅓ cup softened butter and the salt to the flours and mix on medium speed until the butter is evenly distributed, about 2 minutes. Lower the speed and add the cold water to the dough mixture (depending on the level of humidity and other factors, you may need to add additional water). Finish mixing on medium speed until smooth, 5 to 6 minutes.

3. Remove the dough from the mixing bowl and place it on a sheet pan lined with parchment paper dusted with flour. Form the dough into a rectangle of uniform thickness. This is the "water dough." Cover with plastic wrap and refrigerate.

4. Meanwhile, prepare the "fat dough." Using the same mixing bowl, combine the 3 cups of cubed butter and the reserved 1 cup of flour mixture. Beat by hand or with the paddle attachment of a stand mixer until smooth, 1 to 2 minutes. Avoid overmixing; you do not want to incorporate any air into the mixture. Pat or roll this mixture between two pieces of parchment paper to make a rectangle that will cover two-thirds of the rectangle of water dough. Cover it with plastic wrap and place in the refrigerator for at least 30 minutes, or until it is the same consistency as the water dough.

5. Once the fat dough is the same consistency as the water dough, place it on the right side of the water dough, leaving a ½- to 1-inch border around the three edges. Fold the left side of the water dough over and onto the fat dough, just as you would close a book. Lock in the butter by pressing the dough around the 3 open sides with the tips of your fingers. The fat dough is now locked into the water dough and ready for the first fold, which is a 3-fold (letter-fold).

6. Begin with the open end of the fold facing you. Roll the dough lengthwise into a rectangle. Fold the left third of the dough to the center. Fold the right side completely over the left side, as you would fold a letter. When the folds are complete, there should be 3 layers. Mark the dough with the number of turns, cover, and refrigerate for 30 minutes. Repeat the 3-fold procedure up to 5 more times, chilling the dough in between rolling and folding until it feels cool and firm, about 30 minutes.

7. Cover and refrigerate until ready for use. Puff pastry can be frozen successfully. Let it thaw in the refrigerator before using.

See What We Learned: Puff Pastry, page 134.

PITHIVIERS

Pithiviers, a town in the Loire region of France, was once an important center of commerce. It was also renowned for its cakes, thanks to the excellence of the local wheat and the skill of the local bakers. The pithiviers pastry, replete with almond paste and a glazed sugar coating, is said to date back to the eighteenth century.

MAKES 6 TO 8 SERVINGS

½ cup (1 stick) unsalted butter, softened

⅓ cup sugar

⅓ cup almond paste

¾ teaspoon vanilla

2 eggs

1 pound Classic Puff Pastry (page 252)

Egg wash of 1 egg whisked with 1 teaspoon water

1 tablespoon light corn syrup, heated

1. Beat the butter in a bowl with a wooden spoon until creamy, about 2 minutes. Add the sugar and continue to beat until the mixture is light and fluffy. Break the almond paste into pieces and stir in until smooth, then add the vanilla. Add the eggs one at a time, beating well after each addition to prevent curdling.

2. Unfold the puff pastry and cut out two 8-inch rounds. Place 1 round on a parchment-lined baking sheet. Spread the almond mixture over the center of the round, leaving a ½-inch border. Lightly brush the border with some of the egg wash. Place the second pastry round on top of the filling and line up the edges of the circles. Gently press the edges together. Chill the pastry for 20 minutes.

3. Preheat the oven to 375°F. Crimp the edges with the tines of a fork. Brush the pastry all over with egg wash and, using a sharp knife, score a spiral pattern in the top of the puff pastry. Be careful not to slice all the way through the pastry. Bake until golden brown, 35 to 40 minutes.

4. Brush the top of the pastry with the corn syrup. Raise the oven temperature to 425°F, return the pithiviers to the oven, and bake until the top is golden, 2 to 3 minutes more. Be careful not to overcook, as corn syrup burns easily. Let the pithiviers cool slightly before slicing and serving, or serve at room temperature.

See photo on page 165.

CREAM PUFFS

For the puffiest cream puffs and the best texture, put these pastries into a hot oven, then reduce the temperature to finish baking. The high initial temperature makes the puffs expand rapidly, while the lower temperature dries them out so that they emerge from the oven crisp and light.

MAKES 20 CREAM PUFFS

1 cup milk

½ cup (1 stick) unsalted butter, cubed

2 tablespoons sugar

½ teaspoon salt

1 cup sifted bread flour

3 eggs

Egg wash of 1 egg whisked with 1 tablespoon milk or water

½ cup sliced blanched almonds, optional

2 cups Pastry Cream (page 261) or Diplomat Cream (page 261) or Chantilly Cream (page 266)

Confectioners' sugar for dusting

1. Preheat the oven to 375°F. Line baking sheets with parchment paper.

2. Combine the milk, butter, sugar, and salt in a saucepan over high heat and bring to a boil. Add the flour all at once and stir in well. Cook, stirring constantly, until the dough begins to come away from the sides of the pan, about 5 minutes.

3. Immediately transfer the dough to a bowl and stir by hand or with the paddle attachment until the mixture cools to body temperature. Add the eggs one at a time, beating well and scraping down the bowl with a rubber spatula after each addition.

4. Pipe the batter using a plain round tip or spoon the dough into 20 balls the size of a golf ball on the prepared baking sheets, about 2 inches apart. Brush the unbaked puffs very lightly with the egg wash. Scatter the sliced almonds over the puffs if using. Place the puffs in the oven and bake until they are puffy and lightly browned, about 20 minutes. Reduce the oven temperature to 325°F and continue to bake until the puffs appear dry and a rich golden brown, another 20 to 25 minutes. Remove from the oven and cool completely before splitting and filling.

5. When the pastry has cooled, slice the top ½ inch off each cream puff. Fill the base of each with pastry cream. Replace the top of the cream puff and dust with confectioners' sugar. Cream puffs can be assembled up to 4 hours before serving; keep refrigerated.

See photo on page 96.

Variation

PROFITEROLES Profiteroles are smaller versions of cream puffs. Prepare the batter as directed above. Shape the profiteroles by piping or spooning out 24 equal size balls (about the size of a large marble) on prepared baking sheets about 1 inch apart. Bake until puffy, lightly browned, and dry in appearance, 30 to 35 minutes. After the puffs have cooled, slice off the top of each pastry as directed above and dip the tops into 1 cup warmed Hard Ganache (page 267). Place the iced tops on a tray and let them set in the refrigerator while you fill each base with Pastry or Diplomat Cream. Then replace the tops and store the finished profiteroles in the refrigerator for up to 4 hours before serving.

CLASSIC NAPOLEONS

The puff pastry for napoleons is baked in such a way that it does not rise. Docking the pastry before it is baked and keeping a weight on top of the pastry results in a thin, crisp layer, perfect to layer with a rich cream filling. Fondant, used to glaze our Napoleons, is a specialty product used in professional pastry shops for which there is no real substitute. You can purchase it from stores that specialize in cake decorating products or through an online source.

MAKES 8 NAPOLEONS (2 BY 3¼ BY 1½ INCHES)

¾ pound Classic Puff Pastry (page 252)
1½ cups Diplomat Cream (page 261)
Apricot Glaze (page 260), warmed, as needed
4 ounces fondant
2 fluid ounces Simple Syrup (page 260)
1 ounce bittersweet chocolate, melted

1. Roll the puff pastry into a rectangle that measures about 9 by 15 inches (about the same dimension as a standard baking sheet) and about ⅛ inches thick. Place on a parchment-lined baking sheet and chill in the refrigerator for at least 1 hour.

2. Preheat the oven to 375°F.

3. Dock the entire surface of the puff pastry generously with the tines of a table fork and top the pastry with a second parchment sheet. Bake for 20 minutes. Rotate the pan and continue to bake until golden brown and dry throughout, 7 to 10 minutes. Cool the puff pastry to room temperature.

4. Trim the edges of the pastry using a serrated knife and cut lengthwise into three strips. Spread half of the diplomat cream in an even layer on one strip, cover with a second strip, and gently spread the remaining cream over the puff pastry. Top with the third strip (it should be upside down so smoothe the sides to remove any excess diplomat cream). Wrap the napoleon and freeze overnight.

5. On the next day, unwrap the napoleon and set on a cooling rack to thaw for 10 to 15 minutes. (Place the cooling rack on a baking sheet to catch any drips of glaze or fondant.)

6. Warm the apricot glaze until it is thin enough to brush and lightly coat the top of the napoleon.

7. Gently warm the fondant over a double boiler to 100°F. Add enough simple syrup to the melted fondant to thin it enough to flow easily. Pour the fondant onto the center of the napoleon and spread the fondant in a thin layer over the entire pastry.

8. Pour the melted chocolate into a parchment paper cone and pipe thin lines of chocolate lengthwise along the pastry about ¼ inches apart. Drag the tip of a paring knife horizontally across the chocolate lines in alternating directions. Let the fondant set completely before slicing. To slice the pastry into individual napoleons, use a serrated knife. Warm the blade of the knife in hot water and wipe it dry before cutting the slices. The napoleons are ready to serve now, or you may keep them in a storage container in the refrigerator for up to 2 days.

CHOCOLATE ÉCLAIRS

The shape of a baked éclair depends upon how it is formed before baking. It is easiest to make a nice, smooth éclair using a pastry bag, but you can also drop the batter from a spoon. Use a table knife dipped in water to smooth out any tails or peaks on the surface of the éclair before it goes into the oven. To be sure that your éclairs are all about the same size, use a pencil to trace templates onto the sheets of parchment paper before you place them, pencil-marked side down, onto baking sheets.

MAKES 12 ÉCLAIRS

> 1 cup whole or low-fat milk
> ½ cup (1 stick) unsalted butter, diced
> 2 tablespoons sugar
> ½ teaspoon salt
> 1 cup bread flour, sifted
> 3 large eggs
> 1 large egg white
> 1½ cups Diplomat Cream (page 261)
> 2¾ cups Chocolate Glaze (page 267), warmed

1. Preheat the oven to 375°F. Line 2 baking sheets with parchment paper. Combine the milk, butter, sugar, and salt in a saucepan and bring to a boil over high heat. Reduce the heat to medium, add the flour all at once, and stir well. Cook, stirring constantly with a wooden spoon, until the dough begins to come away from the sides of the pan, about 5 minutes.

2. Transfer to the bowl of a stand mixer fitted with the paddle attachment and beat at medium speed until cooled to room temperature. Add the eggs one at a time, beating well and scraping down the bowl with a rubber spatula after each addition. Beat in the egg white. Transfer the dough to a pastry bag with a plain round tip. Pipe the dough into 5-inch-long cylinders on the parchment-lined baking sheets about 2 inches apart.

3. Bake the éclairs until they are puffed and light golden brown, 20 minutes. There may be beads of moisture on the sides. Lower the oven temperature to 325°F and continue to bake until the éclairs look dry, 20 minutes more. Transfer the éclairs to wire racks and let cool completely before filling.

4. Pierce a hole in both ends of each cooked éclair using a skewer or chopstick. Fit a pastry bag with a ⅛-inch plain tip. Fill the pastry bag with the Diplomat Cream and pipe into the éclair from each end. Dip the top of each éclair in the warm glaze, removing any excess with a small metal spatula, and transfer to a rack set over a baking sheet. Refrigerate until the glaze firms, then serve.

Note

An alternative method for filling the éclairs is to slice them in half horizontally and pipe the Diplomat Cream in a spiral over the base of the éclair using a plain pastry tip. Dip the top of the pastry in warm glaze, removing any excess with a small metal spatula, and place it on top of the cream. Chill to firm the glaze as directed above.

PARIS-BREST

MAKES 1 PASTRY (8 SERVINGS)

1 cup whole or low-fat milk

½ cup (1 stick) unsalted butter, diced

2 tablespoons sugar

½ teaspoon salt

1 cup bread flour, sifted

3 large eggs

1 large egg white

Egg wash of 1 egg blended with 2 tablespoons milk, optional

½ cup toasted slivered almonds, optional

1½ cups Diplomat Cream (page 261)

Confectioners' sugar for dusting

1. Preheat the oven to 400°F. Mark an 8-inch circle on a sheet of parchment or eight 3-inch circles. Line a baking sheet with the parchment paper, pencil-marked side down.

2. Combine the milk, butter, sugar, and salt in a saucepan and bring to a boil over high heat. Reduce the heat to medium, add the flour all at once, and stir well. Cook, stirring constantly with a wooden spoon, until the dough begins to come away from the sides of the pan, about 5 minutes.

3. Transfer to the bowl of a stand mixer fitted with the paddle attachment and beat at medium speed until cooled to room temperature. Add the eggs one at a time, beating well and scraping down the bowl with a rubber spatula after each addition. Beat in the egg white. Transfer the dough to a pastry bag with a plain round tip. Pipe the dough onto the marked circle directly on the line you drew. Pipe another ring of pastry directly inside the first one so that you have a thick ring. Pipe another two circles on top of the first two and continue building up, until all the pastry has been used. Brush the ring with egg wash and sprinkle with the toasted almonds, if using.

4. Bake the ring until puffed and golden, 30 to 35 minutes, reduce the temperature to 350°F, and bake until the pastry is crisp, light, and a good brown color, another 20 to 25 minutes. Remove from the baking sheet and place on a wire rack. Immediately slice the ring in half horizontally, making the base twice as deep as the top. Take off the top and scoop out any uncooked pastry from the base. Cool completely.

5. Spoon the Diplomat Cream into the bottom of the ring and cover with the top. Dust with confectioners' sugar and serve.

See What We Learned: Paris-Brest, page 98.

Sauces, Glazes, and Creams

RASPBERRY SAUCE

Good-quality frozen berries make a respectable sauce, so you can enjoy summer fruit flavors throughout the year. Pastry chefs often store fruit sauces in squeeze bottles so that they can easily squirt the sauce in a pattern on a dessert, pool it onto plates, or add a few drops as garnish for another sauce.

MAKES ABOUT 2 CUPS

> 1 pound fresh or frozen raspberries (3½ cups)
> ¾ to 1 cup sugar
> 1 to 2 tablespoons freshly squeezed lemon juice

Combine the raspberries, ¾ cup sugar, and 1 tablespoon lemon juice in a saucepan and bring to a simmer over medium heat. Cook until the sugar has dissolved, about 10 minutes. Taste the mixture and, if necessary, add more sugar. Continue to heat until any additional sugar is dissolved. Strain the sauce through a fine-mesh sieve. Adjust the flavor by adding additional lemon juice if necessary. The sauce can be served warm or cold; it will thicken slightly when stored in the refrigerator, and keeps for up to 10 days.

Baker's Note: If you find that your sauce separates after you have finished it, you can add a cornstarch slurry (2 teaspoons cornstarch blended with 2 teaspoons cold water) to thicken it. To add the slurry to a cooled sauce, pour the sauce into a saucepan, bring to a boil, and gradually whisk in enough slurry to thicken the sauce slightly. Bring the sauce to a boil a second time after adding the slurry, then allow the sauce to cool.

Variations

STRAWBERRY SAUCE Substitute fresh or frozen strawberries for the raspberries.

MANGO SAUCE Substitute diced fresh mango for the raspberries. If desired, substitute lime juice for the lemon juice.

BLUEBERRY SAUCE Substitute fresh or frozen blueberries for the raspberries. If you use blueberries, you will need to add the cornstarch slurry.

MIXED BERRY COMPOTE Add about 1 cup of a combination of raspberries, strawberries, blueberries, and blackberries to the sauce and simmer just long enough to warm the fruit.

LEMON BUTTER SAUCE

To make beautiful lemon zest julienne, use a vegetable peeler to cut away long strips of the skin, making sure that you don't cut deeply into the bitter white pith. Choose organic lemons to avoid any residues from pesticides or herbicides. It is best to remove the peel before you juice the lemons.

MAKES 2 CUPS

> 1 cup lemon juice
> 1 cup sugar
> ¾ cup plus 2 tablespoons water
> 1 vanilla bean, split in half
> 1 cup (2 sticks) plus 2 tablespoons butter, cubed
> 2 tablespoons lemon zest, cut in fine julienne

1. Combine the lemon juice, sugar, water, and vanilla bean in a saucepan and bring to a rapid simmer over medium heat. Continue to simmer until the mixture is lightly thickened and reduced to about one-third its original volume, 25 to 30 minutes. Remove the pan from the heat to let the mixture cool slightly. Take out the vanilla bean and scrape out the seeds with the tip of a paring knife and stir them back into the sauce.

2. Return the saucepan to low heat and add the butter, a few cubes at a time, whisking constantly, until all of the butter has been added to the sauce. Stir in the lemon zest. The sauce is ready to serve now, or cool the sauce and keep it refrigerated until you are ready to serve it. Warm the sauce gently either in a double boiler over barely simmering water or in a microwave on low power, 30 to 50 seconds.

LEMON CURD

Lemon curd makes an excellent filling for tarts and tartlets, or spread it instead of jam between cake layers. I also like its lemony tang on toast. For a lovely citrus curd, replace the lemon juice with the freshly squeezed juice of oranges or limes.

MAKES ABOUT 2 CUPS

> 6 egg yolks
> ¾ cup sugar, divided
> ¾ cup (1½ sticks) unsalted butter, diced, divided
> ¾ cup freshly squeezed lemon juice
> 1 teaspoon grated lemon zest

1. Prepare an ice bath. Blend the egg yolks with ½ cup of the sugar and set aside.

2. Combine ½ cup of the butter, the remaining ¼ cup sugar, the lemon juice, and lemon zest in a heavy nonreactive saucepan and bring to a boil over medium heat, stirring constantly. Temper the egg yolks by gradually adding about one-third of the hot butter mixture, whisking constantly. Add the tempered eggs to the remaining butter mixture in the pan and continue cooking over medium heat, stirring constantly. As soon as the mixture comes to a boil, reduce the heat to low, and whisk in the remaining ¼ cup butter.

3. Pour the curd through a fine-mesh sieve into a clean bowl and cool over the ice bath. Stir the sauce occasionally as it cools. Store in the refrigerator for up to 3 days.

APRICOT GLAZE

This glaze adds sheen and flavor to baked goods like Danish pastries (pages 244–249) and cinnamon rolls. It holds well, so you can make a double batch and keep it on hand. Try apple jelly instead of apricot jam for a glaze with a subtle flavor. If you use apple jelly, there is no need to strain the glaze. Brush a thin, even coating of warm glaze on cooled baked goods with a pastry brush, wiping away any pools that develop on the surface.

MAKES 2 CUPS

¾ cup apricot jam
¾ cup water
¾ cup corn syrup
⅓ cup brandy

1. Combine the jam, water, corn syrup, and brandy in a saucepan; bring to a boil over high heat, stirring until the jam is completely melted. Strain the glaze through a wire sieve into a bowl.

2. The glaze is ready to use once it has cooled to room temperature, or store it in a covered container in the refrigerator for up to 3 weeks. Warm the glaze over low heat or in the microwave until it is thin enough to brush easily.

ORANGE SAUCE

I like to pool this sweet dessert sauce around a slice of dark chocolate cake. It is also lovely spooned over fresh strawberries. Feel free to reduce the amount of liqueur in the recipe.

MAKES 2 CUPS

⅔ cup apricot marmalade
⅓ cup sugar
3 tablespoons orange zest
2 tablespoons Grand Marnier or apricot liqueur

In a small saucepan over medium-low heat, combine the marmalade, sugar, and zest. Simmer for 2 minutes. Strain into a small bowl. Add the Grand Marnier or apricot liqueur. Allow to cool. Serve at once or store covered in the refrigerator.

SIMPLE SYRUP

For extra flavor, add sliced or halved lemons, oranges, or vanilla beans to the syrup while it is hot and let them steep until the syrup is cool.

MAKES 2 CUPS

1 cup sugar
1 cup water

Stir the sugar and water together in a heavy-bottomed saucepan. Bring the syrup to a boil over high heat and boil without stirring for about 3 minutes. Remove the pan from the heat, cool to room temperature, and refrigerate until ready to use.

PASTRY CREAM

This pastry cream is the base for soufflés and can also be used to prepare a range of fillings for éclairs, cream puffs, or cream-filled pies.

MAKES 1½ CUPS

> 5 tablespoons granulated sugar, divided
> 2 egg yolks
> ⅓ cup all-purpose flour
> ¼ teaspoon salt
> 1 cup milk
> ½ teaspoon vanilla extract

1. In a bowl, blend 2 tablespoons of the granulated sugar, the egg yolks, flour, and salt. Set aside.

2. Heat the milk and remaining 3 tablespoons sugar in a small saucepan over medium-high heat. Bring to a boil and remove from the heat. Whisk in the vanilla extract and let cool slightly.

3. Gradually add the warm milk to the egg yolk mixture, whisking constantly. Return the mixture to the saucepan over medium heat. Whisk constantly until the mixture thickens and comes to a boil, about 1½ minutes. Remove from the heat. The pastry cream is ready to use as the base for a soufflé now, or it may be properly cooled and stored for later use. To cool the pastry cream, transfer it to a bowl and place over a pan of cold water. Whisk until the pastry cream is cool, about 5 minutes.

See What We Learned: Pastry Cream, page 94

DIPLOMAT CREAM

This cream with such an important-sounding name is none other than whipped cream mixed with pastry cream and stabilized with gelatin. Because Diplomat Cream is firmer in texture than simple Chantilly Cream, it is a good choice for cake and pastry fillings.

MAKES ABOUT 4 CUPS

> 1 envelope (2¼ teaspoons) powdered unflavored gelatin
> ¼ cup cold water
> 2 cups Pastry Cream (at left)
> 1 cup heavy cream

1. Sprinkle the gelatin over the cold water in a small bowl and stir to break up any clumps. Let the gelatin soften in the water for about 2 minutes. Heat the softened gelatin over simmering water or in a microwave for about 20 seconds on low power until the granules melt and the mixture is clear. Stir the gelatin into the Pastry Cream by hand with a rubber spatula until evenly blended.

2. Whip the cream in a chilled bowl until it holds a medium peak. Working by hand with a spatula, fold the whipped cream into the pastry cream in 2 or 3 additions, folding just until evenly blended. Use at once.

BAVARIAN CREAM

No one knows exactly why this cream is known as Bavarian, but it is a staple in the classical French pastry kitchen. Firmer than Diplomat Cream, Bavarian Cream may be served on its own, molded in pyramids or mounds, or used as a filling for cakes.

MAKES ABOUT 4 CUPS, OR ENOUGH TO FILL A 9-INCH CAKE

- 2 envelopes (4½ teaspoons) powdered unflavored gelatin
- ½ cup cold water
- 2 cups Custard Sauce (at right), cooled but not chilled
- 1 cup heavy cream

1. Sprinkle the gelatin over the water in a small bowl and stir to break up any clumps. Let the gelatin soften for about 2 minutes. Heat the softened gelatin over simmering water or in a microwave for about 20 seconds on low power until the granules melt and the mixture is clear. Stir the melted gelatin into the Custard Sauce and continue to cool, either over an ice bath or in the refrigerator until the mixture mounds when dropped from a spoon, about 20 minutes.

2. Whip the cream in a chilled bowl until it holds a medium peak when the whisk is turned upright. Working by hand with a spatula, fold the whipped cream into the slightly gelled custard sauce until evenly blended. Chill for at least 2 hours or up to 2 days before serving.

Variations

RASPBERRY OR STRAWBERRY BAVARIAN CREAM Replace 1 cup of the Custard Sauce with 1 cup raspberry or strawberry purée combined with ¼ cup sugar.

LEMON BAVARIAN CREAM Replace 1 cup of the custard sauce with 1 cup Lemon Curd (page 259).

CUSTARD SAUCE

Custard Sauce, also known as crème anglaise (English cream), is like a liquid version of pastry cream. It is extremely important not to allow the mixture to boil. Cook the cream just until it coats the back of a spoon, no longer, or it will curdle. Custard sauce is usually served chilled, as an accompaniment to a wide range of mousses, cakes, and fruit desserts, but I have to confess that I love the way it tastes when still warm.

MAKES ABOUT 2 CUPS

- 1 cup whole milk
- 1 cup heavy cream
- ½ vanilla bean, split lengthwise
- ½ cup sugar, divided
- 4 egg yolks

1. Combine the milk, cream, vanilla bean, and ¼ cup of the sugar in a large, heavy nonreactive saucepan. Bring to a simmer over medium heat. Prepare an ice bath if you plan to serve the sauce cooled.

2. In a medium bowl, combine the remaining ¼ cup sugar with the egg yolks. Whisk until thoroughly combined. Temper the eggs by gradually adding about one-third of the hot cream mixture, whisking constantly. Add the tempered eggs to the remaining cream mixture in the pan, and gently cook over low heat, stirring constantly, until it is thick enough to coat the back of a spoon, 6 to 8 minutes.

3. Strain the sauce through a fine-mesh sieve into a pitcher to serve warm, or into a bowl set over the ice bath to serve chilled. If using the ice bath, stir the sauce occasionally as it cools. Refrigerate for at least 2 hours or up to 2 days.

CHOCOLATE BAVARIAN MOUSSE

This dark chocolate mousse is made dense with the yolks of nearly a dozen eggs. Be sure not to throw away the egg whites. Depending on the size of the eggs you use, you should have just enough to make an angel food cake.

MAKES 6 TO 8 SERVINGS

1 envelope (2¼ teaspoons) powdered unflavored gelatin

¼ cup cold water

1 cup milk

⅓ cup sugar

11 egg yolks

1¾ cups dark chocolate, finely chopped

1½ cups heavy cream, whipped to soft peaks

1. Sprinkle the gelatin over the water and let stand until softened and swelled, 3 to 4 minutes. Heat the gelatin on medium heat over a water bath until it dissolves, 1 to 2 minutes. Set aside.

2. Bring the milk and about half of the sugar to a boil over medium-high heat. Whisk the rest of the sugar together with the egg yolks. Turn off the heat and gradually add about one-third of the hot milk mixture to the yolk mixture, stirring constantly with a whisk. Stir the warm yolk mixture back into the remaining milk mixture, continuing to stir constantly. Cook over medium-low heat, stirring constantly, until the custard coats the back of a wooden spoon, about 5 minutes.

3. Strain the hot custard onto the chopped chocolate. Cover and let stand for 5 minutes, then stir until thoroughly incorporated. Add the gelatin-and-water mixture to the chocolate mixture.

4. Cool the custard to about 80°F, then thoroughly fold in the whipped cream. Use immediately as a filling or pipe or spoon into dessert dishes and refrigerate at least 3 hours and up to 2 days before serving.

CARAMEL MOUSSE

The technique of beating hot sugar syrup into the egg yolks ensures that they are brought to a high enough temperature to destroy any possible bacteria, so this mousse can be eaten with pure delight.

MAKES 8 SERVINGS

1 envelope (2¼ teaspoons) powdered unflavored gelatin

2 tablespoons cold water

⅔ cup Caramel Sauce (page 266)

⅓ cup sugar

5 tablespoons water

3 egg yolks

¾ cup heavy cream, whipped to soft peaks

1. Stir together the gelatin and the cold water in a small bowl and let the gelatin soften and swell, about 3 minutes. Warm the Caramel Sauce, add the gelatin, and stir until it has melted into the caramel sauce. Cool to room temperature.

2. Combine the sugar and water in a small pan and bring to a rapid boil over high heat. Place the yolks in a mixing bowl. While whipping the yolks, gradually add the sugar and water mixture, whipping on medium speed until the mixture cools to room temperature and is thick and foamy. Fold the caramel mixture into the yolk mixture, and then add the whipped cream in two separate additions. Use immediately as filling or spoon into dessert dishes and refrigerate at least 3 hours and up to 2 days before serving.

CHOCOLATE SABAYON MOUSSE

Sabayon is the French version of Italian zabaglione, an ethereal custard made with egg yolks that are whipped with sugar and Marsala over a hot water bath until light and frothy. This recipe includes heavy cream and chocolate, for a denser and more mousse-like texture.

MAKES ABOUT 4 CUPS, OR ENOUGH TO FILL A 9-INCH CAKE

1¼ cups heavy cream

1 package (2¼ teaspoons) powdered unflavored gelatin

¼ cup cold water

5 large egg yolks

⅓ cup Marsala or sweet sherry

¼ cup sugar

4 ounces semisweet or bittersweet chocolate, chopped

1. Whip the cream in a chilled bowl until it holds a firm peak. Cover and refrigerate. Sprinkle the gelatin over the cold water in a small bowl and stir to break up any clumps. Let the gelatin soften in the water for about 2 minutes. Heat the softened gelatin over simmering water or in a microwave for about 20 seconds on low power until melted.

2. Prepare an ice bath. Whisk together the egg yolks, sherry, and sugar in a heatproof mixing bowl and set over simmering water. Continue to whisk as the eggs cook. They will thicken, triple in volume, and become a pale yellow, about 15 minutes. The mixture should fall from the whisk in ribbons that hold their shape on top of the sabayon. Remove from the heat and set directly in the ice bath.

3. Melt the chocolate in the microwave or over simmering water and let cool slightly. Add about one-third of the sabayon mixture to the cooled melted chocolate to lighten it, then add the chocolate mixture to the remaining sabayon. Stir in the melted gelatin. Continue to whisk over the ice bath until the sabayon is cool. Fold the whipped cream into the sabayon and serve immediately.

See What We Learned: Mousse, page 154

ITALIAN BUTTERCREAM

MAKES ABOUT 4½ CUPS, OR ENOUGH TO FILL AND ICE AN 8- OR 9-INCH CAKE

> 7 cups Italian Meringue (see below)
> 2 cups (4 sticks) unsalted butter, diced, at room temperature
> 1½ teaspoons vanilla extract

Just before you are ready to make the buttercream, prepare the Italian Meringue. Once the meringue cools to room temperature and reaches stiff peaks, add the butter a few pieces at a time while continuing to whip on high speed. Once all the butter has been incorporated and the buttercream is thick and very smooth, blend in the vanilla extract. The buttercream is ready to use now, or store covered in the refrigerator for up to a week. Let the buttercream soften at room temperature before beating it on low speed with the paddle attachment to make it warm and soft enough to spread.

See What We Learned: Italian Buttercream, page 138.

ITALIAN MERINGUE

A meringue made with a cooked sugar syrup is known as Italian meringue. This stable foam works well for piping meringue shells or for making Italian Buttercream, above.

MAKES ABOUT 7 CUPS

> ¾ cup sugar, divided
> ¼ cup water
> 5 large egg whites

Grease a heatproof glass measuring cup. Combine ½ cup of the sugar with the water in a heavy saucepan. Cook over medium-high heat without stirring until the mixture reaches 230°F. At that point, place the egg whites in the bowl of a stand mixer fitted with a whisk attachment and whip on medium speed until frothy. Add the remaining ¼ cup of sugar and beat the meringue to medium peaks. When the sugar mixture reaches the soft ball stage, 240°F, pour it into the measuring cup, then into the meringue in a slow, steady stream on low speed. Increase the speed to high and whip until the meringue cools to room temperature and has the desired peak.

CHANTILLY CREAM

The secret to light and billowy whipped cream is to avoid overwhipping it. If the cream begins to take on a slightly yellow cast, it is close to turning into butter. If necessary, fold in a small amount of unwhipped cream to rescue the texture. The ultrapasteurized heavy or whipping cream found on most grocery shelves contains a stabilizer. For better flavor and whipping quality, look for pasteurized (rather than ultrapasteurized) cream.

MAKES ABOUT 2 CUPS

1 cup heavy cream, chilled
¼ cup confectioners' sugar
½ teaspoon vanilla

Chill a stainless-steel bowl and the beaters of a handheld mixer, the whisk attachment of a stand mixer, or a balloon whisk. Pour the cream into the chilled bowl and whip on medium speed until thickened, about 3 minutes. Increase the speed to high and gradually add the confectioners' sugar while whipping. Add the vanilla and continue to whip until the cream has the desired peak according to its intended use. (Soft peaks are good for dolloping cream, while firmer peaks are better if the cream is to be piped, used for topping, or folded into another mixture.)

CARAMEL SAUCE

I love to watch the transformation of sugar from bright white crystals to a golden brown liquid. Be patient as you stir the sugar—don't be tempted to speed up the process by turning the heat up too high.

MAKES ABOUT 2 CUPS

1½ cups heavy cream
¾ cup sugar
½ cup light corn syrup
2 tablespoons unsalted butter

1. Prepare an ice bath. Bring the cream to a boil in a saucepan over medium heat, then remove from the heat.

2. Combine the sugar and corn syrup in a heavy saucepan over low heat and stir until the sugar dissolves. Slowly cook to a golden brown without stirring, 8 to 9 minutes. Remove from the heat and put the saucepan in the ice bath for 20 seconds to stop the cooking. Remove from the ice bath and stir in the butter.

3. Carefully stir in the hot cream, mixing until fully blended. To store the caramel sauce, transfer it to a clean bowl or jar, cover tightly, and refrigerate for up to 2 weeks. Reheat the sauce over low heat or in the microwave before serving.

CHOCOLATE GLAZE

This chocolate glaze stays shiny but soft and is a perfect topping for Cream Puffs (page 254) or Chocolate Éclairs (page 256). Use it to glaze a cake or to drizzle into vanilla ice cream for a chocolate ripple effect.

MAKES ABOUT 1½ CUPS, OR ENOUGH TO GLAZE A 9-INCH CAKE

½ cup plus 2 tablespoons heavy cream

1 tablespoon corn syrup

8 ounces semisweet or bittersweet chocolate, finely chopped

Combine the cream and corn syrup in a heavy saucepan and bring to a boil over medium heat. Remove the pan from the heat and add the chocolate. Let the mixture rest for 2 to 3 minutes. Stir until the chocolate is completely melted and the sauce is very smooth. The glaze may be used at this point, or it may be cooled to room temperature, poured into a clean, dry container, covered tightly, and refrigerated for up to 2 weeks. To reheat chilled chocolate glaze, warm it over very low heat or in the microwave until it is warm enough to flow easily.

SOFT GANACHE

By changing the amount of cream in the ganache, you can vary its consistency from soft to hard. A soft ganache is soft enough to whip, using the paddle attachment of your mixer to make an icing or filling that spreads or pipes easily. A hard ganache for truffles will hold its shape even at room temperature. If you want a filling or topping with a light texture, more like whipped cream, add ⅓ cup of chilled heavy cream to cool ganache before whipping.

MAKES 2¼ CUPS (4 CUPS AFTER WHIPPING)

10 ounces semisweet or bittersweet chocolate, finely chopped

2 cups heavy cream

2 tablespoons unsalted butter

1. Place the chopped chocolate in a bowl. Heat the cream in a heavy saucepan over medium heat, just to a boil. Pour the hot cream over the chocolate and add the butter. Let the mixture rest for 2 to 3 minutes and then stir until the chocolate is completely melted and the ganache is very smooth. Cool the ganache to room temperature, then cover and refrigerate at least 8 hours and up to 2 weeks.

2. To make a whipped filling or frosting from soft ganache, transfer the chilled ganache to the bowl of a stand mixer fitted with the paddle attachment. Beat the ganache on low speed until it softens and lightens, about 3 minutes. Change to the whisk attachment and whip on medium speed until the ganache thickens and lightens in color; it should hold soft or medium peaks, 2 to 3 minutes. The ganache is now ready to use as a filling or icing.

Variations

HARD GANACHE Use this ganache to roll into truffles or to use as a glaze. Decrease the amount of cream to 1¼ cups.

MEDIUM GANACHE Decrease the amount of cream to 1½ cups.

Conversions and Equivalents

INGREDIENT EQUIVALENT

INGREDIENT	DESCRIPTION	VOLUME	WEIGHT (U.S.)	WEIGHT (METRIC)
Apple	1 medium	1 cup sliced	4.2 oz	119 g
Baking powder		1 tsp	0.15 oz	4 g
Baking soda		1 tsp	0.18 oz	5 g
Bread crumbs	5 slices bread	1 cup crumbs	3.5 oz	100 g
Butter	1 stick	8 Tbsp	4 oz	113 g
Cheese				
	hard (e.g., Parmesan cheese)	1 cup grated	3.75 oz	106 g
	medium (e.g., Cheddar cheese)	1 cup shredded	3 oz	85 g
	soft (e.g., fresh goat cheese)	1 cup crumbled	4.75 oz	135 g
Chocolate chips		1 cup	5.5 oz	156 g
Coconut (fresh)		1 cup	2.75 oz	78 g
Coconut (dried)		1 cup	2.4 oz	68 g
Cornstarch		1 Tbsp	0.3 oz	8.5 g
Eggs				
	5 large eggs	1 cup		
	4 extra-large eggs	1 cup		
	7 large egg whites	1 cup		
	14 large egg yolks	1 cup		
Flour				
	all-purpose	1 cup	4.4 oz	125 g
	cake	1 cup	3.9 oz	111 g
	bread	1 cup	4.8 oz	136 g
Gingerroot		1 tsp grated	0.15 oz	4 g
Herbs (dried)		1 Tbsp	0.08 oz	225 mg
Herbs (fresh)		1 Tbsp minced	0.115 oz	3 g
Honey		1 Tbsp	0.75 oz	21 g
Jalapeño				
	1 medium	1 tsp minced	0.10 oz	3 g
	1 medium	2 Tbsp minced (approx.)	0.5 oz	14 g

INGREDIENT	DESCRIPTION	VOLUME	WEIGHT (U.S.)	WEIGHT (METRIC)
Lemon	1 medium, juiced	3 Tbsp	1.5 oz	43 g
	1 medium, zested	2 tsp	0.10 oz	3 g
Lime	1 medium, juiced	3 Tbsp	1.5 oz	43 g
	1 medium, zested	2 tsp	0.10 oz	3 g
Nuts		1 cup chopped	4 oz	113 g
Orange				
	1 medium, juiced	1/2 cup	4 oz	113 g
	1 medium, zested	1 Tbsp	0.25 oz	6 g
Raisins		1 cup	6 oz	170 g
Salt (table)		1 tsp	0.25 oz	7 g
Seeds (sesame, cumin, fennel, etc.)		1 tsp	0.20 oz	6 g
Spices (ground)		1 tsp	0.07 oz	2 g
Sugar				
	brown	1 cup	7.75 oz	220 g
	confectioners' (sifted)	1 cup	4 oz	113 g
	granulated	1 cup	7.1 oz	201 g
	superfine	1 cup	7.5 oz	213 g

Useful measures

3 tsp = 1 Tbsp
4 Tbsp = 1/4 cup
16 Tbsp = 1 cup
1 cup = 1/2 pt = 8 fl oz
2 cups = 1 pt
2 pt = 1 qt
4 qt = 1 gal
1 stick butter = 8 Tbsp = 4 oz = 1/2 cup

Useful temperatures

Water freezes at 32°F/0°C
Water boils at 212°F/100°C

To convert Fahrenheit to Celsius

Subtract 32. Divide result by 9. Multiply result by 5 to get Celsius.

To convert Celsius to Fahrenheit

Divide by 5. Multiply result by 9. Add 32 to get Fahrenheit.

High-altitude baking

At sea level, water boils at 212°F. As you increase the altitude at which you are baking, increase the oven temperature by 15 to 25 degrees and decrease baking time by about 5 minutes.

At 2,000 ft above sea level, water boils at 208°F.
At 5,000 ft above sea level, water boils at 203°F.
At 7,500 ft above sea level, water boils at 198°F.
At 10,000 ft above sea level, water boils at 194°F.

Checking a thermometer's accuracy

To check a probe or candy thermometer's accuracy, let it stand in boiling water for 10 minutes. It should read 212°F, assuming that you are at sea level. (See above for boiling temperatures at various altitudes.) If it doesn't read 212°F, add or subtract the appropriate number to make allowances when using the thermometer. For example, if the water is boiling and your thermometer reads 208°F, it registers 4 degrees cooler than the actual temperature, so you would add 4 degrees to the number showing on the thermometer when measuring the temperature of an ingredient.

You can substitute one pan for another using the following guidelines:

> To substitute a glass or nonstick pan, reduce the baking temperature by 25°F.
>
> To substitute a pan that is shallower than the one specified in the recipe, reduce the baking time by 25 percent.
>
> To substitute a pan that is deeper than the one specified in the recipe, increase the baking time by 25 percent.

Use the following guidelines for filling pans:

> Fill cake pans at least one-half full but no more than two-thirds full. (Deep pans like tube pans and Bundt pans are typically filled half full.)
>
> Fill loaf pans and muffin tins two-thirds full.
>
> Fill soufflé dishes and steamed pudding molds to within 1 inch of the rim.
>
> Fill jelly roll pans at least half full or to within ¼ inch of the top.
>
> Add fruit fillings to the top of a pie pan, mounding them slightly higher in the center.

What went wrong?

Sometimes, despite the baker's best efforts at care and consistency, a baked good does not turn out as expected. While this is a frustrating experience, you may be able to learn something from it. Certain faults in a baked good indicate that ingredients were measured improperly, mixtures were not cooled properly, or the oven temperature was incorrect. The charts below examine some common faults and what might have gone wrong.

COMMON BAKING PROBLEMS

TYPE OF BAKED GOOD	EFFECT	CAUSE
Yeast bread	Didn't rise well	Improper mixing; too much salt; not enough yeast; dough underproofed or too cold; pan too large; oven temperature too high
	Crust pale	Not enough salt or sugar; oven temperature too low; dough overproofed
	Crust dark	Too much sugar; oven temperature too high
	Crust too thick	Not enough sugar; baked too long; oven temperature too high
	Uneven grain	Dough proofed too long or at too high a temperature
	Coarse grain	Improper mixing; dough too cold; improper shaping technique; pan size too large
	Poor taste and flavor	Not enough salt; dough insufficiently risen; dough allowed to rise at too warm a temperature; dough overproofed

TYPE OF BAKED GOOD	EFFECT	CAUSE
Quick breads and cakes	Crust dark	Too much sugar; oven too hot
	Cake shrinks	Mixed too long; batter too wet; cake overbaked
	Crust bursts	Mixed too long; batter too dry; oven too hot; wrong type of flour
	Cake falls	Not enough flour; cake underbaked
	Coarse or irregular crumb	Undermixed; not enough eggs
	Dense texture	Not enough leavener; batter too warm; wrong type of flour
	Tough texture	Not enough sugar; not enough fat; not enough liquid; batter beaten too long
	Fruit sinks	Too much leavener in batter; not enough flour in batter; fruit not dried enough
Cookies	Crumble	Removed from the pan while hot; let cookies cool before lifting from pan
	Dry or hard	Too much flour; baked too long; dough or batter over mixed; dried fruits not properly plumped before mixing; too much salt; not enough fat
	Spread too much	Dough not chilled; pans overgreased; batter portioned onto warm or hot pans; butter too warm during creaming step
	Baked unevenly	Dough not rolled out to even thickness or not portioned evenly; cookies placed too close to each other on the baking sheet
	Stick to the pan	Pan not properly greased or lined with parchment paper; too much sugar; oven too hot; cookies overbaked
	Too crisp	Used all white sugar
	Too soft	Wrong type of baking fat; too much brown sugar, honey, or molasses
Pies and tarts	Dough stiff	Not enough fat; not enough liquid; wrong type of flour; mixed too long
	Dough crumbly	Mixed too long; not enough shortening or butter; not enough liquid; wrong type of flour
	Dough shrinks	Dough mixed too long or overbaked
	Filling boils over	Hot filling added to crust; failed to vent crust; too much acid in filling; oven temperature too low (requires longer baking)
	Bottom crust soaked	Mixed too long; bottom heat in oven not working; wet pie pan; too much sugar in filling
	Meringue topping "weeps"	Sugar not dissolved; oven temperature too low; humid atmosphere

Index

A

Acidity, 83, 123, 142
Active yeast. *See* Yeast
Air, 18, 19, 73, 76, 110, 115. *See also* Steam
All-purpose flour, 30, *71*
Almond Filling, 247
Angel
    Biscuits, 183
    Food Cake, 193
    Food Summer Pudding, 232
Apple
    Filling, 245
    Pie, 223
    Sour Cream Coffee Cake, 188
Apple types
    for coffee cake, 188
    for pie, 43
Apple-Filled Turnovers, 244
Apricot Glaze, 260

B

Baguettes, 199
Bakers' percentage, 129–130
Baking powder, 18, *73*, 74–75
Baking science, 18–19, 40–41, 44, 69–76
Baking soda, *73*, 74
Banana Nut Bread, 178
Basic pastry components, 92, 100
Bavarian Cream, 149–150, 262
Bavarian Mousse, Chocolate, 263
Bear Claws, 247
Bench scraper, 41, *84*, 121
Berry and Pear Crisp, Spiced, 242

Berry Cobbler, Mixed, 241
Berry Compote, Mixed, *232*, 258
Beurrage. See Lock-in methods
Biga, 29, 203
Biscuits, 181
    Angel, 183
    Cheddar Jalapeño, 184
Blind baking pie crusts, 46–47
Blitz Puff Pastry, 133, 244
Block method, 121–122, 164
Blooming gelatin, 149, 153
Blueberry Sauce, 258
Boot Camp focus, 68–69, *87*, 158, 161, 169
Boston Brown Bread, 175
Botrytis, 141, 143
Braiding challah, 63–67, *64–67*
Bread and Butter Pudding, 234
Bread dough, 32–33, 61. *See also* Mixing methods
Bread flour, 30, *129*
Bread Pudding, Pumpkin, 235
"Breaking" dough, 33
Brioche à Tête, 207
Brown Bread, Boston, 175
Brownie, Chocolate, Cheesecake, 216
Brownies, Fudge, 218
Bunnies, chocolate, 122
Buns, Sticky, with Pecans, 208
"Burning", 101, 104
Butter, 18, 61, *71*, 110–111, 112, 129, *129*
Butter Cookies, 117, 214
Buttercream, 136–140, *137–139*
Buttercream Torte, 194
Butterflake rolls, 62

C

Cake flour, 30, *71*
Cake recipes, 192–196
Caramel
    Chocolate Mousse Cake, 196
    Mousse, 264
    Sauce, 266
Caramelizing sugar, 104, 239, 266
Carbon dioxide, 74–75
Challah, 63, *64–67*, 205
Chantilly Cream, 102, *190*, *232*, 266
Cheddar Jalapeño Biscuits, 184
Cheesecake, Chocolate Brownie, 216
Chemical leavening, 18, *73*, 74
Cherry Cheese Danish, 249
Cherry Pie, *49*, 220
Chinois, 46, 104
Chipotle Skillet Cornbread, 179
Chocolate, 118–123, 120, *120*, 164
    Bavarian Mousse, 263
    Brownie Cheesecake, 216
    cake decorations, 164, 166
    Cherry Scones, Glazed, 186
    Chunk Cookies, 27, 211
    Croissants. See Pain au Chocolat
    Éclairs, 256
    Ganache, 100, 100, 266
    Glaze, 266
    liquor, 119
    Mousse Cake, Caramel, 196
    Pots de Crème, 240
    Sabayon Mousse, 264
    Soufflé, 168, 235
    Sponge Cake, 192
    Tart Dough, 226

Ciabatta, 82–83, *84–85*, 204
Cinnamon
    Smear, 210
    Swirl Bread, Raisin, 206
Citrus Tart with Chocolate
    Crust, 226
Classic Napoleons, 255
Classic Puff Pastry, 252
Cobbler, Mixed Berry, 241
Cocoa
    butter, 119
    Dutch-process, 74, 123
    nibs, 119, 123
    powder, 123
Coffee, 160
Coffee Cake, Apple Sour Cream,
    188
Compote, Mixed Berry, *232*, 258
Compressed yeast. *See* Yeast
Conching, 119
Cooked-sugar method, 153
Cookie dough crust, 116, 117–118
Cookie recipes, 211–218
Cookies, 27, 50
Cooling, 27, 95
Cornbread, Chipotle Skillet, 179
Cornstarch, 43–44, 74
Country-Style Corn Bread, 180
Couverture, 119
Cranberry Quick Bread, 191
Cranberry-Pecan Pie, 231
Cream Cheese Filling, 249
Cream puff dough. *See* Pâte à
    choux
Cream Puffs, *97*, 254
Cream Scones, 185
Creaming method, 16–19, 24, 25,
    26, 75–76, 110
Crème anglaise, *92*, 93, 100–101,
    149. *See also* Custard Sauce
Crème
    Brûlée, 237
    Caramel, 239
Crisp, Spiced Berry and Pear, 242
Croissants, 133, 250–251
Curdling, 24, 101

Custard, 88–104
Custard Sauce, 262

D
Danish pastry dough, 133
Danish, Cherry Cheese, 249
Date Nut Bread, 176
Deactivating enzymes, 150
Decorating cakes, 164, 166, *167*,
    195
Decorating comb, 166
Dessert recipes, 232–243
Dessert sauces, 164–166,
    258–267
Dessert wine, 140–144, *142*
Diplomat Cream, 102, 261
Dough
    enriched, 60–62
    fat, 129–135
    lean, 33, 82–85
    rubbed, 40–43
    water, 129–135
    wet, 84–85
Drop cookies, 27
Dutch-process cocoa, 74, 123

E
Éclairs, 96, 256
Egg wash, 33, 62, 157
Eggs, 18, 61, 71, *71*, 93, 110. *See
    also* Air
Emulsion, 18, 165–166
Enriched dough, 60–62
Equipment
    bench scraper, 41, 121
    chinois, 46, 104
    chocolate molds, 122
    decorating comb, 166
    instant-read thermometer, 45
    lame, 33
    offset spatula, 121
    pastry tube, 96, 99, 117, 137
    scales, 22

Silpat, 148
spatula, 166
tamis, 52, 115
transfer sheets, 122–123
turntable, 166

F
Fat, 18, 40–42, 61, *71*, 72, 128
Fat dough, 129–135
Fermentation, 29, 75, 119,
    140–141, 143. *See also* Fester-
    ing
Festering, 82–83, 85
Filling recipes, 258–267
    Almond, 247
    Apple, 245
    Cream Cheese, 249
Flaky pie crust, 40–41
Flaky Pie Dough, 219
Flavorings, 53, 101, 140, 172
Flour, 18, 30, *31*, 70–71, 96, 110,
    129–130
"Flour power", 29–30
Foaming method, 76, 108–115,
    114–115
Focaccia, 203
Fold methods, 132–135, *134–135*
Folding, 117, *155*
Food safety, 45, 91, 93, 150–152,
    154, 225, 264
Frangipane, 117
French meringue, 44
Fresh yeast. *See* Yeast
Fruit strips, 156, 158
Fruit tarts, 116, 118. *See also* Pie
    and tart recipes
Fudge Brownies, 218

G
Galette, Rustic Peach, 229
Ganache, 100, *100*, 266
Gelatin, 149–150, 153
Génoise. *See* Sponge Cake

Ginger Cake, 191
Glazed
    Brownies, 218
    Chocolate Cherry Scones, 53,
        186
Glazes, 53, 118, 244, 258–267
Gluten development, 32, 42, 72,
    83, 134
Greasing pans, 112

H
Ham
    and Cheddar Scones, 187
    and Cheese Croissants, 251

I
Ice wine, 141, 143, 144
Instant yeast. *See* Yeast
Italian
    Buttercream, 138–139, 265
    Meringue, 45, 138–139, 153,
        265

L
Lame, 33
Laminated dough, 128–135
Late-harvest wine, 141
Lattice crust, *48–49*
Lean dough, 33, 82–85
Leaveners, 70, 72–75, *73*, 110
    air, 18, 73, 76
    chemical, 18, 73, 74
    eggs, 110
    organic. See Yeast
    steam, 71–72, 73, 96, 128–129,
        156
    yeast, 31–32, 73, 75
Lemon
    Bavarian Cream, 262
    Butter Sauce, 165–166, 190,
        259

Curd, 259
    Meringue Pie, 225
    Shaker Tart, 228
Liaison, 93, 101. *See also* Tem-
    pering
Lining pans, 25
Liquefiers, 18, 70–72, *71*
Lock-in methods, 128–129, 132,
    134–135

M
Mango Sauce, 258
Mealy dough, 42
Measuring. *See* Scaling
Mechanical leaveners. *See* Air;
    steam
Meringues, 44–45, *45*, 112
Milk, 61, 96
Mise en place, 16, 94, 117, 149,
    150, *154*
Mixed Berry
    Cobbler, 241
    Compote, 232, 258
Mixing bread dough, 32–33,
    61
Mixing methods
    creaming, 16–19, 24, 25, 26,
        75–76, 110
    foaming, 76, 108–115,
        114–115
    modified, 61
    rubbed dough, 40–43, 76
    straight dough, 61, 75–76
Molding chocolate, 122–123
Mousse, 149–155, *154–155*
    Cake, Chocolate Caramel,
        196
    Caramel, 264
    Chocolate Bavarian, 196
    Chocolate Sabayon, 264
Mudslide Cookies, 212
Muffins, Smoked Provolone and
    Thyme, 172

N
Napoleons, Classic, 255
Nappé, 101
Nibs, 119, 123

O
Oatmeal-Raisin Cookies, *213*, 215
Offset spatula, 121, 166
Oil, 18, 82
1-2-3 Cookie Dough, 116
Orange
    Sauce, 260
    Soufflé, 236
Organic leaveners. *See* Yeast
Overbeating, 101, 115, 131
Overmixing, 19, 72, 115, 117, 130,
    132
Overwhipping, 169

P
Pain au Chocolat, 250
Pairing wine with desserts, 144
Palmiers, 156
Pan Smear, 210
Paris-Brest, 96, *98-99*, 102, 257
Parker House Rolls, 200
Pasteurization, 45, 225
Pastry bag. *See* Pastry tube
Pastry components, basic, 92, 100
Pastry Cream, 92, *92*, 93, *94–95*,
    101, 168–169, 261
Pastry flour, 30, *129*
Pastry recipes, 244–257
Pastry tube, 96, *99*, 117, *137*, 166
Pâte à choux, *92*, 96–99, *98–99*
Peach Galette, Rustic, 229
Peanut Butter Cookies, *213*, 214
Pear Crisp, Spiced Berry, 242
Pecan Pie, Cranberry, 231
Pie and tart recipes, 219–231
Pie crust, 41–49
Pie Dough, Flaky, 219. See also
    Pie crust

Pie fillings, 43–44. *See also pie and tart recipes*
Pithiviers, 157–158, *165*, 252
Plating, 102, 164
Poolish, 29, 82–83, 84, 204
Pots de Crème, 104, 240
Pound Cake, 19, 194
Presentation. *See* Plating
Profiteroles, 254
Protein content of flours, 30
Provolone, Smoked, and Thyme Muffins, 172
Pudding
    Angel Food Summer, 232
    Bread and Butter, 234
    Pumpkin Bread, 235
Puff Pastry, 126–135, *129*, *134–135*, 156–158, 252
Pumpkin
    Bread, 177
    Bread Pudding, 235
"Punching down" dough, 33

Q
Quick bread recipes, 172–191
Quick Bread, Cranberry, 191

R
Raisin Cinnamon Swirl Bread, 206
Raisining, 141
Rapid-rise yeast. *See* Yeast
Raspberry
    Bavarian Cream, 262
    Sauce, 258
Recipe conversion, 60
Refrigerator cookies, 27, 50
Relaxation. *See* Festering
Resting
    pie crust, 42, 116
    puff pastry, 132, 135, 156
    yeast dough, 33, 61, 83, 85

Retrograde
    bread, 69, 72, 83
    starch, 43
Rising, 33
Rolling pie crust, 45–46
Rolls, Parker House, 200
Rubbed dough method 40–43, 76. *See also* Pie crust; Biscuits; Scones
Roulade, 110–111
Rustic Peach Galette, 229

S
Sabayon method, 152–153
Sabayon Mousse, Chocolate, 264
Salmonella, 45, 150–151
Salt, 82, 112
Sanitation. *See* Food safety
Sauce
    Blueberry, 258
    Caramel, 266
    Custard, 262
    Lemon Butter, 259
    Mango, 258
    Orange, 260
    Raspberry, 258
    Strawberry, 258
Scales, 22–24
Scaling, 16–19, *17*, 24, 29, 47, 73, 91, 130, 153, 154
Science of baking, 18–19, 40–41, 44, 69–76
Scones, *52–53*
    Cream, 185
    Glazed Chocolate Cherry, 186
    Ham and Cheddar, 187
Scoring bread dough, 33
Scraping bowl, importance of, 24, 32, 75
Seasonality, 102
Seeding method. *See* Block method
"Shaggy" dough, 42, 47, 52, *52*
Shaker Tart, Lemon, 228

Shaping
    bread dough, 33, 62, 63–67, 84
    cream puffs and éclairs, 96, 99, 256
    puff pastry, 156–158
    rolls, 83
    scones, 53
Shortening, 18, 41–42, *71*, 112, 136
Sifting, 19, 52, *115*
Silpat, 148
Simple Syrup, *92*, 101, 260
Skillet Cornbread, Chipotle, 179
Smoked Provolone and Thyme Muffins, 172
Soufflé, 168–169
    Chocolate, 168, 235
    Orange, 236
Sour Cream Coffee Cake, Apple, 188
sourdough, *73*, 75
spatula, 166
Spiced Berry and Pear Crisp, 242
Sponge Cake, 110
    Chocolate, 192
    Vanilla, 192
Stabilizers, 18, 70, *71*, 110
Stale. *See* Retrograde bread
Starch, 43–44
Steam, 33, 71–73, 96, 128–129, 156
Sticky Buns with Pecans, 208
Straight dough method, 61, 75–76
Strawberry
    Bavarian Cream, 262
    fans, 102
    Sauce, 258
Substituting dry yeasts, 31–32
Sugar, 18, 71, 72, 82, 102, 140–141
Summer Pudding, Angel Food, 232
Swiss Meringue, 45, 225

T

Tabling method, 121
Tamis, *52*, 115
Tapioca starch, 43–44
Tart Dough, 222
    Chocolate, 226
Tea, 158–159, *159*
Temperature
    for baking puff pastry, 157
    for baking cream puffs, 254
    of bread dough, 32, 83
    of ingredients, 18–19, 32, 75,
        76, 93, 104, 111, 116–117,
        118, 130, 131, 132, 154
Tempering, 93, *94*, 104, 110–111,
    117, 120–122, 131, 149, 150,
    153
    chocolate, 120–122, 164
Tenderizers, 18, 72, 82
Tenderness, 222
Terroir, 119
Texture, 18, *30*, *40*, 41, 42, 43,
    47, 70, 71, 72, 83, 84, 96,
    100, 102, 117, 119, 121, 122,
    133, 141, 150, 153, 154
Thermometer, instant-read, 45,
    101, 138
3-2-1 pie dough, 47
Tips for
    airy soufflés, 236
    baking bread at home, 33
    baking lean bread doughs, 33
    baking pâte à choux, 96
    baking pies, 49
    beating egg whites, 114
    billowy whipped cream, 266
    blind baking pie crust, 46–47
    braiding challah, 63, 64–65
    beautiful biscuits, 181
    caramelizing sugar, 104, 239,
        266
    crisp cornbread crust, 180

cutting biscuits, 184
delicate scones, 185
filling a pastry tube, 166
filling éclairs, 102
fudgy brownies, 218
gelatin and tropical fruits, 150
glazing tarts, 118
julienning lemon zest, 259
keeping cookies round, 50
keeping cake serving plates
    clean, 194
lofty angel food cakes, 193
matching pie crust to pan size,
    47
mixing batters, 19
molding brioche, 207
perfect pound cake, 28
preparing pans, 112
preventing chocolate seizing,
    121
preventing skin on pots de
    crème, 240
professional-looking Danish,
    249
puffiest cream puffs, 254
pumpkins for pie, 44
reheating bread, 33
repairing buttercream, 139
repairing curdled batter, 24
rolling dough, 118, 219
shaping éclairs, 256
shaping scones, 53
softening dough, 118
softening ingredients, 19, 101,
    117, 157
successful meringue, 44–45,
    225
tempering chocolate, 121–122
troubleshooting puff pastry,
    128, 130, 131, 132
troubleshooting soufflés, 169
unmolding cakes, 115, 116

using leftover egg whites, 263
warming ingredients, 18, 117
Torte, Buttercream, 194
Transfer sheets, 122
Turntable, 166

U

Undermixing, 115

V

Vanilla Sponge Cake, *114–115*,
    192

W

Water, 32, 42, 82, 96, 112, 121,
    129
Water dough, 129–135
Wet dough, *84–85*
Whipped cream, 101
White chocolate, 119, *120*
Whole wheat flour recipes, 174,
    175, 177
"Window" in bread dough, 32–33
Wine, 140–144, *142*

Y

Yeast, 31–32, *73*, 75, 82
Yeast bread recipes, 199–210

Z

Zabaglione. *See* Sabayon
Zucchini Bread, 174

Benefactors

Many of the educational facilities at The Culinary Institute of America are made possible by the generous financial support of the friends and benefactors of the college. We wish to acknowledge and thank the following individuals and companies who have made the facilities pictured in Baking Boot Camp available:

The Anheuser-Busch Foundation for the Anheuser-Busch Theatre in Roth Hall (5); Rich Products Corporation and Robert and Mindy Rich for the instructional bakeshops of The Apple Pie Bakery Café Sponsored by Rich Products Corporation (8); The H.J. Heinz Company Foundation for Heinz Plaza (11); Banfi Vintners for the Banfi Vintners Dining Room in the J. Willard Marriott Continuing Education Center (20, 162); the Family and Friends of John J. Profaci for the Torre John J. Profaci of the Colavita Center for Italian Food and Wine and Joseph P. DeAlessandro for the Joseph P. DeAlessandro Dining Room in the Ristorante Caterina de' Medici (37, 125); Colavita USA/Colavita S.p.A./Ind. Al. Co. S.p.A. for the instructional kitchens of the Colavita Center for Italian Food and Wine (2, 12, 17, 23, 38, 46, 58, 103, 111, 113, 126, 133, 146); Ed Hartley Benenson and Paul Bocuse for the Escoffier Restaurant Dining Room and Escoffier Restaurant instructional kitchen, respectively (57); Franz W. Sichel for the Hilde Potter Room in the American Bounty Restaurant (79, 161); Mr. and Mrs. Paul Elbling for the Mr. and Mrs. Paul Elbling Chef's Table in St. Andrew's Café (106); Dr. Lewis J. and Ruth E. Minor for the Dr. Lewis J. and Ruth E. Minor Skills I and Skills II Kitchens in the J. Willard Marriott Continuing Education Center (80); North American Companies/ABC Affiliated Distributors/Sherman Memorial Fund for the North American Companies/ABC Affiliated Distributors/Sherman Memorial Fund Lecture Hall in the J. Willard Marriott Continuing Education Center (88, 108); H.J. Heinz Corporation for the Storeroom in Roth Hall (170).